PURE GEOGRAPHY

J. G. Grau

JOHANNES GABRIEL GRANÖ

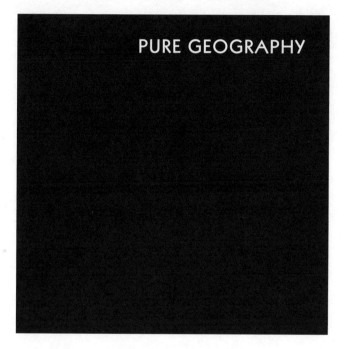

PURE GEOGRAPHY

Edited by Olavi Granö and Anssi Paasi

Translated by Malcolm Hicks

The Johns Hopkins University Press

BALTIMORE AND LONDON

FRONTISPIECE: J. G. Granö, photographed in Turku, Finland, at the time of the publication of *Pure Geography,* in 1929.

Published in cooperation with the Center for American Places, Harrisonburg, Virginia

Pure Geography was originally published as *Reine Geographie* by the Geographical Society of Finland in *Acta Geographica,* vol. 2, 1929, and as *Puhdas maantiede* by Werner Söderström, Porvoo, 1930.

06 05 04 03 02 01 00 99 98 97   5 4 3 2 1

The Johns Hopkins University Press
2715 North Charles Street
Baltimore, Maryland 21218-4319
The Johns Hopkins Press Ltd., London

Library of Congress Cataloging-in-Publication Data will be found at the end of this book.

A catalog record for this book is available from the British Library.

ISBN 0-8018-5591-8

CONTENTS

EDITORS' PREFACE

Pure Geography, by Johannes Gabriel Granö (1882–1956), was originally written in Finnish, although it was first published in German in 1929 under the title *Reine Geographie. Eine methodologische Studie beleuchtet mit Beispielen aus Finnland und Estland,* evidently with an international readership in mind. The original Finnish manuscript was published the following year, as *Puhdas maantiede,* and it is this that has served as the basis for the English translation, now available at last after an interval of almost seventy years. Up to now only brief, fragmentary examples of this work, or indeed of J. G. Granö's geographical thinking as a whole, have been accessible to the English-speaking reader.

Interest in the publication of a complete English version of this work has been aroused by the emergence of "landscape" as one of the keywords in geography during the 1980s and 1990s, as well as in the broader fields of cultural studies and ecology, so that it probably commands more attention now than at any time since the 1930s. Landscape research has gained in popularity in the form of both empirical studies and analysis of the history of the concept of landscape. In the geographical context, this development seems to be part of the general trend distinguishable in the subject matter of the discipline. Interest has also been awakened in many of the phenomena discussed in *Pure Geography,* because of their importance for current research. Inquiries are constantly being made concerning the book's availability, but the truth of the matter is that even the German edition has been unobtainable for years. Morever, references to secondary sources or to brief excerpts reproduced from time to time in English are apt to lead to misinterpretations of the original ideas and to the omission of essential parts of the framework, which have remained quite unknown to modern researchers.

Torsten Hägerstrand, who frequently mentions many notions derived from *Pure Geography,* first raised the question of commissioning an English translation in the early 1970s, and work on it was begun under the direction of Professor Anne Buttimer, but the project, which was based on the German edition, was never completed (van der Vaart 1975). The present translation is based on the Finnish original *Puhdas maantiede,* from which the German version differs only on a few minor points.

Translating a work of this kind is an extremely difficult task, not least because one of its aims in its time was to create a body of geographical terminology in Finnish, for which purpose the author had recourse to the immense capacity of the Finnish language for developing neologisms by means of prefixes and compounds and for adopting words from the vernacular and assigning them specific scientific meanings. In this aspect of his work Granö is known to have consulted philologist friends and scholars specialized in the structure of the Finnish language.

The demanding work of translating *Pure Geography* into English was undertaken by Malcolm Hicks, with the valuable assistance of Sirpa Vellonen, carefully exploring the existing versions in various languages and consulting Finnish experts in order to settle on the best English equivalents for the terms that Granö created for the purposes of his very detailed nomenclature. The present volume also contains a concise bibliography of J. G. Granö's publications in various branches of geography and a list of articles containing evaluations of his scientific work. We have also provided an extensive introduction discussing the position and significance of *Pure Geography* in the history of geographical studies and from the viewpoint of present-day research.

The editors wish to thank all those people who have assisted them at various stages in their work, most particularly Professors Torsten Hägerstrand (Lund), Anne Buttimer (Dublin), and W. R. Mead (London) for their constant help and encouragement. The work of Malcolm Hicks in preparing the actual translation has naturally been decisive for the success of this venture, and we extend our thanks to him and to the Turku University Foundation for its financial support.

The editors have had access to the original negatives of the photographs taken by J. G. Granö and his hand-drawn maps, and the illustrations for this volume have been prepared from this material by Martti Valtonen, of the Department of Geography, University of Turku.

Landscape research would appear to be undergoing a renaissance within geography at the present time, with parallel trends visible in some other disciplines (e.g., anthropology and ecology), propelled forward by the traditions of modern cultural and social theory. One would be justified in claiming that this work of Granö's stands out as an important element in the history of landscape science and in many senses even today offers good ideas for conducting investigations that set out from multidisciplinary perspectives. We hope and trust that the appearance of this English translation will serve as a source of inspiration for many readers with an interest in the history of geographical ideas and in landscape research in general.

At the Department of Geography, University of Turku, where J. G. Granö signed the preface to *Pure Geography* 66 years ago.

OLAVI GRANÖ
Emeritus Professor of Geography
University of Turku

ANSSI PAASI
Professor of Geography
University of Oulu

Pure Geography in the Tradition of Geographical Studies

J. G. Granö belongs to the corps of reformers in geography at the beginning of the present century who believed that it could no longer be content with a role as the general science of the earth or as a science of the interaction between humans and nature. He concurred with the notion espoused by the German methodologist Alfred Hettner that geography should concentrate on examining areal differentiation in the earth's surface in terms of the distributions of causally linked phenomena, but he also shared the conviction expressed by many others (e.g., Herbertson, Passarge, Brunhes, Vidal de la Blache, Berg, Semenov-Tyan-Shanski) that this chorological viewpoint is not sufficient to define the content of the science. Instead, it was held that the essential objects of geographical study were areal units conceived of in some way or other as complexes. This was an allusion to the *Landschaft* doctrine of Otto Schlüter, Siegfried Passarge, and others.

Thus it was German geographical thinking that formed the principal context for Granö's ideas, which in turn provides a natural explanation for why his *Reine Geographie* was published in 1929 in German and not in English, for example. The German connection continued to dominate Finnish geography until the 1950s, as can be seen from the fact that most publications intended for an international readership were written in German.

Granö's landscape science differed fundamentally, however, from the thinking of the German *Landschaft* school, for his notions of the foundation and procedures of geography were derived from a quite different concept of science from those of his contemporaries. The result was an overall system that provides a completely new vision of geography as a field of research and teaching. Thus, it is difficult to discuss Granö on the same dimension of the history of ideas as the other reformers of geography who were active at the same time. As Waibel notes, as an innovator he lies "outside geography as we have known it up to now" (1933:204).

Granö set out from the assumption that no true research method for regional geography had yet been developed—a notion that seems very familiar today in view of current discussions over the new regional geography! The problem, he believed, stemmed from the imprecise use made of the basic concepts in this field—environment, landscape, area, region, and the like. Therefore, the first step was to determine the true nature of environment and landscape and only after that, he maintained, would one have the means to handle the question of geographical regions. For him, regions (*Landschaften*) were not obvious objects of geographical study in their own right, for all regional information is relative, bound in some way or other to the human agent who observes, experiences, and records it. In other words, the "subjective landscape" should somehow be retained as the starting point for geographical procedures and should not be rejected in favor of a regional scientific treatment, as happened when the transition was made to *Landschaftskunde.*

It was from this starting point that he created the doctrine he called "pure geography," the content of which conformed to his view of what should belong to the scientific and pedagogical field of geography in an ideal division of labor between the university disciplines, a division more rational than that prevailing at the time.

The designation "pure geography" was evidently an intentional allusion to the *Vera Geographia* or *Reine Geographie* movement, which had been prominent in German geography for some one hundred years, from the work of Leyser in 1726 to that of its last representative, Wilhelmi, in 1820 (Lüdde 1849). Granö wished to associate himself directly with this significant tradition, which had preceded the emergence of geography as an independent discipline from the 1870s onwards and had eventually been overshadowed by the figures of Ritter and von Humboldt. This school had recommended a classification of the earth's surface to be arrived at through the study of natural features that would yield a set of natural regions with greater permanence than political units. It was the discernment of such natural regions that would give geography its status as an independent discipline. Geography should no longer be merely the tool of the "state geographers" (*Staatsgeographen*) of that time, for use in their definitions of political boundaries on maps and their directories of place names, but it should have its own linguistic content, which would be of value to geography itself and not merely of assistance to other fields or to the exercise of political power, as Farinelli (1997) puts it.

By reviving the term a hundred years later, Granö was evidently attempting under new circumstances to promote the objectives of geography itself in the same way the advocates of "pure geography" had done in their time. We should, he was saying, destroy the barriers that the systematic disciplines have constructed by dividing the geographical whole into areas of study. The choice of this term arose out of a strong desire to emphasize the independence of content and methodology that belonged to an academic subject that constituted a scientific discipline in its own right. As if seeking a motto to this effect, he quotes the German Robert Gradmann in the Introduction to *Pure Geography:* "The highest ambition of every geographer should be to pursue the study of pure geography for its own sake and to produce exemplary, concise, and classically perfect representations of natural landscapes. Then people will begin to understand us better." It must be emphasized, however, that *Pure Geography* has by no means remained merely a milestone in the past history of the discipline, for its content has begun to arouse new interest in many quarters since the 1970s, especially in the English-speaking world. Attention has been attracted both by the possible links between Granö's thinking and behavioralist geography and by his ideas on the significance of sounds and the like as landscape elements and his emphasis on the other senses in the perception of landscape.

His ideas have also been applied in practice in a number of recent empirical studies. Unfortunately, this search for connections, especially in Anglo-American circles, has frequently been founded on no more than superficial observations, in the absence of a full statement of the text in English. The book itself, nevertheless, continues to be an object of considerable interest in many respects. Torsten Hägerstrand argues in favor of its relevance to the modern situation in the following words (translated from the Swedish original):

Reine Geographie has proved to be half a century ahead of its times in the conceptual structures it represents. It aroused contradictory responses when it first appeared, and many people were influenced by it, but the deeper significance of Granö's ideas was alien to his contemporaries, because views on research were utterly different at that time. In more recent times, with the focusing of interest on the man/environment complex, new research trends in the fields of geography, architecture, environmental psychology, the cognitive sciences, etc., have begun to move closer to the issue of the nature of the human being and his environment that was raised in *Reine Geographie*. At the same time it is fascinating to note that *Reine Geographie* is more comprehensive and more logically ordered than the efforts of modern researchers. Finally, Granö was an exceptional methodologist in the sense that he observed his own theoretical principles in the practical research that he carried out.

The Background to *Pure Geography*

J. G. Granö's career as a geographer spanned the first half of this century, the period when geography was establishing itself as an independent university discipline. Granö was very much involved in this process of identification, and it would be no exaggeration to say that his career reflected both the general academic development of geography and features of the contexts in which his own geographical work was taking place. In the course of his explorations in Central Asia in 1906–16, Granö specialized initially in geomorphology, a highly fashionable branch of science at that time, and one regarded by many as the true métier of the geographer. He was engaged in studying southern Siberia and Mongolia, undoubtedly motivated by the fact that he had spent his childhood and the summers of his student years in Omsk, in western Siberia, his father having moved there as Lutheran pastor to the Finnish expatriate community.

Granö made his first acquaintance with geography during his early years as a student at the University of Helsinki. In the autumn of 1901, when attending the lectures of Professor J. E. Rosberg (1864–1932), who had just been appointed to the first chair in geography, Granö decided to adopt this as his subject rather than botany and zoology, which had been his main interests up to that time. J. A. Palmén (1845–1919), professor of zoology, and Wilhelm Ramsay (1865–1928), professor of geology, also exerted a strong influence on Granö. Palmén was at this time active in the Geographical Society of Finland, founded in 1888, and Ramsay was working on problems of glacial geology, with which Granö's early research was to be closely connected.

Geography had only recently been accepted as a university discipline in Finland, and its position was a weak one relative to that of the Geographical Society of Finland, which united a broad spectrum of representatives of different branches of science whose work was devoted to the then highly esteemed patriotic cause of increasing people's knowledge of Finland as a country. It should be remembered that Finland still had the status of an autonomous Grand Duchy of the Russian Empire at that time and gained its independence only in 1917.

Through Rosberg, Granö became interested in geomorphology and in the diversified regional geography that his professor practiced, including the branch known as *Heimatkunde* (home area studies). The first object of study for Granö was the settlement geography of the Finnish communities in Siberia (1905).

Although his first published work on Central Asia was concerned with the archaeology of northern Mongolia, the principal focus of his attention came to be the Altai Mountains, the glacial geology and geomorphology of which he discussed in numerous papers published in German, Russian, and French. The methods he followed in this work were very much those used by Albrecht Penck in his research into the glacial history of the Alps and William Morris Davis in his peneplain theory.

He also depended greatly on Russian geographical research, with which he had become acquainted while living in Omsk in 1913–16. Granö's views on the extensive glaciation of the Altai region during the Ice Age had been influenced by the thinking of Pyotr Kropotkin (1842–1921), secretary of the Russian Geographical Society, and of the explorer G. N. Potanin (1835–1920). Both these men moved over later from studying the physical laws of nature to investigating social geography, which led them to espouse revolutionary ideas and ultimately caused them to be exiled. Kropotkin, who was regarded as an anarchist, emigrated to Great Britain, and Potanin, who was accused of being a "Siberian separatist," had spent a short time in the 1870s in a labor camp at Sveaborg, a fortress on an island off Helsinki. One of Granö's publications in Russian appeared in the 1915 commemorative volume of the *Proceedings of the Russian Geographical Society* dedicated to Potanin. The two largest glaciers in the Mongolian Altai are named even on modern maps after Potanin and Granö.

It would indeed be quite reasonable to assume that it was his childhood acquaintance with the magnificent landscapes of Siberia and the uniform areal structure of this vast region that led Granö later to place so much emphasis on the environment as perceived by the senses and to form synthetic regional entities. The mosaic structure of Central Europe and its *Landschaften* did not provide the same opportunities for a young researcher as could be found in the Russian tradition of recognizing broad, homogeneous geographical zones (Dokuchayev, Berg, see Bassin 1991). Many of the illustrations in *Pure Geography* are from Siberia and the Altai Mountains. A further background element in this is the Finnish national tradition, part of the eventual drive for independence, that assigned a prominent role to landscapes in the creation of a national identity, as has been the case in many other countries at various times.

It was not long, however, before theoretical themes began to emerge in Granö's work. Apart from empirical research, geography for Granö was a field that raised important philosophical and methodological questions, and he began from the 1920s onwards to develop an original methodology of landscape geography. The real object of geographical research, he argued, should be the environment that a human being perceives with his senses, and environmental observations made in this way should be the basis for defining regions.

The radical reorientation that took place in Granö's research work and teaching in the early 1920s may be attributed to his leaving Finland for the newly independent state of Estonia, where he became the first professor of geography at the University of Tartu (Dorpat). It was this position and the new academic context in which he found himself that led him to wrestle with problems concerning the independent status of geography and its significance as a university discipline. One additional factor in this reorientation was naturally the interruption in his research brought about by the Russian Revolution, together with the fact that the University of Tartu had its own ancient, cosmopolitan academic traditions, which fostered close connections with both Russia and Germany. As an application of his landscape geography, with elements of a sociological approach, he organized and led a program of home area studies (*Heimatkunde*), which he termed "human ecology." This activity was motivated by a spirit of national fervor on the part of ordinary people in Estonia. As in Finland, the landscapes of Estonia formed an essential basis for the development of a national identity.

Granö expressed his new view of geography for the first time in a paper written in Tartu and dated 1919. In it he was extremely critical of the general outlook of the Geographical Society of Finland at the time, as publicized by the well-known geologist J. J. Sederholm (1912), with references to C. F. Close (1911) and others. Sederholm maintained that geography was the sum of a number of sciences and not a science in itself, whereas for Granö general (systematic) geography was an essential part of geography as a whole but there was no justification for regarding geography as a general science for studying the earth. A new type of general geography, landscape geography (*Landschaftskunde*), had to be created from the ruins of the older, wider concept. In addition, he advocated a new approach, which he called "regional science," to replace regional geography (*Länderkunde*), which did not satisfy the criteria for a science.

Granö did much in his teaching and in the papers that he published in Finnish, Estonian, and German in the 1920s to develop the new body of theory, and his principal work, *Reine Geographie,* published on his return to Finland, contains a compendium of his ideas on geography and geographical research.

The Content of *Pure Geography*

The starting point for Granö's landscape science was the environment as perceived by the human senses and not regional entities directly, as many other thinkers in regional and landscape geography at that time would have preferred. In this geographical setting he distinguished between the immediate environment, the term for which is translated here as *proximity,* and the distant environment, or *landscape.* He also devised a precise, purpose-built, pragmatic terminology for making generalizations about each of these. The distinction between proximity and landscape was based on the empirical results of physiologists regarding the nature of human perceptions. Thus Granö's landscape science does not in principle set out merely from the investigator's own intuitive experience as is often the case with research in this field.

This means, however, that pure geography calls for a "pure geographer," an investigator who has fully internalized the methodology and terminology of geographical research as suggested by Granö. It should be noted that although Granö's geography is profoundly human-centered, he is speaking of environmental observations made by an experienced scientist, a "pure geographer," and not by a casual bystander. It is important to realize this when comparing Granö's thinking with the perceptual geography of the 1960s, for instance, in which the object of interest was ordinary people's perceptions of their environment. Granö then emphasized certain cartographic methods by which the experienced scientist could move from the human-centered perspective of pure geography to the geographical regions required for teaching and research purposes, the purpose of these methods being to ensure that the regions would be defined and delimited in an accurate, sufficiently generalized, and appropriately concise manner.

By setting out from the environment as perceived with the senses, pure geography was thus able to address the initial cognitive phase of the geographical research process, a phase generally passed over in the geography of that period as being in the nature of a truism. This was the approach adopted by Granö for discovering the fundamental nature of geography, which meant understanding the way in which a geographer transforms and structures information on the "real," physical world principally as sensory data formulated "on the spot" and not as an "after-image" or memory. His attempt to remove such "after-images" from geographical studies was derived from his governing principle that every geographer should have a generally accepted, "objective" perception of the real environment rather than giving priority to personal values, attitudes, and aesthetic emotions when reporting results or even transmitting geographical data in general.

Granö obviously considered the perceptual environment to be our basis for acquiring our entire *Weltbild,* since he believed that we are bound to our senses, even though we may place all manner of magnifying or clarifying instruments between our senses and the objects that we are examining. He clearly felt that it was only through measurable conceptual descriptions shared by all that it was possible to teach, inform, and communicate. Such a demand for objectivity is a utopian one, of course, for the observation of a landscape is always a subjective act, as is the representation of landscapes in cartographical form, where the investigator's own subjectivity and imagination are always present. By limiting himself to the environment as perceived with the senses, Granö, nevertheless, managed to create a logical foundation for the order of magnitude of geographical regions and what things should be included in the description or excluded from it. By simplifying the background to the description, he was able to adopt a whole system of coded symbols for landscapes.

The earth's surface, in Granö's view, consisted of a plurality of environments bound by the senses of the person perceiving them. He had, therefore, to consider very carefully the relationship between perceptual experience and external objects, and to find a way for insights from psychology and the natural sciences to be integrated within the discipline of geography. Such an idea had not been considered by geographers at that time, but certain psychologists and philosophers had given thought to the problem. The main issue for Granö was to place one's "subjective" perceptual environment in a real "objective" environment. The environment that encircles a human being everywhere and continually, both the immediate environment (proximity) and the distant environment (landscape), and that moves with the observer has to be fixed in space to the surface of the earth, to areal units as homogeneous complexes. These Granö called not landscapes but geographical regions. Thus his landscape is a concept for the visual environment only and does not correspond to the German *Landschaft,* which apart from this visual meaning, refers primarily to an area distinguished by a more or less uniform aspect.

Expressed in this way, the task of delimiting regions was a process of definition rather than discovery: the regional units were not given but had to be determined arbitrarily to serve the purpose of the research. In order to do this, Granö further developed Passarge's cartographic "overlay" techniques of 1908, which allowed him to define core areas and transition zones (see figure). The regions might vary considerably in size, depending on the extent to which he wished either to generalize or go into detail, those corresponding to landscapes being referred to with a term translated into English as "locality," and being grouped together to form larger areas translated as "districts" and "provinces." The small area corresponding to a proximity is named here "vicinity."

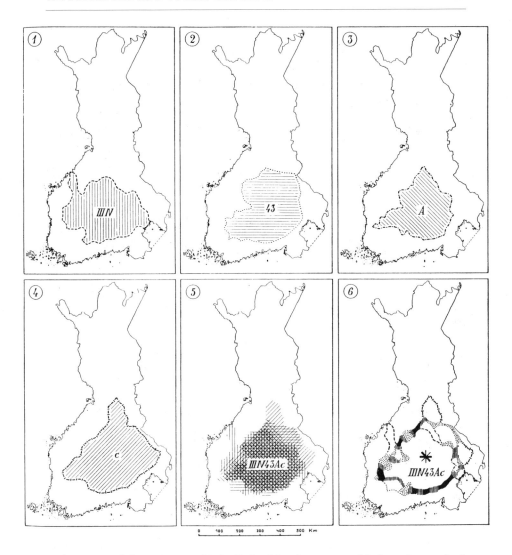

Delimitation of the province of Lake Finland by the cartographical overlay method. The analytical maps 1–4 denote regions that are homogeneous in terms of landforms (*III IV* = mound and hillock terrain), water forms (*43* = lake system and lakes), vegetation (*A* = forest), and artificial matter (*c* = isolated dwellings). Map 5 is a synthetic map combining the analytical regions of maps 1–4 and assigning it the composite code *III IV 43A c*. Map 6 depicts the manner in which the resulting region stands out from its surroundings (degree of individuality) and includes the boundaries given by the analytical maps 1–4, thereby serving to distinguish a homogeneous core area for the region and a transitional zone. From J. G. Granö, "Geographische Ganzheiten," *Petermanns Geographische Mitteilungen* 1935.

For Granö, geographical research should not be limited only to visual features, however, but should also take account of the interrelations between phenomena and functional processes and the genetic changes that these bring about. The often deductive examination of the latter he refers to as "geographical physiology." The first step in any geographical study, however, was inevitably to determine the facts by describing the visible characteristics of an area without attempting to explain them in advance, as Granö himself did in his early work, following the model of W. M. Davis (for details, see O. Granö 1990).

Geographical methodology was not just a matter of conjecture for Granö as it was for so many geographers before and after him. The goal of his theoretical discussions was always to develop methods applicable to practical research carried out in real environments. These applications are manifested in two ways in *Pure Geography:* first, in the presentation of landscape-scale regions for Estonia, and, second, in the illustration of his methods of studying proximities, which take all sensory impressions into account, not just visual ones. Granö prepared in minute detail a series of cartographic plans of all these sensory impressions and the corresponding vicinities on the small island of Valosaari in the lake region of Finland, but he did not develop or apply this method, which was perhaps his most original one, anywhere else, although he discussed landscapes and their corresponding regions in many of his later works.

The question for Granö was thus not one of the interrelation between the human being and his or her environment in a causal, possibilistic, or cognitive sense, but rather one of reciprocity between the geographer's mind and his surroundings. But as the text of *Pure Geography* demonstrates, his classification of the elements of the environment represents a quest for analytical precision and objectivity that bears a great resemblance to the nomothetic approach that gained currency later.

The discussion and problematization in *Pure Geography* of aspects of the geographical investigation process that had previously been regarded as self-evident aroused serious criticism among other geographers. Granö's discussion of geographical complexes and wholes was felt to be problematic just because of its anthropocentric starting point. It has been said, for instance, that Granö did not make any explicit distinction between wholes in nature and in our minds. In the words of Hartshorne (1939:277):

> Starting from the sensory landscape, a psychological unit phenomenon, he (Granö) attempts to analyze and synthesize the objective earth phenomena that have produced that result in the observer. In doing so, however, he apparently transfers the concept of the Whole back to the earth phenomena, over-

looking the fact that these represent a Whole only in the psychological reaction in the observer, not in the reality outside him—and they do not produce the same Wholes in different observers.

On the other hand, the logical manner in which the method is applied in practice and the innovatory cartographical techniques and means of processing regional data gained wide acceptance in their time, and many adherents (see references).

Although Granö refers in the last chapters of his book to the importance of the social environment for landscape geography, the discipline was for him very much one of the natural sciences, and for this reason he attempted to create a strictly scientific, analytical body of theory. But the social environment was for him also a part of nature and therefore amenable to being observed "objectively." In this respect his attitude reflects the spirit of his times, the Zeitgeist, and also the institutional context under which geography was pursued in Finland at that time, that of the natural sciences. Thus, in contrast to many of those who have worked to develop landscape geography and regional geography, he categorically rejected any role for subjectivity and the artistic element in research, distancing himself in this respect from many of the German and French landscape geographers, for instance. If a sociological aspect is included in the geographical study of the environment, the result is a branch of science referred to by Granö as "human ecology."

At the same time, Granö was already involved in writing his extensive popular geography of the Altai, running to more than seven hundred pages, which appeared in Finnish and Swedish (1919–21, new Finnish edition in 1993). This serves as an example of a different methodological orientation, adopting a more literary form, and its description of the physical conditions in terms of regions and its ethnographic accounts of human activity rely heavily on the writer's inner experiences and interpretations of the environment. It is as if he were in this way evading the limits that he had set on strict scientific research in the spirit of pure geography and opening the door to a more subjective approach, which in a sense resembles the landscape descriptions provided by later humanistic geographers. Unlike them, however, he offers no justification for such an approach in his theoretical writings, but quite specifically excludes the subjective, artistic element from his concept of geography proper (Paasi 1984).

The following quotations also prove that he understood that people perceive landscapes in different ways and see different things in the same landscapes. In pure geography the perceiver is *Homo Geographicus,* for whom the landscape presents itself objectively through a strict classificatory scheme. This is his description of the upland plains that are typical of the Inner Altai:

What does it look like there, above the forest? There are alternative answers. A Russian peasant who is bound to the land would tell you about it in the following way: "There are few forests. The area is so flat that one can drive by carriage wherever one wishes, except for the steep-edged river valleys in some places and the evil marshes. It is sad, but the grain does not grow there. There are often snow-storms in summer and the ground is white with frost at night even during the warmest season."

A Kirghiz who is used to going up to the alpine meadows on the hills with his cattle in summer, would say: "An excellent area. There are no gnats or gadflies. The cattle get fat. There is a fresh wind blowing and one develops an excellent appetite."

A hunter from the Altai would tell you about the elk and wild reindeer, about the steinbock and bear that linger on the snow patches on the hills on warm summer days. He might recall the brilliance of the flowers on the alpine meadows and the enchanting moonlit nights. He may lose himself in meditation and ask, in the words of an old nuptial poem: "Are the golden flowers still shining on the hills of Altai? Is the pale moon still shining on the slopes of the golden mountains? . . . " Yes! Yes, the alpine meadows still dress themselves in the golden brilliance of their flowers for the short summer. The yellow alpine poppies nod on the edges of the springs, the alpine buttercups open their shining blooms on the soft carpets of moss, the violets follow the movement of the sun in the sky with their gaze, and the moon still casts its light on the nocturnal landscape. It shines down on hundreds of pools where the waterfowl spend their nights, and on the light-colored patches. Its silver beams peep into the dark bushes of alpine birch and caress the grass, which is white with frost. Everything is as before. The loveliness of the hills will be preserved! (Granö 1919: 33–35).

In this next quotation Granö describes the landscape of the Swan River, which lay in front of the wanderers when they arrived on a high ridge.

Far away in the north, on the horizon, there were some hills with snow patches, and down below us was the Swan River, curving in a bright belt. The landscape was covered with a light, bluish veil. Complete silence! We could not hear the cuckoo calling, nor the whistle of the golden oriole. We could not feel any breath of air. We were surrounded by a great sanctuary of flowers, cast in wax, as it were. It was like a fairy tale, a dream! I don't know what day of the week it was by the calendar, but that is of secondary importance. It is certain that the virgin nature far away in northeast Altai was spending a summer Sunday (Granö 1919: 260).

Soon after the publication of *Reine Geographie,* Granö completed an extensive work on the geographical regions of Finland, *Die Geographischen Gebiete Finnlands* (1931), determined in accordance with his new methodology and corresponding to the set of regions arrived at by the same means just previously in the third edition of the *Atlas of Finland* (1928). This was the first time that geographical regions of Finland had been defined, and it was done precisely in terms of landscape characterizations such as "Archipelago Finland" and "Lake Finland," a style that was to become typical of Finnish regional geography in subsequent years. This system also served to describe the physiological features of the same homogeneous landscape regions without any separate functional definitions. As editor of the *Atlas of Finland*, Granö was able to implement many of his ideas on regional studies and compiled singlehanded the first large-scale dot maps showing the distribution of population and vegetation in Finland. Granö's regions as such have been preserved even in the current fifth edition of the *Atlas of Finland* (1993).

The same method was duly applied in his extensive geography of Mongolia and the related landscape profiles in later years (1938, 1941), in accordance with their author's general theoretical views as contained in his *Geographische Ganzheiten* (1935, new ed. 1973). He returned to questions of regional analysis and the recognition of regions in many of his later writings, his last treatments of the subject being in a paper presented in French at the International Geographical Congress in Lisbon in 1949 and his contribution to the *Handbook on the Geography of Finland* in 1952. Granö was also one of the first Finnish geographers to suggest that the subject could serve as a valuable tool for regional planning.

Influence and Dissemination of Granö's Ideas

The evolution and application of the research methods associated with pure geography were closely linked with academic teaching. It should be remembered, of course, that at the time when Granö was putting his ideas forward geography as a discipline conformed to the "Humboldtian" notion of the university, its purpose being to describe and interpret the world by the combined means of teaching and research. Granö was an enthusiastic and charismatic teacher and organizer of university teaching, holding chairs at three universities (Tartu 1919–23, Helsinki 1923–26 and 1945–50, Turku 1926–45). He had, in fact, been the first assistant in geography at the University of Helsinki and had taught courses as early as 1902.

In Estonia, Granö established his own school of geographical thought. He organized intensive local and regional research in both the countryside and the towns, and a significant research program in urban geography was begun under his leadership in Tartu. Thus Granö was already studying internal differentiation in an urban environment and the problems of urban hinterlands in the early 1920s. Followers of his ideas in Estonia were distributed over many parts of the world following the Second World War; one of the most outstanding of these scholars was perhaps Edgar Kant, Granö's pupil and close colleague, who moved to Sweden in 1944. He amassed a considerable reputation as a representative of the Lund school (see Buttimer 1987, 1994, Kurs 1992). Granö also founded his own schools of geographers in Helsinki and Turku, although his influence was no longer so marked during his last years as a university teacher, spent in Helsinki.

Granö's ideas on the philosophy and methodology of geography spread rapidly throughout Finland and Estonia and also to Central Europe, but they only sporadically found their way to other parts of the world. His work sparked lively discussions at the International Geographical Congresses held in Warsaw and Amsterdam in 1934 and 1938. His ideas were received most favorably in the German *Landschaftskunde* circles, but even there hardly anybody accepted unreservedly his view that the perceived environment should be the basis for geographical studies, which was considered to be too much influenced by the psychology of perception. In other respects, however, his approach to landscape as a synthetic object of study and cartographic analysis was widely approved (see statements by A. Penck 1928, Hassinger 1930, Passarge 1931, Lautensach 1933, Schrepfer 1934, Bürger 1935, Winkler 1938). But there were also scholars who were critical of his work in other respects, including representatives of the *Landschaftskunde* school such as Jaeger (1931), Waibel (1933) and later Lehmann (1950) and Paffen (1953) as well as those of other schools (among whom the most critical were Ahlmann in Sweden and Leiviskä in Finland). The use of his method of defining regions spread beyond Finland and Estonia to some extent, as far afield as Hungary and Switzerland (cf. Mészáros 1938, Schaffner 1946, Capt 1947, Windler 1954), and he had an obvious influence on the polemic regarding geographical theory in the 1930s (see the detailed survey by Schmithüsen 1976).

With the exception of his contribution to the *Atlas of Finland,* which attracted broad attention, Granö's ideas spread much less readily in English-speaking areas. It is understandable that they should have met with a sympathetic response on the part of the Sauer school at Berkeley (e.g., Broek 1938). His code of symbols for landscapes was taken into use in a modified form (e.g., by Finch 1933), and his works were also reviewed in English (e.g., van Cleef 1932, Jessen 1936, and later Freeman 1961, etc.). As we saw above, Hartshorne (1939) reviewed Granö's ideas in some detail in his *Nature of Geography,* but he could not bring himself to accept the view of the perceived environment as the basis for geographical study. In Italy, too, Granö's views gained a certain amount of approval (Bertacchi 1930, Renier 1935).

Although Granö's ideas were closely associated with psychology, they did not receive much acclaim from workers in that field. The professor of philosophy at the University of Helsinki, Eino Kaila, a well-known logical empiricist who spanned the border between philosophy and psychology, discussed Granö's theory briefly in his lectures in the academic years 1934–35, obviously concentrating on those presented in *Reine Geographie*. This has been reported by the Finnish philosopher Georg Henrik von Wright, who was a pupil of Kaila's.

As far as Granö's thinking is concerned, it is interesting that Kaila emphasized the importance of the distinction between a phenomenal and a physical space. The former is self-centered, because we always experience ourselves at its center, and it contains a great number of objects of perception that have no physical counterparts (e.g., the vault of heaven), whereas a physical space is not self-centered, and we can talk about it only because most things maintain their relative positions: "if there were no 'geography' in the broadest sense of the word, there would not be any physical space" (Kaila 1939: 231). This "geographical space" differs from our common-sense view, in which space is not the same as the ordering of physical facts. In Kaila's terms, the aim of Granö's geography is in fact to make a transfer from anthropocentric phenomenal spaces to the physical space of science (and of pure geography), which he understands as being formal and independent of the subjectivity of the researcher. Granö's influence can also be seen in Kaila's posthumously published works (1960, 1979).

The Relevance of *Pure Geography* for Contemporary Geography

Looked at from a modern perspective, *Pure Geography* occupies a critical position in the history of geographical studies because for the first time it provided the regional complex that had emerged as a major object of study for geography with an analytical research method of its own, a method which could be applied operatively in practice in the form of verbal and cartographic means of representation. It therefore constitutes a method which goes further than mere intuitive description or the implementation of a regional geographical model (*Länderkundliche Schema*) procedure as determined by the accepted content of the systematic sciences à la Hettner.

The impact that *Pure Geography* had on the subsequent development of geography may be appreciated from later reviews (e.g., Schmithüsen 1976). Schultz draws attention to one aspect that had previously been ignored, namely, that in the context of the history of geography Granö tends to be grouped erroneously among those outdated geographers who restricted themselves to the visual features of the landscape, although in practice he emphasized both in *Pure Geography* and particularly in his later works the importance of paying attention to the physiology of regions and "provided a clear formulation of the multiplicity of meanings attached to physiological landscape indicators in a way in which more recent social geography has only gradually been able to do" (1980:158).

The position and significance of *Pure Geography* in the history of geographical ideas in the German-speaking world may be appreciated from the

INTELLECTUAL AND SOCIAL CONTEXTS

fact that Beck's *Zeittafel der Geographie 1859–1945* (1960, 1964) mentions only two events occurring in Finland, the publication of the *Atlas of Finland* in 1899 and the appearance of *Reine Geographie* in 1929.

As far as the traditional way of dealing with landscapes and the new landscape and regional geography are concerned, *Pure Geography* is relevant in that it represents a combination of elements that later achieved prominence in two of the main trends in geographical thought, the systems analysis trend from the 1950s onwards and the behavioralist-humanistic trend that began in the 1960s. Granö succeeded in (1) treating landscapes in a revealing manner as perceptual environments, and (2) developing an analytical method for defining regions, attempting to combine these two as consecutive stages in the same research process. Thus, Granö was in a way a forerunner of both the behavioralist-humanistic and the systems analysis approach, even though to overemphasize these connections would be a gross error of presentism. These connections have, nevertheless, been subsequently pointed out. The problem of presentism has been discussed in connection with the ideas of Granö in Paasi (1984), where attention is drawn to a danger that can easily arise in the history of ideas: that when the past is studied in modern terminology, things are perceived which may not even have been in existence at the time.

These two trends in landscape research—contrary to the situation in the work of Granö—have, nevertheless, gone in separate directions. The systems analysis trend attempted to penetrate directly "behind the landscape impression," without stopping to consider questions of subject and object, employing systems thinking and quantitative methods to determine scientifically the "real" structures of a landscape and its ecological correlations (see Uhlig 1971, Schmithüsen 1976, Leser 1978, for example). It was E. Markus who brought the theories of L. S. Berg to Estonia from St. Petersburg to act as a counterbalance to those of Granö, and he was also the first person (in 1925) to use the concept of a "natural complex" in the context of landscape ecology, in the same sense as it was used later (in 1939) by C. Troll (Roosaare 1994). Alienation from the human environment as such emerges most clearly in the adoption as scientific terminology of words that do not exist at all in the standard language, for example, geoecology, geosynergy, compage, geomer, geotop, idiochor (see Whittlesey 1954, Carol 1956, Troll 1971, for example). On the other hand, modern landscape ecology, in the form of "human ecosystem science" (Naveh 1982, Furman and Godron 1986) bears a closer resemblance to Granö's landscape geography. Quite separate from this, humanistic and behavioral circles within geography have contemplated the significance of landscape and environment in ordinary people's cognition and environmental experiences.

Ideas derived from *Pure Geography* have been used in recent times mainly when considering architectural theory (see Pietilä 1968, Rapoport 1992) and the perceived environment other than in a visual sense (see Kaups and Mather 1968, Ohlson 1976, Nemeth 1984), and authors such as Buttimer (1976, 1990), Mead (1977, 1993), and Hägerstrand (1991) have emphasized other innovations to be found in the work. Porteaus (1990) and Rodaway (1994) have recently noted the relevance of Granö's ideas, and his notion of soundscape, for instance, seems to have become a topic of interest in modern social geography (Smith 1994).

Landscape research acquired a prominent position in Anglo-American geography in the course of the 1980s, as well as in other forms of research into society and culture, and at the same time the new regional geography became a major topic of discussion. It could very well be said, in fact, that culture, symbolism, and power are key words that characterize the new viewpoints adopted by geography over this period in the case of both the new regional geography and the interpretation of landscapes.

Likewise it could be said that, just as J. G. Granö attempted to develop the methods and concepts of landscape research in accordance with the methodology of the natural sciences, the most recent views to be expressed in geography—and other fields—have emphasized the textual nature and social construction of landscapes and simultaneously the appreciation of landscape research as a part of the study of culture and society. Rather than simply asking what a landscape is, what it means, or how it is observed, more and more scholars today are showing an interest in "ways of seeing" or how a landscape "functions" as a form of cultural praxis. Other questions that have more frequently aroused interest are the relation between power and landscapes, the ideological significance of landscapes, the importance of landscapes for cultural and social identity, landscapes and gender, the relation of landscape research to architecture, the relation between landscapes and representations, and the ontology of landscapes (see Olwig 1984, Cosgrove and Daniels 1988, Zukin 1991, Rapoport 1992, Rose 1993, Matless 1992, Duncan and Ley 1993, Mitchell 1994, Farinelli 1997). All these matters of social or cultural theory have naturally tended to steer landscape geography away from the neutral notion of landscape that places emphasis on observation and objectivity. In the same way the new, or reconstructed, regional geography stresses the historical nature of regions and the manner in which they come into being as the products of social, cultural, and economic processes and struggles.

In spite of the fact that both landscape research and the theoretization of regions have proceeded toward new problems and tasks within geography, and did so particularly markedly during the 1980s, we believe that the publication of *Pure Geography* in English at this juncture will not only serve to give new prominence and depth to our knowledge of the tradition of research into landscapes and regions but also stimulate ideas for still more questions that these branches of geography should be prepared to investigate. Those currently engaged in developing landscape geography will of course also come up against many questions of the kinds that are touched upon in *Pure Geography,* including that of the relation between representations and the world and that of the nature of the language through which these representations should be constructed.

References

Aalto, Pentti (1991). "Old Turkic epigraphic materials, gathered by J. G. Granö." *Journal de la Société Finno-Ougrienne* 83:1–72.

Allix, A. (1913). "Exploration du J. G. Granö dans la Mongolie occidentale." *La Géographie* 26:293–95.

Bassin, Mark (1991). "Russia between Europe and Asia: The ideological construction of geographical space." *Slavic Review* 50:1–17.

Beck, Hanno (1960). "Zeittafel der Geographie von 1859 bis 1905." *Geographisches Taschenbuch 1960/61*. Wiesbaden, 1–14.

——. (1964). "Zeittafel der Geographie von 1905–1945." *Geographisches Taschenbuch 1964/65*. Wiesbaden, 1–18.

Bertacchi, Cosimo (1930). "Reine Geographie." *Rivista Geografica Italiana* 37:66–67.

Broek, J. O. M. (1938). "The concept landscape in human geography." *Comptes Rendus du Congrès International Géographique* 2:103–9.

Bürger, K. (1935). "Die Landschaftsbegriff." *Dresdner Geographische Studien* 7:1–131.

Buttimer, Anne (1976). "Grasping the dynamism of lifeworld." *Annals of the Association of American Geographers* 66:277–92.

——. (1987). "Edgar Kant 1902–1978." *Geographers: Biobibliographical Studies* 11: 71–82.

——. (1990). "Geography, humanism, and global concern." *Annals of the Association of American Geographers* 80:1–33.

——. (1994). "Edgar Kant and Balto-Skandia: Heimatkunde and regional identity." In David Hooson, ed., *Geography and National Identity*. Oxford, 162–83.

Capt, A. (1947). *Die Anwendung von Granö's Methode zur Landschaftsgliederung am Beispiel des Kantons Zürich*. Diss., Zürich.

Carol, Hans (1956). "Zur Diskussion um Landschaft und Geographie." *Geographica Helvetica* 11:111–32.

Close, C. F. (1911). "On the scope and position of geography." Paper presented at the British Association.

Cosgrove, Denis, and Daniels, Stephen, eds. (1988). *The Iconography of Landscape*. Cambridge. 317 p.

Davis, W. M. (1921). "Morphology of the Altai Mountains." *Geographical Review* 11: 155–56.

Duncan, James, and Ley, David, eds. (1993). *Place/Culture/Representation*. London. 341 p.

Farinelli, Franco (1997). "The wit of the landscape and the astuteness of the representation." In A. Buttimer and S. Brunn, eds. *Beiträge zur Regionalen Geographie* (Text and image: Social construction of regional knowledge). Leipzig.

Fickeler, Paul (1925). "Der Altai." *Petermanns Geographische Mitteilungen Ergänzungshefte.* suppl. 187. 202 p.

Finch, Vernor C. (1933). "Montfort: A study in landscape types in Southwestern Wisconsin." *Geographic Society of Chicago Bulletin,* vol. 9. Entire issue.

Fischer, Eric, Campbell, Robert D., and Miller, Eldon S., eds. (1967). *A Question of Place.* Arlington, Va., 304–10. 446 p.

Forman, Richard T. T., and Godron, Michel (1986). *Landscape Ecology.* New York. 619 p.

Freeman, T. W. (1961). *A hundred years of geography.* London. 334 p.

Granö, Olavi (1979). "Johannes Gabriel Granö." *Geographers: Biobibliographical Studies* 3:73–84.

——. (1990). "The spread of the peneplaine concept to Finland. An example of a paradigm's relation to an institutional structure." *Striae* 32:37–42.

Hägerstrand, Torsten (1991). "The landscape as overlapping neighbourhoods." Carl Sauer Memorial Lecture. In G. Carlestam and B. Soube, eds., *Om Tidens Vidd och Tingens Ordning.* Byggforskningsrådet, 47–55. Reproduced in G. Benko and U. Strohmayer, eds. (1995). *Geography, History, and Social Sciences. The GeoJournal Library* 27:83–96. Kluwer Academic Publischers.

Hartshorne, Richard (1939). "The Nature of Geography." Dordrecht and Boston: *Annals of the Association of American Geographers* 29 (no. 3 & 4):171–658.

Hassinger, H. (1930). "Zur Methode der Landschaftsbeschreibung und Landschaftsgliederung." *Geographische Zeitschrift* 36:293–96.

Hildén, Kaarlo (1956). "Hommage á la mémoire de J. G. Granö." *Terra* 68:2–13. (Includes a complete bibliography.)

Jaeger, Fritz (1931). "Granös Reine Geographie." *Petermanns Geographische Mitteilungen* 76:67–68.

Jessen, Jorgen (1936). "A Finnish geographer." *Baltic Countries* 11:1–6.

Juntunen, Alpo (1993). "The influence of the Russian Empire on Finnish geography." *Fennia* 171 (2):137–58.

Kaila, Eino (1939). *Inhimillinen tieto, mitä se on ja mitä se ei ole.* Helsinki. 271 p.

——. (1960). "Arkikokemuksen perseptuaalinen ja konseptuaalinen aines." *Ajatus* 23:50–115.

——. (1979). "On the system of the concepts of reality: A contribution to logical empiricism." In R. S. Cohen, ed., *Eino Kaila, Reality and Experience: Four Philosophical Essays.* Dordrecht, 59–125.

Kant, Edgar (1933). "Géographie, sociographie et l'écologie humaine." *Publicationes Seminarii Universitatis Tartuensis Oeconomic-Geographici* 4:1–61.

——. (1956). "Johannes Gabriel Granö. In memoriam." *Svensk Geografisk Årsbok* 32:163–72.

Kaups, Matti, and Mather, Cotton (1968). "Eben: Thirty years later in a Finnish Community in the Upper Peninsula of Michigan." *Economic Geography* 44:57–70.

Kurs, Ott (1992). "Scientific heritage of Edgar Kant." *Estonia, Man, and Nature.* Estonian Geographical Society, Talin, 108–28.

Lautensach, Hermann (1933). "Wesen und Methoden der geographischen Wissenschaft." *Handbuch der Geographischen Wissenschaft.* 1:23–56.

Lehmann, Herbert (1950). "Die Physiognomie der Landschaft." *Studium Generale* 3:182–95.

Leser, H. (1978). *Landschaftsökologie.* 2d ed. Stuttgart. 433 p.

Lüdde, Johann Gottfried (1849). *Die Geschichte der Methodologie der Erdkunde.* Leipzig. 130 p.

Matless, D. (1992). "An occasion for geography: Landscape, representation, and Foucault's corpus." *Environment and Planning D: Society and Space* 10:41–56.

Mead, W. R. (1977). "Recent developments in human geography in Finland." *Progress in Human Geography* 1:361–375.

———. (1993). *An Experience of Finland.* London. 164 p.

Mészáros, O. (1938). "Kunhalom. A tájleirás Granö szerint" (Referat: "Die Anwendung von Granö's Methode"). Diss. *Acta Litterarum ac Scientiarum Universitatis Hungarica Fransisco-Iosephinae.*

Mitchell, W. J. T. (1994). *Landscape and Power.* London. 248 p.

Naveh, Zev (1982). "Landscape ecology as an emerging branch of human ecosystem science." *Advances in Ecological Research* 12:189–198.

Nemeth, David (1984). "Prolegomenon to a geographic study on the subjective quality of inner-city space." *Cheju National University Academic Journal Korea* 19:151–162.

Ohlson, Birger (1976). "Sound field and sonic landscapes in rural environments." *Fennia* 148:33–43.

Olwig, Kenneth (1984). *Nature's Ideological Landscape.* London. 115 p.

Paasi, Anssi (1984). "Connections between J. G. Granö's geographical thinking and behavioural and humanistic geography." *Fennia* 162 (1):21–31.

Paffen, Karlheinz (1953). "Der Landschaftsbegriff als Problemstellung." *Forschungen zur Deutschen Landeskunde* 68:17–43.

Passarge, Siegfried (1931). "Die Metode der Landschaftsbestimmung durch Symbole." *Geographische Zeitschrift* 37:227–30.

Penck, Albrecht (1928). "Neuere Geographie." *Sonderband Zeitschrift der Gesellschaft für Erdkunde zu Berlin,* pp. 31–56.

Pietilä, Reima (1968). "Maisema ja rakentamismuodot." *Arkkitehti* 65:30–31.

Porteaus, J. Douglas (1990). *Landscapes of the Mind: Worlds of Sense and Metaphor.* London. 227 p.

Rapoport, Amos (1992). "On cultural landscapes." *Traditional Dwellings and Settlements Review* 3:33–47.

———. (1992). "On regions and regionalism." In F. G. Sturm, ed., *Pueblo Style and Regional Architecture,* 272–94. New York.

Renier, Stefano (1935). "Un maestro e una scuola: J. G. Granö e l'Istituto geografico dell'Università di Abo." *Rivista Geografica Italiana* 42:24–28.

Rodaway, P. (1994). *Sensuous Geographies: Body, Sense and Place.* London. 198 p.

Roosaare, J. (1994). "Physical Geography of Estonia: Bridging western and eastern schools of landscape synthesis." *GeoJournal* 33:27–36.

Rose, G. (1993). *Feminism and Geography: The Limits of Geographical Knowledge.* Cambridge. 205 p.

Schaffner, Werner (1946). "Die geographische Grenze zwischen Jura und Mittelland." Diss. *Abteilung Geographie Universität Zürich* 15.

Schmithüsen, Josef (1976). *Allgemeine Geosynergetik.* Berlin and New York. 349 p.

Schrepfer, Hans (1934). "Einheit und Aufgaben der Geographie als Wissenschaft." In J. Peterson and H. Schrepfer, eds., *Die Geographie vor neuen Aufgaben,* 61–86. Frankfurt.

Schultz, H.-D. (1980). "Die deutschsprachige Geographie von 1800 bis 1970." *Abhandlungen des Geographischen Instituts für Anthropogeographie* 29. Berlin. 478 p.

Sederholm, J. J. (1912). "Den vetenskapliga geografins mål och medel" (Résumé: "But et méthodes de la géographie scientifique"), *Fennia* 32 (11):1–42.

Serebryanny, L. E., and Gerasimov, I. P. (1956). "J. G. Granö 1882–1956." *Izvestiia Akademiia Nauk SSSR Seriia Geograficheskaia* 6:126–27.

Smith, Susan J. (1994). "Soundscape." *Area* 26:232–40.

Troll, Carl (1971). "Landscape ecology (geoecology) and biogeocenology. A terminological study." *Geoforum* 8:43–46.

Tuominen, Oiva (1988). "Coincidence and continuity in a geographer's life." In T. Hägerstrand and A. Buttimer, eds., *Geographers of Norden.* Lund Studies in Geography, series B (no. 52):130–46.

Uhlig, H. (1971). "Organization and system of geography." *Geoforum* 7:7–38.

Van Cleef, Eugene (1932). "A philosophy of geographical regions." *Geographical Review* 22:497–98.

Van der Vaart, Jacob H. P. (1975). "Granö's pure geography." *The Monadnock,* June, 91–95.

Waibel, Leo (1933). "Was verstehen wir unter Landschaftskunde." *Geographischer Anzeiger* 34:197–207.

Westermanns Lexikon der Geographie (1969–70). (Entries: "Granö, Johannes Gabriel" and "Reine Geographie"), 257, 987–88, Braunschweig.

Whittlesey, D. S. (1954). "The regional concept and the regional method." In P. E. James and C. F. Jones, eds., *American Geography: Inventory and Prospect,* 19–68. Syracuse, N.Y.: Published for the Association of American Geographers by Syracuse University Press.

Windler, Hans (1954). "Zur Methodik der geographischen Grenzziehung am Beispiel des Grenzbereiches der Kantone Schwyz, Zug und Zürich." *Geographica Helvetica* 9:129–85.

Winkler, Ernst (1938). "Zur Frage der allgemeinen Geographie." *Atheneums-Schriften Zürcher Privatgymnasium,* Yearbook 1938:1–19. Reproduced in E. Winkler, ed. (1972). *Probleme der allgemeine Geographie,* 167–190. Darmstadt.

Zukin, Sharon (1991). *Landscapes of Power: From Detroit to Disney World.* Berkeley, Calif. 326 p.

J. G. GRANÖ

Johannes Gabriel Granö was born in Lapua, western Finland, on 14 March 1882 and died in Helsinki on 23 February 1956. After his father was appointed pastor to the Finnish community in Siberia, the family lived in Omsk for the period 1885–91 and then returned to Finland. J. G. Granö passed his school matriculation examinations in 1900 and enrolled at Helsinki University, but he regularly returned to Siberia in the summers while his father continued as pastor there in 1902–13. Granö graduated in 1906 and obtained his doctorate in 1911.

Granö was appointed assistant in geography at Helsinki University in 1902 and became docent in 1911. He was named to the chair in geography at the University of Tartu in Estonia in 1919 and subsequently became professor at Helsinki University in 1923, at Turku University in 1926, and at Helsinki once again from 1945 to 1950. He also served as editor in chief of the *Atlas of Finland* from 1923 to 1926. He was rector of Turku University from 1932 to 1934 and chancellor from 1945 to 1955.

Granö's first published research was concerned with the colonies of Finnish settlers in Siberia (1905) and the archaeology of northern Mongolia (commissioned by the Finno-Ugric Society in 1906, 1907, and 1909). At the same time he surveyed vast areas of Mongolia and investigated the glacial history of the Altai region. This was followed by work on the geomorphology of the Russian Altai in 1913–16, during which time he lived in Omsk. His Asian research came to an end with the Russian Revolution.

During his period in Tartu, Granö was responsible for setting up the Department of Geography and organizing local studies in the towns and countryside. His research interests during this period turned toward landscape studies and regional geography, and it was as a theoretician in these fields that he served as professor at Helsinki and Turku Universities. Granö was an honorary member of thirteen scientific societies and *Doctor honoris causa* of the Universities of Tartu and Turku.

He was married in 1913 to Hilma Ekholm (1882–1965), a graduate of Helsinki University and also a geographer. She took part in his 1913 and 1915 Altai journeys as a research assistant and helped in the production of the *Atlas of Finland* (1923–26). They had three daughters and one son, Olavi, co-editor of this volume.

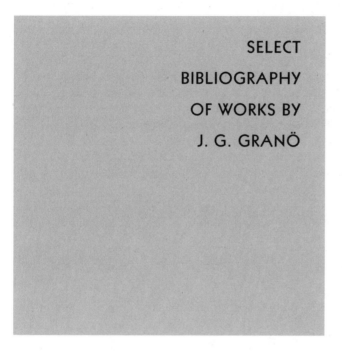

SELECT BIBLIOGRAPHY OF WORKS BY J. G. GRANÖ

A complete bibliography appeared in *Terra* 68 (1956):7–13.

Archaeology

1909 "Archäologische Beobachtungen von meinen Reisen in den nördlichen Grenzgegenden Chinas in den Jahren 1906 und 1907" *Journal de la Société Finno-Ougrienne* 26 (3):1–54.

1910 "Archäologische Beobachtungen von meiner Reise in Südsibirien und der Nordwestmongolei im Jahre 1909." *Journal de la Société Finno-Ougrienne* 28 (1):1–67.

"Über die geographische Verbreitung und die Formen der Altertümer in der Nordwestmongolei." *Journal de la Société Finno-Ougrienne* 28 (2):1–55.

Glacial Geology and Geomorphology

1910 "Beiträge zur Kenntnis der Eiszeit in der nordwestlichen Mongolei und einigen ihrer südsibirischen Grenzgebirge." *Fennia* 28 (5):1–230 (thesis).

1917 "Les formes du relief dans l'Altai russe et leur genèse. Etude morphologique." *Fennia* 40 (2):1–125.

1945 "Das Formengebäude des nordöstlichen Altai." *Publicationes Instituti Ge-ographici Universitatis Turkuensis* 20:1–362.

1952 "Land Forms and Relief, Suomi. A general handbook on the geography of Finland." *Fennia* 72:74–99.

Philosophy and Methodology of Geography and Regional Geography

1919–21 "Altai, vaellusvuosina nähtyä ja elettyä" I–II (Altai, seen and experienced during years of travel), Porvoo, 708 p. (Finnish and Swedish. New Finnish edition 1993).

1920 "Maantieteestä, sen asemasta yliopistossamme ja sitä meillä edustavista seuroista" (Geography and its status in Helsinki University and the Geographical Societies in Finland). *Terra* 32:13–50 (Finnish and Estonian with German summary in *Petermanns Geographische Mitteilungen* 66:229).

1922 "Eesti maastikulised üksused" (Landscape units in Estonia). *Loodus* 1:105–23, 193–214, 257–81 (Estonian with German summary 23 p.).

1923 "Maastik ja ümbrus" (Landscape and environment). *Loodus* 2: 321–27 (Lecture notes by Edgar Kant, Estonian).

1927 "Die Forschungsgegenstände der Geographie." *Acta Geographica* 1 (2):1–15 and *Svensk Geografisk Årsbok* 3:34–46 (German and Swedish, lecture held in Lund, Copenhagen, Stockholm, Hamburg, and Greifswald).

"Suomalainen maisema" (Finnish landscape). *Terra* 39:73–85 (Inaugural lecture, Turku, with German summary 2 p.).

1928 "Geographical regions." *Atlas of Finland* 1925 and *Fennia* 48:116–33.

1929 *Reine Geographie. Acta Geographica* 2 (2):1–202 (German and Finnish).

1930 "Maisematieteellinen aluejako" (Delimitation of landscape regions). *Terra* 42:1–26 (Finnish with German summary 4 p.).

1931 "Die geographische Gebiete Finnlands. *Fennia* 52 (3):1–182 (German and Finnish).

"Altain kasvillisuus" (Vegetation of Altai). *Terra* 43:1–20 (Finnish with German summary 4 p.).

1935 "Geographische Ganzheiten" *Petermanns Geographische Mitteilungen* 81: 295–302 (Reproduced in K. Paffen, ed., *Das Wesen der Landschaft* [Darmstadt, 1973], 3–19).

1938 "Itinerarien und Landschaftsprofile J. G. Granös aus Uranchai (Tannu-Tuwa) und Nordmongolei" (with A. K. Merisuo and Pentti Eskola). *Acta Geographica* 6 (1):1–54.

1941 "Mongolische Landschaften und Örtlichkeiten." *Acta Geographica* 7 (2):1–291.

1952 "Régions géographique et une méthode pour les délimiter." *Comptes Rendus du XVI Congrés International Géographique.* Lisbon 1949, 322–31.

"Geographic regions, Suomi. A general handbook on the geography of Finland." *Fennia* 72:408–38.

Settlement and Urban Geography

1905 "Siperian suomalaiset siirtolat" (Finnish colonies in Siberia). *Fennia* 22 (4):1–86 (Finnish with German summary 22 p.).

1923 "Hembygdsforskning i Estland" (Local study in Estonia). *Terra* 35:131–36 (Swedish and Finnish).

1928 "Vegetation and Distribution of Population." *Atlas of Finland* 1925 and *Fennia* 48:81–91.

1937 "Gehöfte und Siedlungen in Finnland." *Fennia* 63 (6):1–66.

1952 "Settlement of the country, Suomi. A general handbook on the geography of Finland." *Fennia* 72:340–80.

PURE GEOGRAPHY

AUTHOR'S PREFACE

The aim of this work is to demonstrate that the topic of geographical research is the human environment, understood as the whole complex of phenomena and objects that can be perceived by the senses. I will attempt to justify this view in the course of the discussion below and to consider the theoretical and practical consequences arising out of it.

The necessary data regarding this complex of phenomena that we perceive with our senses are provided by *scientific description,* which also forms the basis for its delimitation and definition. Furthermore, the process of formation of the object studied and its stages of development, together with the activity taking place within it—the geographical physiology of its forms in particular—and its significance as a part of a greater whole, can only be determined if we have detailed knowledge of the observable features of an area. It is therefore obvious that an exact and purposeful description of the area concerned from both a physiological and a genetic point of view is absolutely essential for geographical research.

I have been reproached for laying too heavy an emphasis on the descriptive aspect at the cost of the genetic aspect. Such criticism is unjustified. I think I have shown quite clearly in my earlier writings that I consider genetic interpretation an important part of geographical research. I have, indeed, wondered how anyone can think he could describe the genesis of a geographical complex without first having a clear picture of the kind of complex in question, that is, of its physiognomic and physiological nature. My real criticism, however, is directed at the kind of "geographical description" that lacks order and purpose and is often characterized by tedious verbosity. Unfortunately, not everybody seems yet to be convinced of the uselessness of such descriptions.

There are two methods that allow exact, clear, and concise geographical descriptions to be made, with similar determinations and delimitations of the geographical objects concerned based on these descriptions, namely, the use of a *descriptive system* with *exact terminology* capable of adequate generalization and *cartographic representation*. I shall therefore deal with these two methods in ample detail.

I greatly appreciate the valuable assistance I have received from a number of experts in various academic fields regarding the compilation of the terminology used in this book, both Finnish and Swedish, the majority of which was first published in the journal *Terra* in 1924. I wish to express my special thanks to Dr. Y. H. Toivonen, who participated in the work in the capacity of linguist and whose expert advice I have also been able to utilize in my later works.

I also owe a debt of gratitude to the Geographical Society of Finland and to the publishing company Loodus, in Tartu, for providing me with a number of plates originally used in the German edition of this book, some of which had been prepared earlier, and to Oiva Tuominen, student of geography, who compiled the index and helped me in proofreading the manuscript.

Turku, December 1929

J. G. Granö

INTRODUCTION

Pure Geography

From the earliest days of scientific geography, certain methodologists have emphasized that the actual objects of geographical investigation consist of the areas of the earth's surface which are delimited by natural boundaries or that these at least constitute units of major importance. At the beginning of the nineteenth century, the advocates of *reine Geographie* or "pure geography" (Bucher 30,[1] Wilhelmi 292, and others) recommended a classification of the earth's surface into "natural regions" (*natürliche Länder*), which, unlike political states, are not subject to short-term changes. Ritter (e.g., 230, cf. 130) talked about "land individuals" (*Landindividuen*) or "geographical individuals" (*geographischen Individuen*), and the importance of such entities (*Ganzheiten*) was further emphasized in the work of Marthe (163), Beck (16), and Matzat (170).

The branch of geography that studies *landscapes* aims at the same goal,

1. Numbers indicate numerical order in the references at the end of the book.

that is, the scientific description and interpretation of regional entities on the earth's surface (Sapper 241, Passarge 199–207, Schultz 254, etc.), starting out from the first tentative attempts by Oppel (190) and Wimmer (293).

Despite some attempts in that direction, the concept of landscape has not yet been defined in a manner that has gained general acceptance, any more than has that of "natural region" or "geographical individual." In some cases such terms mean only a visible complex, in others a perceived totality, and sometimes a complete entity made up of the perceived and mental environments.

Bryce (29) and Mackinder (156) in their time proposed the human *environment* as the object of geographical research, and Banse (7, 13), the herald of artistic geography, does the same to a certain degree, emphasizing the importance of the "milieu" and "soul" of a region, even though his definitions differ from those of the above-mentioned British geographers. While Bryce and Mackinder (see 278, p. 448) mention the forms of the earth's crust, its waters, the climate, and the resources that industries obtain from the areas concerned as factors which determine our environment, Banse considers all the influences which an area has on its people, although without analyzing them in detail.

These references are perhaps enough to show—despite the differences between the definitions and the weaknesses in them—that in the opinion of many methodologists, geography has a special duty to examine *regional units* regardless of whether they are called geographical individuals, landscapes, environments, or milieus.

This is the view that underlies the following methodological analysis. First of all, however, we should define exactly the purpose of this discussion. As far as we can see, the unit in question is not only of practical significance for the proper organization and classification of geographical material concerned with the earth's surface, but it is also the *essential object of geographical studies* and of the same central and governing importance as the plant in botany, the animal in zoology, a human being in anthropology, or a mineral in petrology. This is the kind of *pure geography* that I have tried to advocate in my published works and university lectures.

In the following section we shall examine in closer detail the direction that geographical research should follow, the matters it should concentrate on, and how geographical individuals and types of geographical systems should be defined and explained. Special attention will be paid to methods for delimiting geographical regions, methods which I have been able to examine in recent years by means of both maps and field studies and which therefore can be illustrated with examples from my investigations in Finland and Estonia.

Difficulties Encountered in Geographical Research

The picture we gain of a geographical entity is coherent and clear, largely because of the manner in which our senses are coordinated, and one might expect that by virtue of this framework of parallelism and synchronism it would also be easy to make qualitative and quantitative comparisons and to explain the significance of the various perceptual phenomena as means of characterizing the environment. The problems encountered are greater than might be expected, however. We are called upon to analyze and describe by the means we have at our disposal—our senses, instruments, words, pictures, and maps—the complex that surrounds us and which, figuratively speaking, exists in each of its constituent parts. This totality must be analyzed without prejudice in such a way that no phenomenon, no quantity, no substance is attributed a significance which it does not possess in the context of the actual environment or environmental group. The synthesis must also be handled just as purposefully. Only in this way can the object of study be presented to the listener or reader as a simplified entity of our making which is characterized by certain qualities, an organism of a certain kind, dependent in a certain manner on certain presuppositions and functions, and which does not rely for its homogeneity or individuality on factors deriving from the analytical process.

It must be openly admitted that in this respect we have more often failed than succeeded, and the task evidently requires further methodological work, but it is also a fact that neither writers of regional monographs nor men with practical experience—writers of textbooks and teachers of geography—have made adequate use of the methodological achievements of our discipline. Often the analysis strays onto the wrong paths and the synthesis is entirely forgotten. Regional geography divides the earth's surface into parts in various manners which take no account of the demands of the task being undertaken. The regional entity selected for examination has seldom led to a systematic description of interrelations, combined effects, and the genesis of the complex. On occasions things have gone so far that regional studies in which the task of description has been assigned to specialists in neighboring disciplines have been acclaimed as the best geographical monographs, overlooking the fact that the central geographical issues have been neglected. When each contributor deals only with his own narrow, specialized field, the coherent overall image characteristic of the area will inevitably receive too little attention, as will its division into regions.

We know, to use a striking parallel, that a given number of bricks and a given quantity of timber, metal, glass, and the like can be used to construct a wide variety of buildings suitable for different purposes and different environments and reflecting the skills of the builders in different ways. Experts on the quality of certain materials can examine the various building materials and scholars of history can say where they came from, how, when, and where they were produced and how and when they were transported to the site where they were found. In doing so, of course, they have not given a description of the actual buildings nor have they indicated whether a particular type of material or complex of materials is characteristic of certain types of building. Other experts are needed who can provide this information. Geography is thus not the sum of the knowledge of all the different disciplines associated with the examination of a certain part of the surface of the earth, nor is the entity surrounding us an indeterminate and featureless agglomeration of material.

The considerable difficulties and shortcomings associated with our work have evidently been the reason why most of us have sought fields of study beyond the limits of the geography described above, which is sometimes referred to, aptly enough, as geography proper as distinct from the kind of "geography" that surrounds it in an indeterminate sphere. We have tended to acquaint ourselves wherever possible with neighboring disciplines and have specialized at as early a stage as possible not in geography but in these other fields, so that our scientific work has only indirectly benefited geography as defined here. When we have occasionally had to deal with questions of regional geography and have been forced to relinquish our familiar and often very simple methodological premises, our helplessness has become all too obvious.

When considering the difficulty and endless variety of the tasks involved in a geography that examines regional units, the geographer certainly has every justification for avoiding research problems that lie beyond his discipline. Gradmann (82, p. 146) has expressed a justified wish that "The highest ambition of every geographer should be to pursue the study of pure geography for its own sake and to produce exemplary, concise, and classically perfect representations of natural landscapes. Then people will begin to understand us better."

Geography and Art

The defects referred to above have recently led to lively discussion and even sharp differences of opinion among geographers. Some (e.g., Banse 7–13, Younghusband 305) have taken the view that *scientific* geography is, at least to some extent, inferior to *artistic* geography. They maintain that scientific geography is unable to portray the environment as a living entity and that it is too tied to material concepts, oversystematized and exaggerated in its attention to exactitude and needless detail, with which it endeavors to disguise the hollowness of its results and the superficiality of the work done. Therefore, away with general geography, exclaims Banse. Regional geography must be raised from the status of a dry, unattainable science to the sphere of art. An accurate description and explanation of the beauty and sublimity of nature is the greatest geographical achievement possible, states Younghusband. "Geography also has to portray the beauty of nature. For my own part, I would go as far as to claim that such a portrayal of beauty constitutes the most important part of geography . . . It is as much our duty to be artists as exact classifiers, cataloguers, and scholars" (305, pp. 228–29).

Banse continues to develop his line of thought (9, p. 17) by claiming that what matters is not what we portray but how we portray it. It is conceivable, for example, that a penetrating examination of the works of Dostoyevsky would provide a more impressive image of Russia than could be obtained by studying the bedrock, soil, water, climate, and so on of the country in the manner we are accustomed to. An exclusively scientific approach to geography can be compared with a careful examination of the individual keys, notes, and strings of a musical instrument. This cannot take us very far, for what we want is to hear tunes and chords. Banse gives an example: We cannot conceive of the Orient as being only made up of limestone, an arid climate, and the flora of the steppes. No, we must also remember the parching heat of the sun, the scents of the sandalwood tree, amber and attar of roses, the wafts of ambrosian air from the blossoming meadows on which squat the black tents of the Bedouins.

Younghusband made the following statement in one of his speeches as president of the Geographical Society of London: "I hope therefore that the Geographical Society will finally realize that the tasks of geography include seeing the beauty of natural forms and events and comparing the special attractions of the various features with each other. This will even become the principal task of geography . . . We have formed a society in order to spread geographical knowledge and I hope and wish that in the future we shall look upon a knowledge of the beauty of the earth as the most important kind of knowledge to be disseminated" (305, pp. 209–10).

The significance of art for geographical description is undeniable, and we are convinced that if we were artists, we could give a much more characteristic portrayal of our objects of study instead of the present destructive and distorting description which arises from our clumsy approach and even our total disregard for the facts. But the fallibility of our approach is to be found in our own limitations, of course, not in those of science. As surely as there is an environment, it will continue to constitute an object of scientific investigation, and sooner or later geography will learn to treat it as such in a correct and scientific manner. It is too early to say that the scientific period in the history of geography is drawing to a close and that an artistic period is approaching before we have a perfectly clear picture of the nature of what we are studying and have developed serviceable methods, and before it has been shown what kind of results can then be achieved.

Would it not be quite inexcusable, however, for us to place principal emphasis on the arousal of aesthetic emotions and praise for the beautiful and sublime when carrying out our investigations and presenting our results to others, since to do so would be to consciously lay the path open to whims and caprices? Let us not be so rash as to believe that we could arrive at an objective concept of harmonies in space and rhythms in time in our description of the environment in the name of art. And would not scientific activity in fact be straying from the true path if the only thing we held as important were *how* we conduct our examination and not *what* we examine, *what* we present and *what* we explain?

1

BASIC CONCEPTS

1.1. The Perceived Environment

The notions that we possess of places and regions gained by personal observation are derived from the overall picture provided by all our senses, the validity of which depends on both the extent of the area we have perceived through our senses at any one time and the duration and degree of detail of this observation. The total impression obtained has a definite extent in both space and time, in that our faculty of sight determines its size and the duration of our lives its temporal boundaries.

In view of the spatially and temporally crucial position of the person who acquires this impression, it is reasonable to refer to it as *an environment perceived by human beings through their senses* or, briefly, *a perceived environment.*

The perceived environment forms the object of geographical research, an object which still belongs to *natural science* even though we also direct our attention to human beings and their activities insofar as these can be perceived with the senses and fall within the complex being studied. For us, nature does not consist only of uninhabited deserts and virgin forests, mountain ranges or open seas, but also of fields, villages, and towns. "Research in natural science examines the whole material world. It studies the products of both 'nature' and 'culture'" (Becher 15, p. 13).[1]

The object of geographical research as defined in this manner forms a special size category in a system into which the universe as a whole can be divided and which it is easy to imagine when examining the structure of this enormous whole. This system begins perhaps (cf. 15, p. 206) with the galaxies of the Milky Way, followed by progressively smaller units: groups of stars with their fixed stars and solar systems; our own solar system; the earth, its atmosphere and crust; continents and oceans; clouds, mountains, rivers, and so on; stones, plants, animals, and human beings; and, finally, the world of the microscope and ultramicroscope.

These "size categories" have to a certain extent influenced the classification and delimitation of the sciences, and we could identify the perceived environment as an important stage in this diminishing series. Its value and significance are in no way reduced by the fact that it embraces a number of smaller objects of study belonging to other disciplines and examined by those disciplines in their own particular way, nor by the fact that it serves as a part of a sequence of larger entities of which only a few fall within the realm of geographical research.

Since the perceived environment constitutes an influential and significant part of our lives, it is as justifiable an object of study as the elements, bounded in one way or another, which are present in it.

1.2. Phenomena

As we now set out to discuss geographically the properties of the perceived environment, we have first to emancipate ourselves from the influence of the neighboring sciences as far as the disposition and planning of the work is concerned. Our object of study is bounded in terms of place, but its observable properties are not dependent on the bedrock, water, or air to the extent that we are forced to use one or more of the systems of the neighboring disciplines as a starting point for our work. Instead, we are faced with the question of whether it would be advantageous to lay aside completely the barriers that our neighbors have used to divide the geographical whole into isolated compartments.

We can form concepts of environments and their objects by examining the features perceived by our senses which form their total image. In the case of the perceived environment, these features may be referred to as *phenomena*.

---

1. This statement does not prevent us from using the word 'nature' in its narrower sense to refer to everything that is not directly related to human activities.

They manifest themselves either as spatial properties, that is, *topological phenomena,* or as temporal properties, that is, *chronological phenomena,* and in both cases they can be either *qualitative* or *quantitative*. Naturally the classification of perceived phenomena must also take into account the senses with which they are perceived.

Without going into a more detailed examination of these phenomena, we can present an outline for a system which meets the requirements of this work:

A. Topological phenomena (existent phenomena)
    I. Qualitative phenomena
       a. General phenomenon: distribution (spatial grouping)
      b. Specific phenomena
         1. Visual phenomena: light sources, colors, forms
         2. Auditory phenomena: sounds
         3. Olfactory phenomena: smells
         4. Tactile phenomena: heat, wetness (humidity, moisture), resistance (pressure, obstructiveness, inclination,[2] bearing capacity)
    II. Quantitative phenomena
      a. General phenomenon: distance (spatial interval)
      b. Specific phenomena
         1. Size (spatial dimensions)
         2. Strength (intensity)
B. Chronological phenomena (occurrent phenomena)
    I. Qualitative phenomena
      a. General phenomenon: rhythm (temporal grouping)[3]
      b. Specialized phenomena
         1. Movement
         2. Change
    II. Quantitative phenomena
      a. General phenomenon: period (temporal interval)
      b. Specific phenomena
         1. Duration (temporal extent)
         2. Speed

2. This does not refer to the visible gradient observed when describing landforms, for example.

3. Geographical rhythm refers to the recurrence of similar phenomena in the course of time, "waves," which we perceive directly by our senses if we stay at the same location as time advances. We could also talk of rhythm in space, but in order to be able to grasp this we should be moving or, in the case of a visual phenomenon, at least let our eyes turn from one place to another. Volz uses the term "rhythm" in both senses (300, 301), while Sander regards the latter as more appropriate to geography (240).

No hard and fast boundaries exist between many of these phenomena and groups of phenomena. Some geographically significant groups will be examined in greater detail below.

1.3. Objects and Elements

When we examine the combinations of phenomena found in the perceived environment and the variations and changes in these, it is possible to detect regular dependence and coherence relationships existing within a given region. This enables us to observe certain *things,* the reality of which is proved by "the permanence of an affinity that follows given laws" (Winderlich 295, p. 7) and which we shall call *objects,* since they are characterized by the phenomena. Phenomena vary according to the time of day or season of the year, while objects are more permanent; the garden behind our house, for example, exists even if we cannot see it and the stones on the beach do not cease to exist even though they are covered by the tide or by snow in winter.

As pointed out above, the perceived environment as a whole is the object of geographical research. It comprises the objects of study of the various natural sciences so that we may expect to find exact definitions and terms for them in these sciences, and the most important of them have also acquired special names in our spoken language. It would be quite absurd not to use these achievements, of course, regardless of how important phenomena are as a basis for geographical research and as observable *properties* of objects.

The perceived environment is thus primarily a complex of phenomena that provides us with knowledge of the corresponding combination of objects, the actual focus of interest in our research. The different aspects and parts of this complex are for the most part already so well known to us on the basis of our experience and education, however, that the phenomena as properties that supply us with information on the objects are often only of theoretical significance. In practice our task becomes the observation of spatially and temporally changing phenomena, which are manifestations of familiar objects, in order to be able to define the geographical complex. It is here that the achievements of the neighboring disciplines are indispensable.

The same situation as for objects applies to the *substance* of which the entity under examination is composed, which is as essential for it as time and space. The examination of phenomena leads us to the achievements of physics and chemistry. For the present, it is enough for us to distinguish seven types of substance, or *geographical elements,* in accordance with the traditional classification, namely, *the earth's crust, water, air, vegetation, animal life, human beings,* and *artificial matter,* that is, the element composed of matter which has been processed or manufactured by human or animal agency. In contrast to artificial matter, all the other elements are composed of *natural matter.*

1.4. Object Location and Phenomenal Space, Object Duration and Phenomenal Duration

The objects whose properties we have termed phenomena have a geographical *location,* as do their specialized phenomena (see system of phenomena, above), occupy a given space, their *object location,* and exist for a certain time, their *object duration.* An object location is not, however, always the same as a *phenomenal space,* that is, the area or space in which the characteristics of the object can be observed, nor is object duration the same as *phenomenal duration,* the time for which the properties of the object are observed. In other words, object location and phenomenal space are not always syntopical, existent in the same place, nor are object duration and phenomenal duration always synchronic, existent at the same time.

Figure 1.1. Visual phenomena of the perceived environment.
(Lake Teletskoye in Altai, photographed by the author in July 1915.) The photograph conveys data mainly on the forms and their grouping, distances and size. The forms represented here are landforms (mountains, valley), water (the lake surface as a "water plain," snow and ice in the ravines on the slopes), vegetation (trees, herb terrain) and air, which includes clouds and the mist hanging over the water. The black-and-white photograph does not provide a correct impression of the sources of light (sky, the gleaming mirror of the water).

Sometimes it may happen that the object locations corresponding to certain phenomena are situated entirely beyond the region being studied, perhaps even beyond the limits of the earth. These are termed *distant phenomena* in contrast to *local phenomena,* which are situated within the region under examination.

The concepts of "object location" and "phenomenal space" differ slightly in meaning from one group of phenomena to another. Sight is the principal sense used for orientation, and it is with this that we primarily determine the position of objects. Because of the special nature of perception by the sense of sight, visual phenomena can be said to possess not only a phenomenal space but also special *occurrence locations.* Lights (sources of light), colors, and forms exist in certain locations as if bound to objects, in which they can be observed and seen at a certain distance. And especially in the case of forms it should be noted that the phenomenal space does not always begin at the limit of its occurrence location, for the larger the form is, the further away from it one has to move in order to be able to see it.

It is regarded as self-evident that an object location or occurrence location should be indicated on a map or profile representing a visible entity, but have optical phenomenal spaces ever been represented cartographically?

Auditory, olfactory, and tactile phenomena constitute a rather different group. We cannot say without recourse to experience or sight what object it is that causes them or where it is, and neither can we differentiate the occurrence locations of these phenomena from their phenomenal spaces. What interests us in this case is the phenomenal space itself, and it is this which is indicated on a map.

1.5. Quantity of Phenomena, Geographical Value, and Characteristics

An impression of the *quantity of phenomena* can be obtained by examining phenomena of a *quantitative kind* (see sec. 1.2). Temporal and spatial alterations in quantity can be illustrated by drawing lines, *phenomenal isopleths,* on a map or profile to connect points at which the quantity of a phenomenon is the same at the same point in time. This enables quantitative variations in phenomena to be portrayed over time and space, provided that we have appropriate measures for them.

When determining phenomena quantitatively it is important to bear in mind not only their size, strength, and duration, which directly affect their quantity, but also the distance between the observer and the thing observed, since the greater the distance, the smaller or weaker the phenomenon usually is. This significance of increasing the distance between the object and the observer is particularly obvious when using phenomenal isopleths on a map, as is the dependence of sensory perceptions on the quality of the air on

Figure 1.2. Characteristics, object location, and phenomenal space.
(The Oigur Valley in Altai, Mongolia, photographed by the author in July 1909.) The
water and vegetation are in reality characterized by color rather than form. The object
location of the mountain rising in the background is delimited by the bottom of the
valley at the foot of the mountain, while its phenomenal space begins only at the first
rider in the caravan (for definitions, see secs. 1.3 and 1.4).

different sides of the object location, for example (clarity, mistiness, etc.). In
some cases it may also be useful to make a cartographic representation of the
effect of increasing time intervals by the same method.

A comparison of the quantities of phenomena constituting geographical
factors in a region provides information on the *geographical value* of each feature. This kind of evaluation is a necessary part of geographical research.
Evaluation means distinguishing between what is important and less important, what is essential and less essential. When this geographical value is
taken into account, larger, stronger, more general, longer lasting, and more
frequent factors are regarded as more important and more essential than
those which are smaller, weaker, less general, more transient, and less frequent. There would be no need to emphasize this principle, which should be
followed in all purposeful research, if it were not that the nature of our object
of study all too easily tempts us to violate it.

The determination of value thus requires comparison. It tells us which phenomenon or phenomena, object or objects are characteristic and representative of the region being studied, in other words, what factor or factors constitute its *characteristics,* no matter whether these are temporal or spatial properties.

1.6. Field of Vision, Medium, and Substrate

It has become customary in geographical studies to structure the material and the presentation broadly speaking according to the material involved and to treat objects almost exclusively as forms. Such a method entails some degree of bias, however, if an examination of regional entities has to be carried out, since the environment as a perceived complex is not demonstrated to its full advantage.

In the following we shall attempt to develop a procedure with its principal structure based on phenomena which only secondarily takes account of material.

Once the necessary empirical material has been collected regarding the area to be studied, starting most conveniently with the specific, qualitative topological phenomena (see sec. 1.2), the treatment of the phenomena, objects, and material is structured in such a manner that the representation reflects as exactly as possible the spatial and temporal changes occurring in the entity perceived and that visual perceptions retain their leading position.

The perceived environment and its representation can first be divided into three parts by considering the qualitative phenomena, or actual perceptible phenomena, associated with the place. The first part, which is decisive for the purposes of geographical orientation and which in a sense governs and unites the entity under consideration, is the visible complex that makes up the environment, the *field of vision.* The second includes the aspects of heat, humidity (in certain cases wetness), pressure (wind, water, etc.), sounds, and smells that we connect with the matter surrounding us, mostly air and to some extent water, combining them into a complex which we call a *medium.*[4] The third and last part is the *base* or *substrate,* the significance of which as a

---

4. Just as we talk of a field of vision, we could of course use the term field of hearing as a particular major part of the perceived environment, as Seppä does in a popularized work *Luonnon löytöjä. Lintunäkymiä ja -kuulumia.* (Findings in nature: Ornithological sights and sounds) (Porvoo 1928), in an attempt to apply our system to the perceptual world, in which bird song is recognized as a significant element. We could treat touch in a similar manner, of course, but as geographers, we will be assessing the value of the various elements in the environment in a more correct manner if we place field of vision and medium in equal positions in our system.

Figure 1.3. An open natural field of vision.

(The Katun Valley in Altai, photographed by the author in September 1914.) The field of vision (see sec. 1.6) is characterized by landforms and forms of water and vegetation to roughly equal extents.

factor in the geographical whole is reflected especially in features of wetness, resistance, bearing capacity, and inclination.

The field of vision, which is covered by the canopy of the sky above, may be termed the *outer field* to distinguish it from the *inner field,* which is covered from above, at least for the most part, by parts of the earth's crust, vegetation, or artificial matter (e.g., in a dense forest, jungle, cave, or human dwelling). In an *open field of vision* we can see the sky to the side in most directions, while a *closed field of vision* is more or less clearly bounded. A *natural field of vision* is mainly composed of natural matter while an *artificial field of vision* is dominated by artificial matter.

A medium is *open* if it does not possess any *hindrances* that obstruct our movement; otherwise it is more or less *bounded.* It becomes a *closed medium* when it is isolated in such a manner that its phenomena differ from those "outside" in terms of heat, humidity, wind, and so forth, that is, when it is separated from the open air by special transparent (windows) or nontransparent *isolators* (walls, ceilings, floors).

Media are on the whole always *natural media,* while substrates, like fields of vision, can be either *natural or artificial substrates.* As in the case of media, substrates can also have hindrances that hamper movement.

1.7. Proximate and Distant Fields of Vision, Proximity and Landscape, and Milieu

The perceived environment was divided above into three parts on the basis of the nature of the phenomena: field of vision, medium, and substrate. Distance and the resulting variations in the quantity and quality of phenomena in space are so important, however, that we should now try to classify and divide the perceived environment into smaller areas defined in *space*.

The examination starts from a purely anthropocentric standpoint, that is, what a person, forming the center of his perceived environment, can observe at various distances. His perceived environment surrounds him to form a *perceptual space* in the same way as the objects he observes are surrounded by the phenomenal space as defined above.

As far as the field of vision is concerned, it is a well-known fact, and one which has been explained more precisely in certain investigations to be discussed below, that sources of light, patches of color, and forms can be perceived by the observer plastically and in their "correct," "real" size in places closest to the observer, who will also form a clear impression of the variation in distances radiating from the point of observation, so that his field of vision is perceived more or less "life-size" and "in perspective" in a plastic sense. This part of the perceived environment may be called the *proximate field of vision.*

We can acquire a direct, "true" conception of the size of objects only up to some tens of meters, and the plastic view will also become obscure at greater distances. The proximate field of vision will gradually give way to a picture-like *distant field of vision,* in which the sources of light, colors, and forms exist in "apparent" sizes and about which the perspective, shadows, and even our experience provide only indefinite information, so that we cannot formulate a "real" concept of the greatest of these "depths," for example, the distance to the horizón or celestial bodies.

It must be noted here that medium and substrate are obvious proximate complexes, as are auditory perceptions. We hear a sound in our ears, but to determine its origin we need experience and the other senses, as mentioned above. In this way, medium and substrate with their phenomena are located in the proximate field of vision, forming together with it a geographical whole which we shall call the *proximate environment,* or *proximity.*

This proximity is a close, intimate world, which we always inhabit and in the context of which we perceive our geographical object with all of our senses. This arena of our lives and activities is surrounded by *the distant environment,* or *landscape,* nothing more than a field of vision more or less tinged with blue by the air. We can see forms, light, shadows, and colors there in the distance, but we cannot hear, feel or smell anything from there, since we are inseparably here, in our proximity, although able to receive sounds, smells, heat, or humidity effects from beyond. Two main parts may be distinguished in the landscape: the *sky* and the *earth* (i.e., a combination of the earth's crust, water, vegetation, and artificial matter), which are separated by the horizon.

The small proximity of which we are the center is thus surrounded by a landscape in a zone several kilometers deep. No matter when or where we are making observations or what we are doing, we are always in this proximity. We perceive it constantly, day and night, whether we are "inside" or "outside," on the open sea, in the desert, or in the forest. We do not always perceive the landscape, however, be it an endless desert or a mountain range reaching to the skies, since that requires a certain minimum lighting and distance.

The perceived environment can thus be divided quantitatively into two major parts on the basis of distances in the field of vision, that is, the proximity, which we perceive with all our senses, and farther away the landscape, which extends to the horizon and which we perceive by sight alone.

When we take into account the fact that the proximity can be divided qualitatively into the proximate field of vision, the medium, and the substrate, we obtain the following classification, which also applies to phenomena:

Figure 1.4. An open natural proximity and natural landscape.
(A view northwards from Mt. Bobyrgan in the northern part of Altai, where the plain of western Siberia spreads out 500–600 m below. Photographed by the author in September 1914.) The picture provides data on the natural proximity, in the foreground (see sec. 1.7), including the proximate field of vision and the substrate with its obstacles. An open steppe plain looms in the distance, beyond the "gate" in the rocks, extending as far as the eye can see, to form an open landscape.

Figure 1.5. A natural closed landscape.

(The Bashkaus gorge in Altai, photographed by the author in June 1914.) The closed landscape (see sec. 1.7) is delimited by steep cliffs almost 1000 m in height.

I. Proximity (proximate environment)
    1. Proximate field of vision
    2. Medium
    3. Substrate
II. Landscape (distant environment)
    1. Distant field of vision
        a. Earth
        b. Sky

The decisive significance of visual perceptions justifies the use not only of the terms *open* and *closed landscape* but also of *open proximity, closed proximity, outer proximity,* and *inner proximity* (see sec. 1.6), while from the point of view of the quality of the matter involved we may speak of *natural* and *artificial landscapes* and *natural* and *artificial proximities.*

Although the above elements of the perceived environment were defined as complexes of phenomena, since only phenomena are directly perceivable, geographical research must naturally explain these wholes in terms of combinations of objects and matter as well. The order of discussing these various factors of the perceived environment depends mainly on practical considerations.

"Landscape" (*Landschaft*) is one of the favorite words for geographers at present. Passarge has developed a "landscape science" (*Landschaftskunde*) in a number of his investigations (199–207) and Obst takes the categorical view that landscapes constitute the actual object of study of geography (188, p. 21): "We are of the opinion that the geography of the future has an object of study of its own, namely, the landscape complex, which does not belong to any other discipline." I expressed similar ideas some years before Obst, but similarly did not provide any detailed definition of the concept of landscape. I wrote as follows (86, pp. 22–23 and 28–29):

> As a geographer, my most important, ultimate task is the explanation of nature . . . as a totality. By totality I do not refer to the whole surface of the earth, but the regional parts of this enormous field of investigation as landscape entities—wild natural landscapes or cultural landscapes, certain areas of land or sea . . . Geographical methods can and should change in many ways depending on my qualifications, the conditions under which I work and many other factors, but I must pursue the major goal, the total picture, a scientific synthesis, with unflagging consistency and using the shortest scientifically valid route, without allowing my interest to shift to tasks that do not actually belong to me and are probably of no use to my discipline. I thus have a special object of study, an objective of my own, an idea behind my work, and I can develop methods suitable for my purposes. I therefore possess all the facilities on which creative investigation, the highest level of scientific work, is based.

And again:

> The author is . . . convinced that general geography is an integral and necessary part of geography, but there is no reason to tie the entire general geography, in the form in which it is mostly defined nowadays, to geography at the present stage of the discipline . . . Up to a certain degree of profundity it belongs entirely to the geographers' field of study, and it may even be practicable to bundle up all this knowledge in one volume impregnated with the geographical approach from the point of view of propaedeutic instruction, but as far as I can see, only a part of it belongs to the geography of the future. This part is *landscape science,* by which I mean *a systematic classification of the geographical elements of the landscape, the examination of their origin and distribution, and the definition of landscape types based on this examination.*

Unanimity has not been reached, however, regarding the meaning of "landscape" in geography. The most common opinion seems to be that landscape begins *immediately* with the observer. Does this opinion claim that a person in a room or a dense forest sees a landscape around him? Opinions differ, however, about the phenomena contained in the landscape. Some writers, including Passarge, call the field of vision as defined above a landscape,[5] others the field of vision and medium, and there are still others who talk about the spiritual qualities of landscapes as relevant factors.

The psychologist Hellpach has defined the concept of "landscape" more accurately than have geographers (109, p. 348): "By landscape we understand the total sensory effect which a piece of land and the sky above it arouse in us." A landscape thus defined corresponds to the whole perceived environment, not only as a perceived entity but also, and mainly, as an "experiential environment."

Hellpach (109, p. 3), like some modern philosophers, talks about a social and a natural *milieu* but does not characterize in any further detail the relationship between the latter and landscape. I have earlier referred to the perceived environment as a geographical milieu (93). This term could also be used of the proximity, unless we consider it more correct to follow Taine and regard the entity composed of the perceived and mental environments as a milieu.

Banse, who emphasizes the central position of milieu as a geographical object of study, is as far as we know the only geographer who has attempted to examine this concept. According to him (8–13), milieu is "the soul of a landscape," the primary object of geographical research. It lies dormant in every landscape as a mysterious, structuring force, but it is impossible to define. It can only be experienced and felt. Such an object of study is naturally beyond the boundaries of the kind of geography we advocate here.

1.8. Immobile and Mobile, Invariable and Variable

Apart from topological phenomena of the environment, we also have to pay attention to chronological ones. We must not regard our discipline so exclusively as a spatial science that we entirely forget things that occur or are arranged in a temporal succession or lay these qualities of our object on one side as matters of secondary importance. It should also be kept in mind when planning fieldwork that one would obtain a more complete picture of the site

---

5. "Landscape is naturally what we see," defines Passarge in the introduction to the fourth volume of his *Vergleichende Landschaftskunde* (203, p. v). It must be pointed out, however, that Passarge discusses landscape in a much broader manner than this definition requires. We do not refer here to his concept of "natural landscape," a geographical entity with certain properties, which we will discuss later.

if one had the opportunity to make observations not only in as many parts of it as possible, but also *as frequently as possible,* at all seasons and in the course of a number of years.

Even in this case we are naturally interested in the whole site as an object and as a combination of objects, and it is the task of the neighboring sciences to examine the chronological phases of various materials and organisms.

This chronological discussion of the environment raises the question of "time scale" and the appropriate unit of time for such an examination, since nothing around us is actually permanent or invariable if we observe the environment in sufficient detail and over a sufficiently long period.

If we consider the significance of the seasons of the year, it may be most expedient to examine to what extent changes occur in the phenomena making up a complex in the course of one year. It is the geographical value of each occurrence that determines what should be taken into consideration.

We observe both immobile and mobile things, both invariable and variable things in our environment in the course of the time unit we select for examination. We also notice that both immobile and mobile things can be either invariable or variable, or conversely, both invariable and variable things can be either immobile or mobile. All this is relative, however, since these properties operate on a continuum, although in spite of this they are of great practical value as concepts.

To take an example, we see that although landforms are stationary, they are covered with snow and ice in winter, or we notice how the various forms of the vegetation are immobile and yet they grow, break into leaf, bloom, bear fruit, and wither. But we know that there are places where these immobile forms are far less variable and far more stable as *factors in the perceived environment* than in our northern land. The forms of artificial matter are perhaps more or less invariable in terms of our time units, but some of them, namely, vehicles, are capable of moving from one place to another at varying speeds within our perceived environment. Human beings and animals are invariable in the distant field of vision, despite their great mobility.

The perceived environment can thus also be divided into major parts by classifying its temporal phenomena, so that we obtain the *immobile,* phenomena that are tied to a place, the *mobile,* formed of constituents moving from one place to another, the *invariable,* being the same the whole year round, and the *variable,* which change in appearance.

1.9. Cause and Activity, Events and Formations

The temporal variation in the perceived environment analyzed here is proof of vital functions and development, so to speak, occurring in the complex. What we actually observe during a certain period provides only a partial, incoherent idea of this activity, however, since our object has many things about it that we cannot directly observe with our senses but nevertheless cause changes in phenomena and often lead to the development of new phenomena.

The various parts of the environment are connected by the tightest conceivable network of causes and activities, and innumerable threads of causality, interaction, and cooperation are intertwined in the geographical complex.

When the research worker concentrates on cause and activity, the phenomena assume a different character and become rather the results behind which we look for certain prerequisites that have brought them about. The threads of activity end in phenomena, and our task is to investigate where these threads come from. Our innate tendency to search behind properties for objects having these properties is activated. We look for them behind the curtain of phenomena as something more stable and real than the variable outer form, and in our opinion each of them is a distinct center of activity, so that together they form a kind of working community. We hold on to this even at the risk of allowing philosophers examining causality to claim that science has passed beyond such a stage of primitive thinking. And since we are now setting out to examine cause and effect from this point of view, it is reasonable to examine the *structure* and *composition* of objects in order to obtain a correct picture not only of the functions of these objects but also of their capability for resistance when various forms of activity come to bear upon them.

A variety of *agents* thus operate in our environment, and these interest us as the primary causes of phenomena. Each of them has its own *sphere of influence,* which can vary considerably in size, up to the whole surface of the earth, for instance.

We know, however, that the existence and quality of phenomena must depend not only on given agents but also on the *targets of their activity.* The nature of a temporal phenomenon and the result of an activity depend on the properties of both the agent and target. This also means that the perceived environment can be regarded as a *physiological entity,* the various factors involved in which are in a relationship in which the concepts "agent" and "target" are only relative, dictated by the practical situation.

Be that as it may, the result of the interaction between an agent and a target can be defined as an *event in time and a formation in space,* the latter in particular being taken to mean a perceptible result. Psychological agents, or *stimuli,* targets, and intellectual *achievements* do not belong to our field of study as such, although they must be taken into consideration in geographical investigation, of course, to the extent that they have an influence on the perceived environment.

The facts presented here regarding the physiology of the perceived environment are mainly concerned with the parts played by the objects in the complex. Analysis of these contributions is a highly important task for geography, and its successful completion calls for a knowledge of the natural laws and forces that form the basis for the geographical whole with its agents and targets, to which each tenable genetic investigation leads. But there is no reason to examine their significance in this connection.[6]

1.10. Geographical Harmony and the Interaction Cycle

No matter how independent and unique the activities of many objects functioning as geographical agents may seem, these activities are still tied in various ways to the spatial and temporal environment. Such aspects should be considered when describing activity, that is, first, activity in the form in which it is characteristic of an agent anywhere and at any time and, second, the significance of a given location, which changes or directs the activity. We know, for instance, that the functions of elevations in the surface of the earth are in some cases characterized by a dissipating force: water flows, snow slides down, and soils move in different directions on account of gravity on the slopes. Depressions, on the other hand, gather water and loose material from different directions into their lowermost parts because of this same force. This dissipating and collecting activity, nevertheless, varies in nature from one place to another, depending on precipitation, wind direction, weathering, and many other factors.

When researchers have familiarized themselves with the events and formations associated with the site, they can state the extent to which the phenomena observed are products of the present time. Everything that is a result of recent activity is *harmonious,* and the more a geographical whole possesses such elements, the more harmonious it is. But a research site may also have formations that cannot be the creations of modern activity. They are *disharmonious* and can be *ancient formations* as opposed to *modern* ones, or *foreign formations,* originating in other places and formed either in modern times or earlier, as opposed to local ones.[7]

Just as the environment has special spatial and temporal characteristics, these also apply to the *interaction* occurring in it. This interaction, which is

6. Hettner discusses geographical causality in detail (125, pp. 252–75). Spethmann's *Dynamische Länderkunde* (260), which emphasizes the physiological aspect, also includes some interesting opinions.

7. These terms have been adopted in the geographical literature mainly under the influence of Passarge. The terms harmonious and disharmonious are used by many writers in a sense different from that above, however.

special in one or more respects, has certain boundaries in time, in that it arises, develops to its climax, weakens and ceases. A period characterized by a certain kind of interaction is called an *interaction cycle,* or simply a *geographical cycle.* The well-known American geographer, William Morris Davis, who was the first to define the concept of cycle with respect to erosion of the earth's crust, has examined a number of *natural interaction cycles* (36–38). With appropriate adaptations and supplements, this method can also be used to deal with geographical interaction of other kinds.

1.11. Geographical Regions

We have indicated that as observers we are surrounded by two concentric areas that have no exact boundaries, namely, the small proximity adjacent to us and the much larger landscape delimited by the horizon. The circles defining these areas move from one place to another as we move, so that new elements continuously emerge in our field of vision as others disappear from it. Our proximity and landscape move in the direction of our movement to new phenomenal spaces, and the anthropocentric spaces of our perception cover new areas bound to objects and the surface of the earth and affecting our senses in various ways.

It is, nevertheless, obvious that in our geographical work we cannot be satisfied with these anthropocentric entities or with the typology of the perceptual environment, which geography is probably capable of establishing. We need entities that have fixed boundaries, are definable with regard to their phenomena and objects, and are earthbound, that is, "natural regions" or "geographical individuals," as discussed in the Introduction.

What route do we have to take to progress from the anthropocentric entities to ones with fixed boundaries, from a world of types to that of reality? We have in Finland, for example, not only an enormous number of anthropocentric environments but also some easily definable landscape types, such as a lake landscape or an archipelago (Granö 93). How should the geographical individuals of Finland be defined? Do we possess a rational method for doing this, or do we have to divide the country into regions in a more or less instinctive manner? Do geographical individuals of different size categories exist, or are their dimensions determined in advance?

It easy to answer these questions from a purely theoretical point of view, no matter how complicated the practical side of the matter is, as we shall see later on. A simple abstraction will lead us from anthropocentric environments to complexes related to the surface of the earth, which possess fixed boundaries, that is, to *regions and areas which constitute uniform complexes in some way as far as their landscape or proximity features are concerned,* but the average size of which can at least to some extent be determined by practical needs, although bearing in mind that the degree of unity diminishes as the size of the region increases, as a result of the greater variability in perceived environments. The largest possible geographical entity is the whole surface of the earth, while the smallest has the size of the minimum part of a proximity which can exist as an entity. We are especially interested in size categories that correspond in area to an open landscape or an open proximity.

It is not a great step from this to the idea that our principal task is to determine and delimit particular small areas corresponding to proximities but having fixed boundaries, each with its own specific proximity characteristics, and particular larger areas corresponding to landscapes and characterized by specific landscape features. We take all phenomena in our immediate environment into consideration when examining the former areas, but only a distant field of vision observable from a given minimum distance when examining the latter.

We could refer to areas defined in this manner and corresponding anthropocentric areas as proximities and landscapes. I have done so earlier, and the words *landscape* and *natural landscape* are common currency in our discipline in this sense. But in order to avoid confusion and misunderstandings, it is better to introduce other terms for these "fixed" entities. As a general term we could thus propose the expression *geographical region,* the area corresponding to proximity could be called a *vicinity,* and that corresponding to landscape a *geographical locality,* or in brief, a *locality.*[8]

We can thus formulate the following definitions:

A vicinity is an area corresponding to a proximity but having fixed boundaries and characterized by environmental phenomena.

A locality is an area corresponding to a landscape but having fixed boundaries and characterized by phenomena related to the distant field of vision.

The scientific observation, description, and thorough examination of these and other entities, which are in some sense coherent in terms of their perceived environment, is the primary task of geography. This is the meaning of our highly generalized definition of the perceived environment as the object of geographical research. All phenomena of the proximity and landscape should, of course, be dealt with systematically when examining these entities, but even so, not all such phenomena are always directly taken into ac-

---

8. Sölch (268) uses the term *chora* (Greek Χωρα or Χωροσ, region, landscape) for regions that are geographically uniform, and distinguishes between "physiochora," which are uniform in their nature, and "cultural chora," which are homogeneous in their culture, using the term "geochora" to refer to a region that is uniform in its nature and culture to a certain extent. He maintains (268, p. 27) that attention should also be paid to the various causal combinations of factors when determining these chora. Marthe talks of "choros regions" (163) in approximately the same sense as Sölch speaks of "geochores."

count when defining them. These spatial entities are coherent to a certain extent, that is, they have a variable number of characteristics, but it is necessary to insist on there being more than one characteristic, since otherwise we could not regard the area to be defined as geographically coherent to any extent. It is also obvious that we cannot regard an area characterized by phenomena perceived with only one sense as a vicinity. The phenomena to be considered in each case are determined by their geographical value.

It follows from the definition of landscape that a geographical locality is at least as large in area as that part of the earth's surface that is delimited by the horizon of an open landscape and can often be considerably larger if its characteristics are uniform over an extensive area. Our assertion that locality corresponds *roughly* to landscape in area must therefore not be taken too seriously. The size of the area is not the decisive point here, but the *degree of uniformity.* In this sense we have to make similar demands with respect to a locality to those that can be made regarding a landscape, which is situated within the boundaries of a locality. The boundary of a locality is the point at which this uniformity of landscapes ends, for it should be noted that uniformity can be understood on a more detailed scale or on a broader one depending on the area concerned, since as mentioned earlier, small areas can be more uniform than large ones. In other words, the crucial factor in the determination of localities is the degree of uniformity that the landscapes of an area possess. In the same way, actual surface area is a secondary factor in the determination of vicinities, the decisive factor being the *degree of uniformity of the corresponding proximities.*

Various small *sublocalities,* which constitute homogeneous entities, and even smaller parts of these, can be distinguished in a locality, particularly by reference to phenomena that do not characterize the entire locality, regardless of the degree of uniformity of the locality *as a whole.*

Geography also needs larger units than the locality, however. Any number of relatively similar localities can be combined into *geographical districts,* and these again into larger units, *geographical provinces,* and even into *continents.* With respect to chronological phenomena, the earth's surface can be divided both horizontally and vertically into *landscape zones.*

Large and to some extent homogeneous neighborhoods can be defined in a similar manner by examining the degree of uniformity in proximity phenomena. When one bears in mind the significance of climatic elements in the medium, it is easy to understand how instructive a comparison between *proximity zones* defined in this manner and climatic zones can be.

In the determination of large geographical entities the uniformity of as many phenomena as possible should be regarded as more important than detailed near-perfect homogeneity with respect to a few properties.

For some geographical tasks, particularly divisions into regions, as discussed later, we need knowledge of the extent to which *various phenomena* characterize areas that differ in size and degree of uniformity. The region to be examined is then divided into parts with reference to its size, the degree of uniformity, and the variations in each phenomenon. We can then talk about *phenomenal spaces* when examining proximity phenomena and *phenomenal regions* in the case of landscape phenomena, and the term *phenomenal zone* can also be used if necessary.

It is perhaps relevant for comparison purposes to explain here how the leading landscape specialists Sapper and Passarge understand geographical entities with permanent boundaries. The former points out (241, pp. 5–6) that a geographical landscape differs from an artist's landscape in that it is "the sum of essential impressions of the landscape which the senses acquire by observing from one or more places . . . A significant difference between the landscape of an artist and that of a person who is describing the natural environment is that the former is only a snapshot in a way, while in the latter case movement occurring in nature during the examination can and must be taken into consideration." He thus also emphasizes the significance of temporal phenomena as characteristics of landscape but does not distinguish between an anthropocentric landscape and a geographical region with fixed boundaries.

"Natural landscape" (*natürliche Landschaft*) in the principal terminology of Passarge roughly corresponds to locality, "partial landscape" (*Teillandschaft*) to sublocality, "part of landscape" (*Landschaftsteil*) and "form element" (*Formbestandteil*) to parts of the locality, and "landscape region" (*Landschaftsgebiet*) to geographical province, but only in terms of *size,* as is implied by the term "form element," emphasizing only one phenomenon. Passarge defines a "natural landscape" as follows (201, p. 13 and 202, I, p. 165): "A natural landscape is an area which is uniform in terms of climate, vegetation, surface structure, water, geological structure, and soils." Although "natural landscape" and "geographical locality" are similar in size, certain crucial differences still exist between them. First, we have taken into consideration *only the distant field of vision* in the definition of localities, but Passarge also includes climate, geological structure, and soil in his definition of "natural landscapes," the geographical significance of which we do not emphasize when determining regions, and second, we also consider visual phenomena representing the animal kingdom, human beings, and artificial elements essential and significant within the landscape, whereas Passarge does not include these in his "natural landscape."

Besides these geographers who have discussed questions of landscape profoundly in their works, many others have also expressed their views on this matter. Friederichsen includes the genetic aspect in his definition of a "natural landscape" (60, p. 13), which also involves the cultural features of the geographical complex. In his opinion, these areas "are uniform in terms of climate, vegetation, surface structure, water, geological structure, and soil, and in terms of features of cultural geography dependent on the former." Even before this definition, Schultz had defined the regions of Russian Turkestan taking features of human geography into consideration as well (254). Hettner places even higher genetic demands on geographical regional entities in his investigation into the *geographical division* of the earth's surface (121, pp. 95–96): "Each natural regional division should aim at being genetic, that is, it must reproduce the causal relationships that exist in reality."

1.12. Unit, Individual, and Type

The terms "unit" and "individual" are used in various senses in the geographical literature. Some emphasize the uniformity of a region, while others focus on the explicitness of its boundaries, and still others attempt to consider not only the perceptible degree of uniformity and the boundaries but also function and genesis, and the terms have been used side by side in all these cases.

To avoid misunderstandings we would actually need three terms: (1) for uniform regions, (2) for entities with distinct boundaries, and (3) for uniform regions with distinct boundaries. It would be a victory of sorts if it could be agreed that the term "unit" should be used in all these cases and that "individual" would be reserved only for uniform regions with fixed boundaries. Units would thus include islands, lakes, and mountains, for instance, even when not uniform in terms of their landscapes and proximities, since they are entities with distinct boundaries. But we would call them geographical individuals only if they were also homogeneous.

From the point of view of geography, which treats the perceived environment as a whole, it is individuals that are considered interesting in the first place. These include localities, districts, geographical provinces, and vicinities, for example.

By comparing geographical phenomena and various entities and by examining the quantity and quality of the characteristics of the latter, we can define *geographical types* that form the *geographical system*. The types are in a way ideal formations that we never find in nature in such a form. Despite this we use type names when speaking of the formations we have seen in nature, since this is a brief and clear way of describing their characteristic features. The system of types is a model with which reality can be compared. We need it just as we generally need purposeful definitions and systematized concepts, although geographers sometimes consider this unnecessary. "For system is the form in which a whole is grasped and mastered in as detailed and coherent a manner as possible . . . It entails comprehensiveness, clarity, and simplicity" (Vannerus 285, pp. 1–2).

2

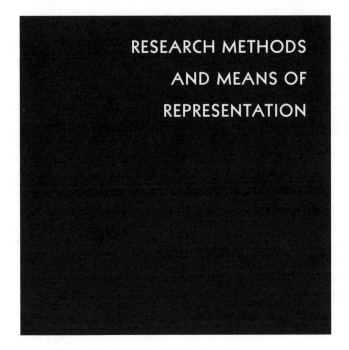

RESEARCH METHODS AND MEANS OF REPRESENTATION

2.1. Significant Viewpoints

In our opinion *geography is a theory of human perceived environments and of regions on the surface of the earth which are uniform in this respect.* We do not regard our object of study as extending to the psychological or social environments created by the varied activities of human societies in the fields of economics, religion, science, the arts, and administration or by family life.[1] Our methods of research and presentation depend in each case on the nature of the demands set for the scientific treatment of these objects.

We mentioned above that even the first methodologists of geography aimed at an understanding of the perceived whole, and some of them also seem to have realized that geographers must familiarize themselves thoroughly with the region they are studying and examine not only one phenomenon characteristic of it or a selection of such phenomena, but all of them. They understood that the earth's surface is an enormous mosaic of environ-

1. Our point of view is similar to that of Schlüter (242–49) and Penck (210).

ments but also realized that these innumerable "individuals" are separated by indeterminate boundary and transitional zones.

The following citation from a work of Wilhelmi from 1820 is highly illustrative in this sense (292, p. 50, compare 179, pp. 14–15):

> Nature's influence is beneficial everywhere, and therefore it is soft and easy; it offers its bounties silently and in an unpretentious way; its features change gradually, its pictures and images mostly merge like the colors of the rainbow so that they can be distinguished only where they occur separately and not where they occur side by side. Such is the transition from one zone to another, the distribution of animals, the mixing of tribes. Seldom are opposites in direct contact. Despite this, the creations of nature are clear and distinct, provided we examine them in their perfect forms and not those occurring in the boundary or transitional zones. The nature of a picture separated from its environment cannot depend on one single feature but on the peculiarity of all its features or the most significant ones and on the special nature of their cooccurrence. These areas thus cannot be distinguished on the basis of height or depth, which are the least significant properties as such and become significant only if they have an effect on the living conditions of the fauna and flora. Therefore height and depth, mountains and rivers, soil and temperature, the light or dark color of the sky, the cheerful blaze of colors among plants, or their dark shadows, the abundance or scarcity of vegetation, cultivated areas or deserts, and the variable forms of humans and animals which affect their environment and shape it; it is only the combination of all these features together that makes the picture complete by enlivening it and characterizing it in a variety of ways.

But it is naturally not enough to appreciate the perceived environment in this way, nor to observe the cooccurrence of phenomena alone. We must aim at a comprehensive understanding of this whole, even though we are not yet able to manage this difficult task, the importance of which was first emphasized by Mayr (172, compare 289, p. 545) and especially Matzat (170, see 290, p. 552). In order to find the right approach we need concepts and a system, we need investigations that concentrate particularly on the perceived environment as a whole and that are carried out in a natural environment. And expedient methods must also be developed, since our object requires, at least in part, different methods from those employed in the other sciences in order to lead to any results.

It is significant that statements about the need for methods for dealing with entities also occur in the philosophical literature. Neeff distinguishes three main methods in his study *Der Geist der Wissenschaft* (The spirit of science, 180): (1) formation of rules, (2) formation of history, and (3) formation of wholes. The last of these, the "teleological investigation of entities," sets the "awareness of the *whole* composed of forms of reality as the aim of investigation. Then it is no longer a question of mathematically defined relationships between various parts or dimensions, nor of historical agents . . . , but of how the parts, the *members,* are united into a harmonious whole" (p. 69). A research method that forms entities thus supplements the above two methods of the mathematical and historical sciences in significant ways. We can agree with Neeff that "a hasty and biased restriction of the theoretical organization to one field of activity alone, for example, to an 'exact,' or mathematical discipline, would not lead to the universality desired but to the narrow outlook of the theorists" (p. 113).

The development of a method that forms entities is also necessary to fend off the danger lurking on the other side, since it may easily happen "that the unbridled 'synthetic' desire for seeing, which is found in confused, fantastic heads especially in our times, may abandon methodological certainty and consistency and go astray, which will not lead to a synthesis of what is observed but rather will cause confusion and chaos, which disturb successful progress toward the clear goals of the investigation" (p. 113).

According to Neeff, an entity can be of various kinds. It can be an organism, for instance, or a culture, and among the scientific disciplines it is ecology that "forms entities." The way in which Neeff understands an entity becomes clear from the following:

> A whole as such is not a law or a history . . . Each whole is, as the term already suggests, something complete, confined as such. Parts cannot be easily removed from it without disturbing or eliminating it. We want here to emphasize the restricting "easily," since an organism may lose parts during its development, or parts may be removed from it without changing its nature as a whole. Elements may also disappear from cultural entities and despite this, or perhaps precisely for this reason, the culture may begin to flourish, since these elements may have been disturbing factors. It is important to bear in mind this relativity attached to a whole, in order to avoid regarding it as something absolute that might exist alone. Every whole is relative and composed of the relationships between its parts. It is only this peculiarity that makes it a whole" (pp. 105–6).

We can also agree with this point of view when considering the perceived environment and geographical entities with fixed boundaries. We naturally comprehend and describe our environment in the manner in which every healthy person sees it. This must be mentioned to avoid misunderstandings, although it is known that we are restricted to our senses, no matter how mathematically accurate may be the methods or instruments we use in our work, and that "nature" is nothing but "the variegated, ever changing play of our perceptions" (97, p. 289). Despite all speculations about what is real and existent, the perceived environment that we observe and comprehend with our "common sense" is of crucial and central importance. Or, as Becher admits (15, pp. 108 and 109) after a profound discussion of these problems: "Ultimately, we have only one way . . . , which the logicians and critical philosophers are not ready to accept: Only a reliance on the natural belief that arises from human common sense can help us forward here." And further, having stated that a belief in reason can be corrected to some extent through the medium of scientific achievements, for example: "In spite of this the natural belief of common sense remains a necessary prerequisite for our sense of reality."

The daily interpretation of our environment, which is familiar to everybody, is tied to movement and—if we may say so—to the use of time. We move from one place to another, making observations from various points, on various sides and at different times. Our field of vision is bounded by the horizon or by closer objects on the surface of the earth, but the celestial bodies in immeasurable space shine their light on our environment from huge distances. We hear different voices from varying distances, and olfactory and tactile perceptions often complement our concept of the environment in a significant manner.

Science specifies this total picture by means of comparisons, measurements, and a systematic concentration on topological and chronological aspects in order that the object of study can be described, defined, and analyzed according to its nature and with a sufficient degree of accuracy. Geographical description and explanation will be examined below, but it should be noted here that we are discussing the regional entities that we have defined in roughly the same manner as that in which the biological sciences treat their objects. When *determining* geographical individuals and *describing* them we take into consideration the perceivable features of the environment in the same manner as a botanist who writes down the form and size of a plant, its color and smell, growing season, and flowering and fruiting times. And in just the same manner as a botanist starts to examine the vital functions and stages of development of his plant, utilizing the achievements of certain neighboring disciplines, we set about *interpreting* geographical entities. Neither we nor the botanist will ask how the various perceptions and total impressions arise, since that is the task of psychology and human physiology. "The idea of the whole guides us on our way from one part to another and leads us to perceive those parts as members of the whole. The teleological method thus attempts to understand the significance of members as agents in the whole, that is, it looks for a harmonious relationship, since none of the members is a whole in itself . . . By structuring the organic whole methodologically, it both separates and unites phenomena. This enables the feature that unites the whole to be recognized as running through all of its parts" (Neeff 180, p. 111).

The main factors of the perceived environment are soon revealed in such a treatment, not only space, which is of fundamental significance to geography—the *power of place*—and the value of location and distribution, which our methodologists from Ritter and Fröbel onward have emphasized in their definitions of its nature and tasks, but also the *power of time,* which has attracted much less attention.

The significance of space was emphasized by von Richthofen in the following words in the first part of his voluminous study of China (224): "Geography is a science of the power of place on the earth, manifested in local variation." Similar claims have been heard lately, especially from Krebs (143, p. 94): "Geography is the science of place: it is above all from place and spatial location that our investigations must set out." An inquiry by Sölch into "natural boundaries" (268) and the paper "Landscape units of Estonia," published by the present author some years ago (88), are also worth mentioning in this connection, since they concentrate on place in particular. Davis (38, pp. 7–8) regards geography as "the geology of the present," as only "one present day in a long series of present days, by means of which the past, which knows no beginning, is pushed into an endless future." The definition of geography formulated by De Geer (41, p. 2) assigns priority to *distribution*: "Geography is the science of the present-day distribution of phenomena on the earth." Huntington represents a similar point of view (128, p. 1), as do Mackinder (156, compare 278, p. 447) and Herbertson (111), to mention a few earlier scientists. De Martonne also considers distribution significant (168, p. 24): "La géographie moderne envisage la répartition à la surface du globe des phénomènes physiques, biologiques et humains, les causes de cette répartition et les rapports locaux de ces phénomènes." According to Hettner, the object of study of geography consists of local conditions on the earth's surface, but he points out in a later publication: "Geography should not be a science dealing with the distribution of various objects, but the 'content' (*Erfüllung*) of places. It is *spatial science,* just as history is temporal science" (125, pp. 124–25). Fröbel formulated his view in the following way in the 1830s (quoted by Müller 179, pp. 15–16): "One should apparently regard the examination of the grouping of things on the earth as the principle of geography."

When we consider the fact that distribution is also a spatial phenomenon, it is clear that all the above definitions emphasize the power of place in a stricter or broader sense. Only Davis and De Geer also outline the task chronologically, in that according to the former geography examines the *present-day* surface of the earth, and according to the latter the *present-day* distribution of phenomena.

2.2. Description and Interpretation, Evaluation and Comparison

The methodological literature discusses extensively the significance and value of analysis and synthesis, induction and deduction, and description and interpretation. Leutenegger (149) provides an overview of the situation. However passionate the debate over the advantages of an exclusively or pre-dominantly inductive or deductive approach may have been, most geographers now usually agree that all of the above methods can be appropriate depending on the stage of our work and that in many cases the application of various methods side by side leads to the best results.

The latter claim does not apply to *description* and *interpretation,* since most of us apparently want to keep these two apart,[2] and in our opinion for good reason. No clear boundaries actually exist between these two methods, since interpretation is also description in a way, and scientific description, which requires a wealth of knowledge and a purposeful and methodical approach and which is often also based on measurements that call for skill and the use of various instruments, is undoubtedly also interpretation at the same time. Such is the geographical description that aims at delimiting uniform regional entities and constructing definitions of these, for instance. Stadler may well be right in saying: "All science is descriptive; there is no distinction between interpretive and descriptive science" (quoted by Leutenegger 149, p. 5).

On the other hand, it is apparent that description and interpretation are at least different stages of scientific operation which it is expedient to keep apart for practical reasons. We should therefore *first* describe the geographical object as it exists in time and space, and this can *then* be followed by an interpretation based on this description and, if necessary, on material from other sources. It should be borne in mind that description, if performed properly and systematically, has perhaps a more permanent value than an interpretation based on assumptions of various kinds, no matter how much the latter may reflect the scientist's power of deduction and ample scientific imagination. Despite all its dryness, exact description deserves more respect, since it bears the stamp of reality, even though it is true that the human mind celebrates its greatest triumph only in interpretation. Description should therefore be impoverished by neither a historical analysis resting on more or less flimsy grounds nor genetic systems of a kind whose validity cannot be vouched for. When drawing up a type system to be used for geographical

2. Passage in particular emphasized this in his landscape science studies, but Wimmer (293) already distinguished between interpretive geography, a special kind of "geosophy," and descriptive "geography."

description, for example, it is more correct and safer to hold fast to directly observable facts.

If we regarded the task of geography as being the *complete* description of the perceived environments of the earth, precisely in the form in which they exist and in every detail, our demand would be impossible to meet, since although reality is continuous in time, it is also endlessly heterogeneous in space down to the smallest detail. "Try just once to 'describe' reality exactly 'as it is' and to include it and all its details in concepts in order to obtain a representation of it, and you will soon be convinced of the irrationality of such an operation, since the reality you have observed will prove to be *endlessly diverse,* and will seem to increase in diversity the more we examine it and its details, since even the smallest element will contain more than any human being will be able to describe, even to the extent that the totality of what he can include in his concepts and thus appreciate in his consciousness is absolutely nothing by comparison with everything that he has to omit" (Rickert 228, p. 33).

Although we thus restrict our task to perceived environments, it is not possible to provide a complete description of these either. The task must be further reduced and the corpus to be studied selected. We therefore try to discover that which is *characteristic,* the geographical *essence* by *evaluation* and *comparison.* We examine nature from a certain point of view, we define concepts and formulate entities. To quote Rickert (228, p. 37), we cut sections through the continuum of reality, perfectly aware of the fact that everything that is left between the lines of these sections will be lost. "For no matter how close to each other we try to place the lines, the continuous and inexhaustible variety of reality will disappear between them without our realizing it. Our concepts can thus be used only to build bridges across the stream of reality, regardless of how short the individual spans are."

Hence, at best, geographical description can only present a small number of traits of the real environment. We are therefore entitled to claim a significant achievement if it is able to *draw the outlines correctly,* that is, if it is *a result of scientific consideration, a correctly characterized simplification.*

Our methodologists, having realized the purpose and possibilities of geographical description, have emphasized the significance of this *essence.* According to Hettner (125, p. 227), the decisive point is then "the aspect of *significance,* or geographical *efficacy,* not in the anthropocentric sense but in terms of all natural phenomena." Gradmann writes (81, p. 613): "The geographer must therefore pay attention to everything that is essential in the perceptible landscape, which we can say is of landscape significance . . . Thus there are a number of facts which are not perceivable in an environment, but which exercise a more significant influence than any other series of phenomena . . . This is what we mean by geographical efficacy." Marthe (163, p. 444) wrote in the late 1870s that "The geographer must above all attempt to find out what is *characteristic* and *influential* in every *choros,* or region.[3] The former (what is characteristic of a region) reflects simultaneity of cooccurrence, in eternal peace and stability, as it were, while the latter (what is influential in a region) reflects the eternal dynamic movement of cooccurrence."

It is not necessary to discuss geographical *interpretation* in any more detail for the present, as it has gained recognition as a generally acknowledged *scientific* method, and in the opinion of many also as the only *scientific* method in geography. It is also methodologically easier to implement than descriptive geography, in that its material can be utilized without any comprehensive preliminary work and is easy to define, although it admittedly makes great demands on the research worker.

2.3. Generalization and Individualization

The concept of *essence* is a relative one in two respects. First, it is dependent on the extent of the area being dealt with and mastered as an entity, or on the distance, figuratively speaking, from which the object is being examined, and second, it is dependent on where we draw the line between what is typical and what is individual. Both types and individuals naturally possess their essential characteristics. The more detailed the type system is in its classification of topological, chronological and physiological features, the less there is to be examined in the context of individuality.

From the point of view of the presentation of geographical information, what is essential can also be said to depend on the space at our disposal. The question of essence is then a matter of either *generalization* or *individualization.* The first procedure is well known to all cartographers. The smaller the scale and the larger the area, the more details have to be omitted and the more the determining characteristics are then emphasized. Cartographic generalization thus means individualization of the remaining parts of the entity to some extent at the same time.

Generalization is usually regarded as involving both the removing of "disturbing" details, that is, "smoothing of curves" and "rounding off of corners" and the more or less obvious accentuation of the individuality of various elements within the whole to the extent that it allows these to continue to be included or even emphasized. As seen from this point of view alone, the two methods merge together.

It is reasonable to draw a clear boundary here as well, however, since the

---

3. That is, in a uniform regional entity (see chap. 1, n. 8).

purposeful exploitation of both methods is necessary. We have to be aware of the fact that their goals are not identical. We place them in a permanent state of interdependence in our geographical system, since it is clear that *individualization means accentuation of the features characteristic of an individual* and *generalization means accentuation of the features characteristic of a number of individuals, or types.*

The more extensive the geographical complex under examination, the more important it is as an area possessing individual features. The size category of locality (see sec. 1.11) still contains so much that is individually significant that the various localities require special treatment as *individuals* in a detailed regional monograph. Vicinities are so small that it would often be no use trying to characterize them individually. It is usually enough to determine what *proximity types* characterize the vicinities of a region.

The scientific value of generalization is commonly accepted, while for many the significance of individualization is questionable. Since individualization occupies a central position in our science, we must be able to state the grounds on which we regard geographical individualization, the formation of individualizing concepts, as belonging to scientific research.

If we want to make rigid demands in this respect, we may, as Rickert does (228, p. 150), consider individualization to be scientifically justified only when it leads to a "scientific result" and possesses a certain "cultural value," without following him so far as to regard the achievement of that result as impossible other than where cultural value is concerned.

Every regional examination which leads via description and interpretation to an understanding of the entity in question naturally fulfills the first demand, although the results, like those of any work, can vary considerably in quality, reflecting the skills of the person carrying it out. Neither do we need to suspect the cultural value of the work, since we are dealing with the *human* perceived environment, the area in which the human being lives and works. I doubt whether there are any objects in perceptible nature which are as worthy of our attention as *individuals* from the point of view of the general culture as is a perceived environment. Unless the various "countries" of the earth were significant in this manner, geography would never have developed, it would never have acquired a position in the universities—as it has done now despite its deficiencies—and scarcely any specialized geographical societies would have been founded.

An awareness of the cultural value of geography should not lead us to replace the already abandoned view which espouses the mere representation of material and bare description with the temptation that lurks on the opposite flank, the idolization of the utility principle into which we have been enticed during the post-war period.

2.4. Topology and Chronology, Physiology and Ontogeny

We suggested above that perceived environments change both spatially and temporally and that they therefore possess certain features, or phenomena, manifest in space and time. The branch of our discipline that examines the former is called *geographical topology,* and the one that examines the latter *geographical chronology.*

Topological and chronological features mark various stages in the development of the perceived environment and the geographical individual and refer at the same time to a certain "life function," a certain physiological structure of that complex. The branch that studies this aspect is known as *geographical physiology.*

Topology and chronology are descriptive in approach, while physiology is mainly interpretive.

The temporal properties of environments, for example, mobility and variability, are naturally reflections of that life function, but geographical chronology and physiology still cannot be regarded as identical concepts, since many things occurring in the environment which lead to a tangible result are not directly perceivable. Geographical chronology does not record this kind of occurrence, while the physiology that examines environments also deals with factors in the complex which we do not include in the perceived environment whose features we are using to define our object of study but which we usually find out by means of deduction, assessing their significance on the basis of their consequences or results.

It is usually the case that both the activities that take place in environments and the objects of these activities are sometimes perceivable and sometimes only indirectly observable, but sooner or later they will lead to consequences which can be perceived as phenomena, which in connection with the *interpretation* of environments may lead us on to factors which do not interest us as such.

From this we can conclude that *topological and chronological material suffices for the determination and description of the geographical object of study, whereas physiology requires more comprehensive and varied material, which is independent of the boundaries between disciplines.*

We must therefore also consider the *psychological* or *social environment,* which is not our object of study (compare sec. 2.1), when examining the life processes of the perceived environment, for it bears a direct causal relationship to that environment, sometimes causing changes in it and sometimes itself changing through the action of the perceived environment.

Our method does not differ in this respect from that of the other natural sciences. Becher, who lays particular emphasis on the fact that only the material world (*Körperwelt*) forms an object of examination, points out that the natural sciences should not disregard psychosocial factors if their operation leads to a perceptible result (15, p. 14).

The interpretive aspect of our discipline also includes *geographical ontogeny*, which examines the origin and stages of development of geographical objects. Like physiology, it is independent of the boundaries of geography in its selection of evidence.

Geographical-physiological and geographical-ontogenetic research enable relationships to be revealed between geographical entities. In this way we obtain the necessary data for drawing up a *genetic system*.

2.5. Proximics and Landscape Science, Geographical Optics, Chromatology, and Morphology

The field of geography that deals with proximities and areas that are uniform in terms of their proximities may be termed *proximics*. It studies the entity that lies within the boundaries of the proximate field of vision and examines all environmental phenomena. Landscapes (see sec. 1.7) and areas uniform with respect to their landscapes are the domain of *landscape science*, which operates within the framework of the distant field of vision and concentrates only on visual phenomena.

Likening geography to botany, we could regard proximics as a kind of cytology or histology of the perceived environment and landscape science as botany proper, that is, as a theory of the plant as a whole, its organs, and the species of plants. It is clear that both proximities and landscapes can be examined in terms of topology, chronology, physiology, and ontogeny, but it should be noted that our comparison breaks down in three respects. First, the individual is far more important in geography than in botany, in which an individual plant and its features are virtually insignificant compared with the *species* as a whole. Second, cells and plants are visible and definable by eye or by means of a microscope and can thus be described and explained without further substantiation, whereas a geographical object of research cannot be directly observed as an entity. It is different in its structure and it is often so large that its scientific examination requires special reduction methods, for example, *land surveying* and *cartography*, and the resulting *plans* and *maps*, that is, correctly proportioned, reduced, and generalized diagrams. Third, individual plants in nature are of a defined size, while the size of geographical individuals depends on what is regarded as a suitable degree of generalization and the scale selected in each research case. Geographical objects of study correspond rather to such objects of botany as forests, meadows, and bogs, which cannot be examined as individuals or units until they have been defined and delimited. This task, that is, *the delimitation of regions,* is one that is particularly characteristic of geography.

Among the phenomena of the perceived environment, it is thus the visual phenomena that belong to both proximics and landscape science. The only difference is that proximics examines the location of phenomena from much closer quarters. The question thus arises of whether it would not be most convenient to consider the field of vision as a whole and not partly in connection with the proximity and partly with the landscape. It should be noted first, however, that distance is considered a significant factor only in the definition of the object and in topological and chronological description. It would be quite absurd to consider only the features lying outside the boundaries of the proximity when interpreting the landscape and to ignore the evidence provided by the microscope and the proximity. Second, it should be remembered that the proximity and the distant field of vision differ from each other to a considerable extent from a practical point of view. As a result of the short distance, the sources of light, colors, and forms of the former are assessed in a different manner from those of the latter, on a far "larger scale," whereas they seldom occur independently and prominently in a landscape as seen from a distance. They either disappear totally or are visible only as insignificant details in the light, color, or form units of larger entities. On the other hand, many phenomena of the landscape, especially those of the earth's surface, cannot be examined visually within the context of the proximity at all. We can see surfaces inclined in various ways, tussocks, stones, holes, and grooves, for example, but not mountains, plains, and valleys.

It is a question of secondary importance which of the branches of geography, proximics or landscape science, should be given priority in the scheme of an investigation. One might perhaps be of the opinion that the reader or listener should be led via the proximity to the landscape, according to the "anthropocentric method." But since entities that are uniform in terms of landscape science are regarded as the main units in our individualizing discipline, it is best to begin with landscape science. We do not walk into the proximity with our eyes closed and move further away to examine it later, but rather we first interpret the general picture of the area from the point of view from which we can see it as a whole and where only visual phenomena characterize the entity seen at a distance, and go on to scrutinize the details after that.

Geography can naturally be divided into parts according to the various phenomena described. It would be pointless, however, to add the names of all these branches of geography to our list of concepts, which is long enough already. It will suffice to mention the most significant branches which examine phenomena in the field of vision, which we shall also discuss below: *geographical optics,* or *photology,* that is, the theory of the sources of light in the perceived environment, the *geographical theory of colors,* or *chromatology,* and the *geographical theory of forms,* or *morphology.*

2.6. The Delimitation of Regions and Scales of Working Maps

The determination or delimitation of regions is the first task in our research work. This important aspect of geography has remained somewhat under-developed. The geographical individual, both as an entity uniform in terms of its perceived environments, as we defined it above, and as an entity homogeneous on the basis of its nonmaterial features, which is the way geographers often see it, is such a difficult object to comprehend that it is dangerous to try to delimit and define it at random, by means of a more or less sophisticated "geographical instinct."

We will go into this neglected section of geography in greater detail later, but it should be mentioned in this connection that our regional division is based on the field of vision. The method rests on the crucial significance of visual phenomena for orientation and the natural tendency of man to divide the earth's surface into uniform areas according to distant fields of vision in particular. A distant field of vision provides us with our first impressions of the location to be defined in greater detail, for example, when approaching an unfamiliar coast, or when the surrounding area unfolds before us as we climb a church tower or reach a mountain top. Observation and experience enable us to combine the distant scenes into a locality, a multiple, colored, shaded, spacious entity with changing and moving parts. But it is when we disembark from the ship or descend from our vantage point to the fields, forests, or dwellings that we come face to face with the innermost geographical nature of the area. The proximate field of vision, the medium, and the substrate form the proximity of that area, in which the details of geographical structure, the pulsation of life and the activities of the organism are revealed to us and enable us to define vicinities at the same time.

The larger the regional individuals to be determined are, the more dependent the researcher is on maps in his work. Bearing in mind that the various hierarchical systems of regions correspond to the degree of generalization of the size category under examination (province, district, locality, sublocality, or proximity), in that the larger the regions to be determined are, the higher is the degree of generalization, it is easy to understand that maps should correspond in scale to the level of generalization adopted. Topographical maps on scales of 1:20,000 to 1:50,000 are therefore suitable for the determination of localities, while sublocalities require field maps to a scale of 1:1000 to 1:2000 and proximities are difficult to map on a scale of less than 1:200 to 1:300. The maps we use as illustrations for our description, both those that present absolute distributions, classifications, and sizes and those that present sets of regions, can be considerably smaller, since the various phenomena are represented on different maps.

2.7. Geographical Systematics

As mentioned above, vicinities and localities are geographical *individuals,* each with a definite location, size, and boundaries. They are not types or species. They do not correspond to *Betula alba* or *Pinus silvestris,* for example, but can be likened to certain birch or pine trees growing at given locations, which have not only the characteristics of their species but also a number of other distinguishing features such as habitat, height, trunk thickness, density of branches, or density of leaves. This individuality is reflected in place names, "geographical names."

Proximities and landscapes can be defined as *types* or *species* that are independent of locations and boundaries on the earth's surface. We can draw up *systems* comprising proximities and landscapes of various types, compare the areas we are studying with the types in this system and examine what proximities and landscapes occur in it.

It has become common practice in geographical publications to use terms for regions and places that indicate not only this individuality but also their position in a rough "system" of this kind. The names "the Enontekiö fjeld region" and "the city of Berlin" provide information on the individuality and location of these units ("Enontekiö," "Berlin") and their general nature ("fjeld region," "city").

Phenomenal spaces and regions (see sec. 1.11) are not types any more than are vicinities or localities. They are areal units characterized by certain phenomena, that is, individuals. But we can create systems in which types are represented by different fields of vision, media, and substrates or phenomena consisting of various substances. The terms that we use again provide information on both individuality and location, and a definite, but often superficially defined type. Thus we speak of the drainage basin of the Elbe, for instance, the forests of the Congo, the lights of Helsinki, or the red glow of the eastern sky.

The special nature of a geographical object of study, nevertheless, means that the proximity and landscape types must be defined in a manner different from that used in the biological sciences.

It would be possible to obtain a suitable *geographical system* by using *immobile phenomena* as a starting point, since the characteristic features of the environment most often occur in what is immobile. The most significant of the chronological phenomena are *duration* and *rhythm,* and in practice this means mainly that annual and daily variations in these must be considered and their value assessed. By remaining within these limits and employing exact evaluation techniques, one could obtain systems for phenomena by taking different elements into consideration in the subclassification, for example, landforms, water, vegetation, artificial forms, sources of light, colors, and other phenomena. It would then be possible to start creating a final system of environments. This could be most easily done, once the systems of phenomena have been generalized for this purpose, by deducing the combinations of the various elements and their phenomena, for it should be kept in mind that a system is of a considerable advantage for a science like geography only if it is concise and concentrates on the most essential features.

A comparison of the combinations of phenomena thus obtained would indicate that the same phenomena can vary considerably in value in different combinations and should therefore vary in the emphasis given to them in different parts of the system. It would be erroneous to regard this feature, which characterizes geographical complexes to a high degree, as an inconsistency in the system. What is important in the classification of marine landscapes, for instance, can be of secondary importance in the definition of other landscapes.

The drawing up of a geographical system, or geographical systematization in a narrower sense, is thus concerned with phenomena and then with environments as entities. A division into regions, that is, a definition of individuals, is different in nature and can best be compared with floristic and faunistic research.

The system outlined above is *descriptive* and, if drawn up correctly, *natural* as well, since it takes into consideration all the phenomena characterizing environments. Naturally it does not provide any information on relationships or origin, so that such terms as genus and family should not be used of its type categories, but instead expressions such as main type, type group, and category.

Geographers usually regard *genetic* systems as the only acceptable ones. While we do not want to deny the significance of such a system for the *interpretive* part of our discipline, we consider it obvious that only what is directly observed can serve as the basis for the *descriptive* part, since our conception of the environment is based on observation and not on relationships or stages of development deduced in one way or another.

No system of the kind proposed here exists as yet, and the task of creating one would require an investigation of its own, but it could probably be carried out without any difficulty. The development of a genetic system will certainly be a question for the more distant future, since it will require extensive physiological and ontogenetic preparatory work. The words of Wagner written in 1885 when defining his point of view in the face of a growing demand to take the genetic principle as the determining one in geographical classification are still true today: "Easy as the formulation of such a demand may be, it is probably equally unsuitable for the development of a detailed classification at the present stage of our geographical knowledge" (277, p. 566).

2.8. Choosing the Object of Study and Consideration of the Past

Although our *objects of study* comprise all areas in which people are able to live, our research also has to *take account of* everything that is *observable* as significant in the environment or that *influences* the environment to a considerable extent.

The whole of the earth's surface can be examined, or any part of it, a vicinity, locality, island, continent, or ocean, but such objects as the ocean floor, the core of the earth, or the "environments" and "landscapes" of celestial bodies can be considered only for the purposes of interpretation and comparison if at all.

We can also examine an individual feature of the perceived environment or, as in the present investigation, a problem or series of problems defined in such a manner that research into it will directly enhance or deepen our knowledge of the environment, whereas faults, shorelines, ice structures, the salinity of sea water, migrations of plants, or forms of civilization are not objects of geographical study. This may be clear without further substantiation on the basis of the facts presented above, but the reader may regard the chronological definition of the object of study as more obscure. We have demonstrated that it is necessary to take the past into consideration in all geographical investigation, but we have not discussed the question of how far the geographer can go back in time when choosing his object. And yet geographers have zealously maintained that their objects of study are *bound to the present.*

Chronological definition is in no sense of any greater importance for environmental geography, which has its explicitly defined objects and an indisputable right to existence, than it is for zoology or botany, for example. Rather the opposite is true, since the organisms of the past are examined by paleontology, while the environments of the past have not been studied by any discipline up to now. The limitation of botany and zoology to the present is regarded as so self-evident that there is no need to emphasize this, and the same is also true for geography. Our objects are modern in the same sense as those of botany and zoology, but as far as we understand, the definition of the "present" is something of a practical question that mainly depends on where the boundaries between geography and the historical disciplines are to be drawn.

2.9. General and Special Geography

In one of his most recent methodological reviews, Hettner again brings up the question of general geography as he defined it around the turn of the century. He writes (124, p. 47): "General geography consists of two closely interdependent elements. It is not only a branch of science that examines species and laws, as most people seem to think, but it also deals with large telluric phenomena, which occur all over the earth or at least on several continents. But we cannot manage without the investigation of types and laws, or rather, we can dispense with them only if we renounce causal theories and content ourselves with description alone." And in his book *Die Geographie, ihre Geschichte, ihr Wesen und ihre Methoden* (Geography: its history, nature, and methods), published in 1927, he condemns the idea of geography as "general earth science" as impossible (125, pp. 121, 122). Hettner regards it as a fault of this "general science" that geography has expanded into fields that were originally foreign to it, that this has led to superficiality, and that the neighboring sciences have not always been favorably disposed toward it. A general science concerned with the earth is "logically impossible, historically unfounded and harmful in practice. Only geophysics can escape from it as an independent science. But this does not belong to the core of geography, nor even to geography at all, but is an independent neighboring branch of science."

Geographers probably generally accept Hettner's point of view, although the authors of textbooks and handbooks still talk about "general earth science." Hettner is undoubtedly right, since in this way general geography becomes an integral and significant part of geography. This also holds true for the most part if the object of study is defined in the manner suggested by us, since although the task of general geography, by analogy to that of general botany and zoology, will then be to deal with everything that is essential in the object of study regardless of its location, that is, the perceived environment in this case, it must direct its attention to various environments in different parts of the world when attempting comparative or evaluative reviews. And although it defines geographical concepts, generates geographical methods, and presents the geographical system, it must inevitably pay attention to entities occurring in given locations.

The present methodological discussion can thus be regarded, even though only within certain limits, as an outline of general geography. Broadly speaking, the plan is clear to the extent that it is reflected in the structure of this book, but the details are still mostly vague and uncertain. We could also emphasize the significance of some issues on which we cannot yet define our standpoint, namely proximity and landscape, and, correspondingly, proximics and landscape science, for instance, although the subject matter could first be divided between topology, chronology, and physiology, and only after that should we deal with the elements of environment related to distance. It may perhaps be unnecessary to discuss proximity and landscape in separate chapters within chronology and physiology (see sec. 2.4), since the greatest and most significant differences are topological in nature.

Special (regional) geography, or *regional science,* deals with geographical individuals (see sec. 1.12) and units consisting of these individuals. *Where the principal method in general geography is generalization, that of special geography is individualization.* The delimitation of regions, as defined above, thus belongs to special geography. But the outline of special geography can be of two kinds once the regions have been defined: it can either follow the system of general geography, that is, deal with geographical individuals by landscape or proximity types, or be based on these regions.

Just as generalization is by no means the sole method of general geography, so individualization is not the only direction in special geography, since no matter how strictly defined the area concerned may be, every regional examination has a section in which the general nature of the object and its position in the system are discussed. It is in the nature of the tasks of special geography that *the delimitation of regions* often accounts for a considerable amount of the material that also belongs to their description. We must therefore be able to answer a question that is entirely foreign to the biological sciences: what position must be reserved for the delimitation of regions and how extensive should this be?

It is obvious that the determination of regional individuals requires detailed induction in order to provide adequate substantiation and that it is impossible to know the result of the comparison of characteristics performed in connection with the description when first delimiting the regions. In other words, the research worker must include all the facts that *may* have some bearing on the definition from the very beginning. Unfortunately, we are obliged to use this secondary material in regional division if we want to present a fully convincing induction.

On the other hand, even though all the essential features, some of which may not be necessary for the delimitation of the regions, may have been mentioned in connection with the determination of individuals, a monograph in regional geography should not end with a list of the entities formed but should gather the topological and chronological phenomena together to form a total picture in a special treatment of these entities. In this way material that could not be used at the regional induction stage can be included.

One can also take the results of the definition of regions as known from the beginning, that is, by offering the reader only the information that proved in the original induction to be decisive for dividing the area into regions. This alternative could be recommended for authors of textbooks and handbooks in particular.

3

LANDSCAPE

3.1. Landscape and Landscape Science

Before we go on to examine landscape in more detail, it is first necessary to recall the main concepts defined above.

A landscape is a visible distant environment, or distant field of vision.

In order for a landscape to be perceived, a given minimum amount of lighting is necessary. We cannot see anything of a landscape in pitch darkness, and we can only discern a landscape shrouded in the darkness of night if we can see at least part of the sky and perhaps a spot of light twinkling in the dark or the shimmering surface of a lake or some other body of water.

Moreover, we must be a given minimum distance away from the landscape if we want to see it. We can therefore form an impression of a forest landscape when walking in a forest only if wider views are visible between the trees, and when sitting in a room we see a landscape only through a window or open door, and then only provided that there are no obstacles outside to block our field of vision.

The latter prerequisite for the perception of a landscape, minimum distance, has not been considered earlier, while the former, minimum lighting, has probably been regarded as self-evident in the circles in which landscapes have been considered only as *visible* complexes. But if we follow the recent, now dominant geographical point of view and look upon the whole perceived environment as a landscape, we must take all sensory phenomena into account. In this case the impression we receive of a landscape is always to a greater or lesser extent defective, since we should not only see it, but also hear, smell, and feel it.

Our definition of landscape includes both the combination of visual phenomena and the complex of objects perceivable through these visual phenomena, and it remains for the research worker to decide which viewpoint is the most viable in each case. In the following we shall regard the world of *forms* as the dominant one, classifying it on the basis of materials and examining the extent to which color, light, and other topological and chronological phenomena characterize certain objects morphographically and in terms of their material composition.

The task of landscape science is to examine, describe, and interpret landscapes on the earth's surface and regional entities that are coherent in terms of their landscapes, that is, distant fields of vision bound to the observer and spatially bound regions that are coherent in terms of their properties in the distant field of vision.

Although the views of others concerning these tasks are sometimes conflicting, this branch of science has, generally speaking, become more or less established. It is not a recent invention, as is sometimes claimed, although it was not pursued in as single-minded and intensive a manner earlier as it is nowadays.

The first investigators to deal with landscape science were Oppel (190) and Wimmer (293) in the 1880s. The former defined a landscape, *Landschaft,* in purely anthropocentric terms as an area which, as seen from a specific location, spreads before the eyes of the observer as an entity, and landscape science, *Landschaftskunde* as the physiognomy of the earth's surface, while in the latter's opinion, a landscape is an area of land determined by its location and natural quality, especially in terms of its influence as a visible entity, and landscape science is merely a descriptive element of geography.

Neither of these early landscape scientists was able to implement his plan on the basis of these definitions. Oppel analyzed Europe, for instance, on the basis of the various countries and dealt with the Alps, which form a single geographical entity if anything does, in four different connections, that is, as parts of France, Switzerland, Italy, and Austria. This mode of presentation is, as Wagner points out (277, p. 610), "descriptive geography of the most primitive kind, from which certain important matters have been omitted in an arbitrary manner." Wimmer mentions at the beginning of his book the plasticity of the substrate (including water and soils), forms of vegetation, climatic conditions, and——in the case of inhabited regions——buildings as the "elements" of landscapes, but later he also takes into consideration "the properties of an area as a political entity or part of one."

A more exact definition of *descriptive* landscape science, which also served as a research program, was presented by Wagner in his criticism of the early works of landscape science mentioned above. He writes (277, pp. 608–9):

> On the basis of this we can conclude that we are talking about elements an artist could combine into a landscape painting. And these definitions actually include an outlining of the task of physiognomics. It can either *divide the earth's face into typical landscapes* and describe these systematically, which would actually offer . . . a number of new things and be worth the specialists' interest . . . As a physiognomy of the earth's surface, it could also act in a similar way to synthetic geography and *describe the continents and countries, ordered in terms of regions* by combining those regions and countries that belong physiognomically to the same type to form a total image. This is an enormous task, however, since if the landscape should alter or factors operating within the same natural landscape change, they would need to be described again, and such repetitions are likely to occur ad infinitum. The fundamental initial task would be the drawing of a map on which all the places where landscape changes occur are marked by lines or zones. This presentation should make it clear that the latter method is a special case of the individualization of regions, the examination of geographical entities, in which the visually observed physiognomic nature of these regions is regarded as the key.

This point of view concerning Wagner's landscape science is interesting both in that our current landscape science has not conceded to this statement written as early as 1885 the position of the first "logical definition of the concept" and in that, in a manner similar to the present investigation, it proposes the *visible* features of the complex as the "key" or basis for the definition of regions, regardless of the differences that otherwise exist between the methods.[1]

3.2. Boundaries and Size of a Landscape and Minimum Size of a Locality

As mentioned above, the *outer boundary* of a landscape is the range of vision, which depends on the height of the place of observation and the relief, which

---

1. Wagner's *Landschaft* refers to the same concept as our "locality" or "district."

we assume in this case to be composed not only of the earth's crust but also of water in a solid state, vegetation and artificial matter.[2]

The *inner boundary* of a landscape against the proximity is difficult to define accurately, as we will see later, but a landscape can at least be clearly perceived at a distance of 100–200 meters from the observer.

The distance of the horizon in an *open landscape* (see sec. 1.7) on a flat, horizontal surface, for example, a wide plain or open sea, is dependent only on the height of the eye above this surface. We thus obtain the radius of the view in kilometers from the formula $3.827 \sqrt{h}$ where h is the height of the point of observation in meters (Wagner 280, p. 95). When we bear in mind that when the observer is in the mountains or traveling by airplane or airship, he may be moving at the height of several thousand meters, it becomes obvious that the radius of his view can be many hundreds of kilometers, although in reality our powers of sight can deal with only a fraction of such a vast area in more detail.

Table 3.1 indicates how the radius of view increases with height.

If we assume that a fully grown person's eyes are at a height of 1.5 m from the ground, we obtain 4.7 km as the range of view, and this we can regard as a minimum distance for the outer boundary of an open landscape.

It becomes obvious from the above argument that landscapes can vary in *size* to a great extent. The smallest possible *closed landscape* (see sec. 1.7), the radius of which is 100–150 m when calculated as a circle, is hardly larger than 0.07 km^2, while an open landscape seen from a height of 9000 m would be as much as $413,965 \text{ km}^2$, which is considerably larger than the area of Finland. The minimum area of an open landscape, a flat, horizontal area that can be perceived in its entirety from a height of 1.5 m, is 69.4 km^2, of which we can only see the mid-part up to a distance of about 2.5 km in clear weather, or approximately 20 km^2, since the fringes of the landscape can only be perceived as a narrow line (the corresponding visual angle being less than 50'', and we cannot distinguish its various features.

As the minimum size for a *locality,* the coherent areal complex corresponding to landscape, we have proposed that of an open landscape (see sec. 1.11). Thus, localities should not in general be smaller than approximately 70 km^2, nor should they be narrower than 9.4 km, the minimum diagonal of an open landscape, since the degree of coherence of a locality is dependent on the coherence of its landscapes and since a person moving at the center of a locality narrower than this can see as his landscape a considerable part of the entities lying outside this coherent area. It should therefore be only in exceptional cases that areas with a width of less than approximately 10 km are accepted as localities.

2. Distant phenomena beyond the range of vision naturally need not be taken into account.

3.3. Description in Landscape Science and Structure and Location of Landscapes

Since the object of geographical study is the landscape as a complex not only of phenomena but also of objects, the anthropocentric viewpoint cannot be regarded as the only one, or even the decisive one, in this work, no matter how significant it may be as a starting point. The result of an anthropocentric examination is the concept of landscape and also a definition of what is the minimum size or minimum intensity to be considered in a *landscape analysis,* which must not be restricted to the presentation of phenomena dependent on variable distances. The size of the objects in a distant field of vision must be presented in dimensions independent of the location of the observer, shapes must be described even when they cannot be seen all the time or from every direction, while sources of light and colors should be dealt with as independent of the place of observation and sufficient attention be paid to materials as well.

This emancipation from the anthropocentric approach does not cause any special difficulties as long as we are concerned with visual phenomena (see sec. 1.11), since the goal is the definition of regional entities, not entities bound to the observer. The description must provide complete information on the topological and chronological *structure* of the area, that is, not only of phenomena but also of elements. The task may conveniently be categorized into three main parts, the examination of forms, colors, and sources of light. As mentioned earlier, we regard the environment primarily as a complex of objects characterized by form, which has certain properties of color and light. The presentation is thus primarily morphological and only secondarily chro-

Table 3.1

Height	Radius of View	Height	Radius of View	Height	Radius of View
1.5 m	4.7 km	150 m	46.9 km	1,000 m	121.0 km
2	5.4	200	54.1	1,500	148.2
5	8.6	300	66.3	2,000	171.1
10	12.1	400	76.5	3,000	209.6
15	14.8	500	85.6	4,000	242.0
20	17.1	600	93.7	5,000	270.6
25	19.1	700	101.3	7,000	320.2
50	27.1	800	108.2	9,000	363.0
100	38.3	900	114.8		

matological and photological. This method results from the fact that forms, being more constant and durable factors, have a greater value in the complex than colors and lights.

But we must also pay attention to elements at the analysis stage. We shall first examine the forms, colors, and lights associated with the earth's crust, water, air, vegetation, fauna, human beings, and artificial matter. This procedure is justified in that these various elements and their structures often possess special characteristic phenomena and sets of phenomena.

It is also clear that the *location* of the area to be examined must be determined without reference to the position of the observer. We must find out the geographical coordinates—length and width—and the absolute altitude of the area, but we do not need exact figures in degrees and meters for the first approximate orientation. If we are examining height above sea level, we can use the following classification for the time being:

1. *Depression,* below sea level
2. *Lowlands,* 0–300 (200) m above sea level
3. *Highlands,* 300 (200)–1500 m
4. *Uplands,* 1500–3000 m
5. *Alpine area,* higher than 3000 m

It remains the task of future research to draw up an altitude classification that corresponds better to the viewpoints of landscape science.

When the location of an area on the earth has been defined and its forms, colors, and lights described, the *synthetic evaluation* that follows should show the extent to which the various factors in the landscape influence the *anthropocentrically* defined entity and in what way features dependent on variable distances have to be considered. This will reveal the fact that only some of the matters considered in the analysis are significant in the complex as well, since the value of a phenomenon as a landscape factor is not dependent only on the phenomenon itself but also on the environment.

The crucial significance of form in the landscape and its consequent important position not only in geographical description and the delimitation of regions but also in physiological geography (see secs. 1.9 and 2.4) obliges us to present a morphographic system that concentrates on the main features of the distant field of vision as the starting point for our task and to discuss cartography briefly as applied to the types in this system.[3]

3. The following chapters on the morphography of landscape are based on my publication "Maisematieteen tehtävät ja maiseman muotojen järjestelmä" (90; Tasks of landscape science and the system of landscape forms). Passarge in particular has done creditable work in specifying geomorphographic terms, esp. 202.

Either form alone or, more expediently, both form and size can be considered when drawing up a morphographic system, that is, not only quality but also quantity. It is difficult for the present to apply methods of the latter kind to all elements of landscapes, however, since it requires constant, accurate *size classification* of forms, which has so far been carried out only to a restricted extent.

One of the important tasks of landscape science is the examination of *categorization* and *distribution,* regardless of the phenomenon or object in question. Where forms are concerned, we speak of *complex forms* in situations where *simple forms* (Passarge's *Grundformen*) are combined into double or other compound formations, which arise from a more or less clear common *base.* Actual *form groups* (Passarge's *Gruppenformen*) can be arranged in more or less circular *clusters* or longitudinal, sometimes very narrow, *rows.* When different forms composed of the same material occur side by side in characteristic complexes (e.g., elevations and hollows in the earth's crust, water in rivers, lakes, and glaciers, vegetation in forests and grasslands, artificial matter in buildings and streets), this is termed *cooccurrence* of the forms of each element, leading to the creation of *form complexes.*

A distribution may be either *individual, clustered, scattered,* or *even,* concepts that will certainly be clear without further definition.

3.4. Forms of the Earth's Crust

The earth's crust, which constitutes the basis for all landscapes, is perceived in geographical complexes in terms of landforms. We speak of an *open landform* if there is at least one direction in which it is not bounded by a surface belonging to itself, and a *closed landform* if it is bounded in all directions. Landforms are traditionally divided into three major groups: *elevations,* which rise above their surroundings, *depressions,* lying below their surroundings, and *plains,* which are neutral in this respect. The first two major groups occur in open and closed forms, while plains always occur in open forms.

3.4.1. *Elevations*

If we consider conditions in Finland and Estonia, elevations may be divided into five *height classes,* which can also be regarded as size categories, since the actual morphographic part of the system is concentrated on the relations that prevail between height and other dimensions:

1. *Hummock,* less than 10 m in height
2. *Mound,* 10–20 m
3. *Hillock,* 20–50 m

4. *Hill,* 50–200 m

5. *Mountain,* over 200 m

Form types can be determined either on the basis of their plan view (as I have done earlier, 90), or on the basis of their cross section. The latter method is more suitable in purely geographical terms. We thus obtain the following system of elevations.[4]

I. Summit (convex or pointed) directly merging with slopes
   A. Forms with convex slopes; fairly broad summit
      a. Forms with gentle slopes, gradient usually less than 10 degrees
         1. *Hump.* Roundish plan view (Fig. 3.1, A–C, I, 1)
         2. *Barrow.* Elongated plan view (III, 1)
      b. Forms with steep slopes, gradient more than 10 degrees, especially in the lower parts
         3. *Dome.* Roundish plan view (I, 2)
         4. *Ridge.* Elongated plan view (III, 2)
   B. Concave forms; narrow, pointed summit
      a. Gently sloping forms; gradient over 10 degrees only near the summit
         5. *Cone.* Roundish plan view (II, 1)
         6. *Crest.* Elongated plan view (IV, 1)
      b. Steeply sloping forms; inclination over 10 degrees only in the lower parts
         7. *Peak.* Roundish plan view (II, 2)
         8. *Hogback.* Elongated plan view (IV, 2)
   C. One slope convex, the other concave
         9. *Crescent ridge.* Sicklelike plan view, inner slope mainly concave (V)
II. Summit (flat or level, horizontal or sloping) at a clear angle to the slopes
         10. *Table.* Variable plan view; slopes mainly concave (VII)

The term *round elevation* covers both humps and domes, *conical elevation* both cones and peaks, *ridge elevation* both barrows and ridges, and *crest elevation* both crests and hogbacks. The forms with longitudinal plan views may be either open or closed and either straight, curved, or circular. In the last of these the elevation surrounds a central hollow of variable shape (Fig. 3.1, A, VI).

The diagram represents a system of forms in which the emphasis is primarily on the plan view (A) and only secondarily on the cross section and longitudinal profile (B, C).

4. Our morphographic system deviates at some points from that of Passarge (202), which is not pure landscape science in that it does not restrict itself to features visible in the landscape.

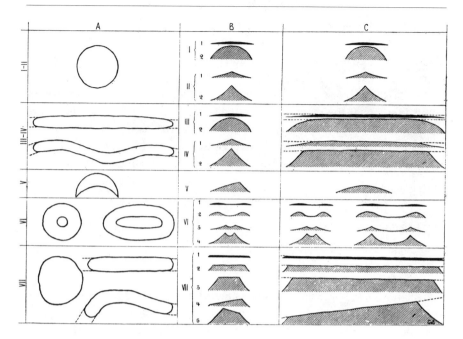

Figure 3.1. Elevations.

A = Plan view; *B* = cross-section; *C* = longitudinal section. *I* = Round elevations; *I,1* = hump; *I,2* = dome; *II* = conical elevations; *II,1* = cone. *II,2* = peak; *III* = ridge elevations; *III,1* = barrow; *III,2* = ridge; *IV* = crest elevations; *IV,1* = crest; *IV,2* = hogback; *V* = crescent ridge; *VI* = circular forms; *VI,1* = circular barrow; *VI,2* = circular ridge; *VI,3* = circular crest; *VI,4* = circular hogback; *VII,1–5* = tables.

3.4.2. *Depressions*

Depressions are not usually regarded as being such significant formations as elevations, since they are most frequently generated by the removal of material in one way or another, and are thus secondary forms. It has also been noted that they are not in themselves features of landforms but merely act to delimit elevations.

Landscape science cannot regard such grounds as significant, since what is decisive in a landscape is that which is larger, more common and more conspicuous from a distance. Elevations are undoubtedly more significant even from this point of view, in that in a way they rise before us in the landscape and attract our attention, while depressions seem to evade our sight since they are below the level of our eyes. The depressions that separate the positive forms that rise up in front of us are not fully visible in the relief. We see only the elevations that delimit them, and therefore they are not as significant as elevations in terms of the delimitation of regions, although it cannot be denied that they are entirely equal to elevations as factors in compound forms. Only depressions separated by very wide flat areas are of interest in their own right for regional divisions, since plains do not necessarily have slopes at their edges and since the value of negative landforms is higher than usual in this exceptional case.

No classification of depressions by size has yet been produced, except for some attempts at the classification of valleys in terms of depth, which have not gained general acceptance. The following depth classification, which corresponds exactly to the above height classification of elevations, can be used for regional division purposes under Finnish and Estonian conditions:

1. *Dent,* less than 10 m

2. *Dip,* 10–20 m

3. *Hollow,* 20–50 m

4. *Bottom,* 50–200 m

5. *Deep,* over 200 m

Differences in plan view are more suitable as a basis for this landform system than for the classification of elevations on account of the manner of occurrence of depressions in the landscape. We distinguish the following types:

I. Closed depressions, or *basins* (Fig. 3.2, A–C, I)

  A. Roundish plan view

    1. *Funnel.* Tapering bottom, slopes connected without any clear, flat bottom

      a. *Flat funnel.* Maximum depth one fifth of the width (I, 1, a)

      b. *Steep funnel.* Depth more than one fifth of the width, maximum depth equals width (I, 1, b)

    2. *Pan.* A clear angle between the flat bottom and the slopes, maximum depth one fifth of width (I, 2)

    3. *Bowl.* With gentle slopes, merging into the bottom with no angle, maximum depth one fifth of width (I, 3)

    4. *Cauldron.* With steep slopes and a more or less flat bottom, depth more than one fifth of width, maximum depth equal to width

      a. *Pan cauldron.* A clear angle between the bottom and the slopes (I, 4, a)

      b. *Bowl cauldron.* Slopes merge into the bottom without forming an angle (I, 4, b)

  B. Elongated plan view

    5. *Furrow.* Narrow bottom, slopes connected without any clear, mediating flat surface (that is, similar in cross section to a funnel, I, 1, a–b)

      a. *Flat furrow.* Maximum depth one fifth of width

      b. *Steep furrow.* Depth more than one fifth of width, but not more than width

6. *Dish.* A clear angle between the slopes and the flat bottom, maximum depth one fifth of width (I, 5)

7. *Trough.* Slopes curve into the bottom without forming an angle, maximum depth one fifth of width (I, 6)

8. *Rift.* With steep slopes and more or less flat bottom, depth more than one fifth of width, maximum depth equal to width

    a. *Dish rift.* A clear angle between the bottom and the slopes (1, 7, a)

    b. *Trough rift.* Slopes curve to the bottom without any clear angle (I, 7, b)

II. Open depressions; open at one or both ends; variable in plan view (III)

    A. Roundish plan view, open at one side: cirques

       9. *Funnel cirque.* Funnellike cross section

          a. *Flat funnel cirque.* Cross section similar to that of a flat funnel

          b. *Steep funnel cirque.* Cross section similar to that of a steep funnel

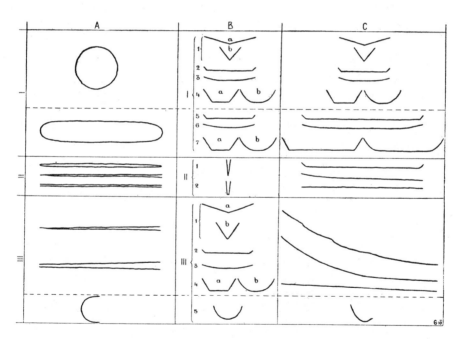

Figure 3.2. Depressions.

A = Plan view; *B* = cross-section; *C* = longitudinal section. *I* = Closed depressions; *I,1* = funnels; *I,1a* = flat funnel; *I,1b* = steep funnel; *I,2* = pan; *I,3* = bowl; *I,4* = cauldrons; *I,4a* = pan cauldron; *I,4b* = bowl cauldron; *I,5* = dish; *I,6* = trough; *I,7* = rifts; *I,7a* = dish rifts; *I,7b* = trough rifts; *II* = gorges; *II,1* = closed gorge; *II,2* = open gorge; *III* = open depressions (valleys, cirques); *III,1* = furrow valleys; *III,1a* = flat furrow valley; *III,1b* steep furrow valley; *III,2* = dish valley; *III,3* = trough valley; *III,4* = rift valley; *III,4a* = dish rift valley; *III,4b* = trough rift valley; *III,5* = bowl cauldron cirque.

10. *Pan cirque.* Panlike cross section
11. *Bowl cirque.* Bowllike cross section
12. *Cauldron cirque.* Cross section similar to that of a cauldron
    a. *Pan cauldron cirque.* Cross section similar to that of a pan cauldron
    b. *Bowl cauldron cirque.* Cross section similar to that of bowl cauldron (III, 5)
B. Often very long, narrow forms with an elongated plan view, open at one or both ends: valleys
    13. *Furrow valley.* Furrowlike cross section
       a. *Flat furrow valley.* Cross section similar to that of a flat furrow (III, 1, a)
       b. *Steep furrow valley.* Cross section similar to that of a steep furrow (III, 1, b)
    14. *Dish valley.* Cross section similar to that of a dish (III, 2)
    15. *Trough valley.* Cross section similar to that of a trough (III, 3)
    16. *Rift valley.* Cross section similar to that of a rift
       a. *Dish rift valley.* Cross section similar to that of a rift (III, 4, a)
       b. *Trough rift valley.* Cross section similar to that of a trough rift (III, 4, b)
II. Open or closed depressions with elongated plan views and often very narrow forms with steep slopes, depth at least equal to width: gorges
    17. *Open gorge.* Open at one or both ends (II, 2)
    18. *Closed gorge.* Closed (II, 1)

Some of the above types (e.g., funnel and furrow) are rare in nature and of only theoretical significance. Combined forms are common in the case of valleys in particular. The most significant of these is the *valley system,* which has often been regarded as a form group.

The often very large extent of valleys makes it necessary to deal with their various parts as individual forms. This is especially true of narrowings and widenings of valleys; the latter are similar to basins if they are large in area and connected only by narrow valley sequences.

3.4.3. *Plains*

The existence of plains as separate forms in the landscape is due to their considerable extent. If a plain is so large in size that it cannot be regarded as part of an elevation or depression and therefore cannot be referred to as a *terrace,* it must be regarded as a simple landform.

A plain is never completely even but always undulates to some extent. Its irregularities can, nevertheless, be distinguished only in its detailed relief, thus being invisible in the landscape, or else they slope so gently that they do not disturb the impression of a plain (Figure 3.3). In the latter case, such a plain can be regarded as a transitional form tending toward a landform complex composed of elevations and depressions.

3.4.4. *Cooccurrence*

Elevations and depressions are relative concepts, and the one cannot exist without the other. The geomorphological reality is always a form complex, but because of the properties of the various types, not all combinations are possible. Gently sloping elevations have gently sloping, open depressions between them, while the larger the variation in altitude, the steeper the forms are. Steep hills and ridges are separated by valleys that are also characterized by steep gradients, and tables occur most often in connection with depressions in which the bottom is at a distinct angle to the slopes.

A typology of complex forms meeting the requirements of morphography can be obtained by starting out from the general nature of the elevation profiles (gentle, steep, convex, concave, flat) and the extent of the relative variations in altitude, that is, the height of the relief:

Figure 3.3. A plain.

(The Kulunda steppe in western Siberia, east of the town of Pavlodar, photographed by the author in August 1905.) This landscape clearly represents a simple form, a perfect plain.

I. Convex elevations
  A. Forms usually with gentle slopes
    1. *Plain.* Such areas have no more than very minor elevations and
       depressions (see the description above of plain as a separate form).
    2. *Flat.* Characteristic forms include humps, barrows, pans, bowls,
       dishes, and troughs and the plains between these. Variations in alti-
       tude are small as far as the eye can see, remaining under ca. 10 m.
    3. *Mound terrain.* This is also characterized by the forms mentioned in
       connection with flats but has relative altitudes in the range 10–20 m.
    4. *Hillock terrain.* The landforms are higher and steeper than in the
       above complexes (average 20–50 m). Dominant elevation types are
       domes and ridges, and elevations with concave slopes sometimes occur.
  B. Forms with both gentle and steep slopes
    5. *Hill terrain.* Average height of elevations 50–200 m, usually with rel-
       atively steep slopes. Convex elevations are the dominant forms but
       concave forms are not unusual, especially if considerable variations
       in altitude occur.
II. Mainly steep elevations, usually with concave slopes and narrow or
     pointed summits
    6. *Mountain terrain.* Differences in altitude over 200 m. The higher the
       relief, the more common are pointed and sharp-edged landforms
       (Figs. 3.4 and 3.8).
III. Table landforms dominant, slopes concave or convex, sometimes de-
     scending in a stepwise manner
    7. *Table terrain.* The elevations vary in height, but are mainly over 50 m.
       A *step table terrain* has stepped slopes.
IV. Plains and flats (and less often mound terrain with very gentle slopes)
    interrupted by depressions
    8. *Basin terrain.* Characterized by large, more or less closed basins
       mainly over 50 m in depth. The slopes are sometimes stepped, giv-
       ing a *stepped basin terrain.* When the basins occur close to one an-
       other this complex form is similar to a table terrain.
    9. *Valley terrain.* Clear, large, steep valleys mostly over 50 m in depth.
       This type also becomes similar to a table terrain if the valleys are
       close to one another.

For the purposes of defining regions, it is useful to denote these various
types with alphabetical or numerical symbols, which can then be inserted
into the landscape code drawn up at the synthetic stage. The complex forms
of the earth's crust are thus marked here with *italicized Roman numerals* in
the following manner: *I*–mountain terrain, *II*–hill terrain, *III*–hillock terrain,

Figure 3.4. A mountain terrain.

(The area around the headwaters of the River Saaskandú in eastern Altai, photographed by the author in July 1916.) Landforms are completely dominant in the landscape. Cirques formed within domes are seen in the foreground, and hogbacks and peaks divided by furrow valleys in the background.

IV–mound terrain, *V*–flat, *VI*–plain, *VII*–table terrain, *VIII*–basin terrain, and *IX*–valley terrain.

This list indicates that the categories are formed on the basis of differences in altitude, which determine their relative position in terms of landscape science. The last three complex forms are variable in relief, in addition to which basin terrains and valley terrains are characterized by depression forms.

3.4.5. *Cartographic Representation*

Topographical forms can be represented by means of landscape maps using different symbols or colors for the above form or form complex types or showing differences in altitude in a similar manner to topographical maps, that is, using contour lines, hatching, or shading. The former method is considerably better when dealing with large areas and/or small-scale maps. It becomes necessary to draw a map representing the distribution of types when attempting to construct a system of regions for an area with unclear vari-

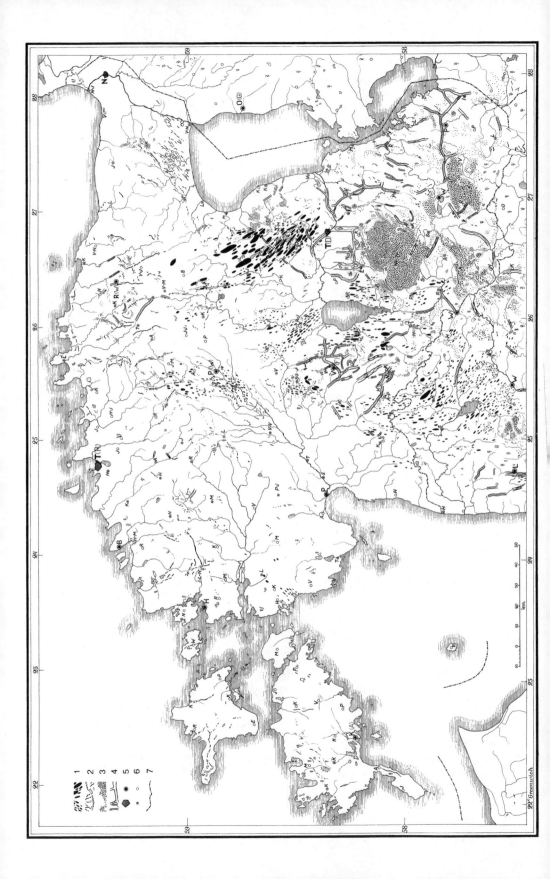

ations in relief which would make the topographical map difficult to read. The forms of the earth's crust can be represented easily by means of contour lines only when examining the smallest geographically uniform areas, for which very large scales can be used.

A morphographic map can naturally be used to record data on the composition and structure of the earth's crust and the manner of formation of the relief. Often the morphographic map as such is so complicated that it is more expedient to represent the other data on separate maps.

The two methods are illustrated by Figures 3.5 and 3.7, the first representing Estonia on a scale of 1:1,000,000 and the second, which was originally drawn to a very large scale of 1:1000, representing a small island known as Valosaari situated close to the town of Mikkeli by Lake Saimaa in Finland (Fig. 3.6). These maps form the basis for geomorphographic definitions of regions, as discussed below.

The following points should be mentioned as explanations to the map of Estonia, which has been discussed in more detail earlier (Granö 88). The local variations in relief that form the basis for an orographic division of Estonia into regions are independent of the bedrock, which is an almost invariable plain with the exception of the islands and cliffs on the coast of the Gulf of Finland and some valleys cut into the substrate in places. The dominant features include accumulation landforms composed of loose deposits and depressions lying between them or cut into them, mostly dating back to the Ice Age, primarily to the deglaciation period.

There is one reliable topographical map of Estonia in existence, on a scale of 1:42,000, that is, sufficiently detailed that it is suitable as a basis for the geographical definition of regions, and it is the data on this map that are represented in generalized form in Figure 3.5, which also considers the genesis of the various forms and form complexes where possible at the same time, so that the map is not only morphographic but also morphogenetic, especially as far as the significance of glacial events is concerned.

Although generalization has been used only where it has been necessary for technical reasons and although only features that seemed absolutely certain were marked on the map, it was naturally impossible to avoid errors. It is

---

(Facing page)

Figure 3.5. Forms of glacial deposits and ancient valleys in Estonia.

1 = Hump and barrow hummocks and mounds (drumlins); *2* = ridge and crest hummocks and mounds (eskers), hump and dome hummocks and mounds (moraine ridges, kames, sand sediments); *3* = hump and dome complexes (hummocky moraine); *4* = dish dent and dish dip valleys (ancient ice-marginal channels); *5* = towns and cities; *6* = village, church; *7* = border.

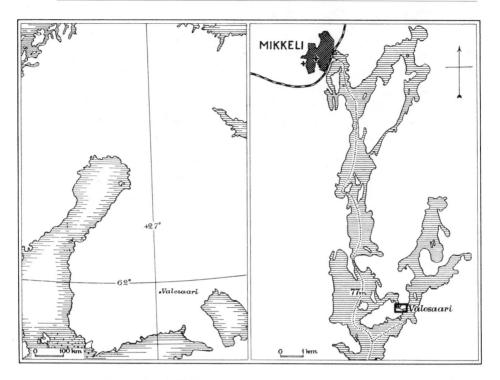

Figure 3.6. Location of Valosaari.

The left-hand map indicates the position of Valosaari in Finland and its geographical longitude and latitude. The right-hand, more detailed map shows the absolute altitude of the site, the extent of the area mapped *(the rectangle),* part of the water system of Lake Saimaa with navigation routes *(dotted lines),* and the town of Mikkeli.

also obvious that our black and white map cannot in every respect meet the scientific requirements set for it where morphology is concerned, since first, very gently sloping ground moraine humps and barrows have not been marked on the map, and second, it was not always possible to distinguish between glacial and glaciofluvial formations or between some later formations such as beach ridges or dune groups and glacial margin formations.

Figure 3.7, the map of Valosaari, is an example of purely morphographic mapping on a large scale. It represents variations in the relief with contour lines at one meter and half-meter intervals, apart from which inclination of the ground was marked between the isohypses by various degrees of hatching perpendicular to the contours. The boundary between land and water was marked on the map only where the shoreline could be clearly distinguished, since the shores are often covered with such a thick aquatic vegetation in summer that the shoreline cannot be seen, and it is still more obscure in winter.

3.5. Forms of Water

If we consider the whole surface of the earth without concentrating on the areas of human settlement, water is the most important of the materials making up landscapes, since most of the earth's surface is sea. But the influence of water is immense on the continents as well, because of its generality and its occurrence in three states, of which the gaseous state actually belongs in terms of landscape science to the formations of the air, or "sky."

We can examine water from the point of view of landscape morphography in approximately the same manner as the earth's surface, in that we can distinguish and define various types of liquid and solid water and can examine their value, groupings, and distributions in order to determine form regions and other regional entities.

Even a superficial examination will indicate, however, that numerous other essential differences also exist between the forms of the earth's surface and those of its aquatic surface.

1. Except for geysers, liquid forms of water are not independent, since their location and shape is determined by the relief.

2. Except for geysers, waves, and surf, the liquid forms of water are usually horizontal or inclined surfaces.

3. The liquid forms of water are partly or entirely mobile, although this movement is only of limited extent as a feature characterizing the landscape.

4. The forms of water are characterized by considerable regional and chronological variability, since, apart from regions with *permanently liquid* or *permanently solid water,* there are vast areas with variable forms, where the forms in which water exists in winter differs to a great extent from that found in summer both in range and manner of influence, and where large areas of the surface of the mainland also change into real water landscapes in winters, that is, other materials are partly or entirely covered with snow and ice. While talking about variability, we should not forget alterations in the amount of water, which often lead to great changes in the landscape. We can thus distinguish *constant* forms, in which the amount of water varies only to a limited extent, *alternating* forms, in which the water regularly dries up at certain times, and *incidental* forms.

The nonindependence of the forms of liquid water, which is manifest in such concepts as lake, river, or bay, is not uncommon in the case of the forms of the earth's crust, since such formations as island, islet, isthmus, cape, and peninsula are equally nonindependent, that is, dependent on another substance, water in this case. We have not found it necessary to discuss these, however, since first, they are as much geographical complexes as features of

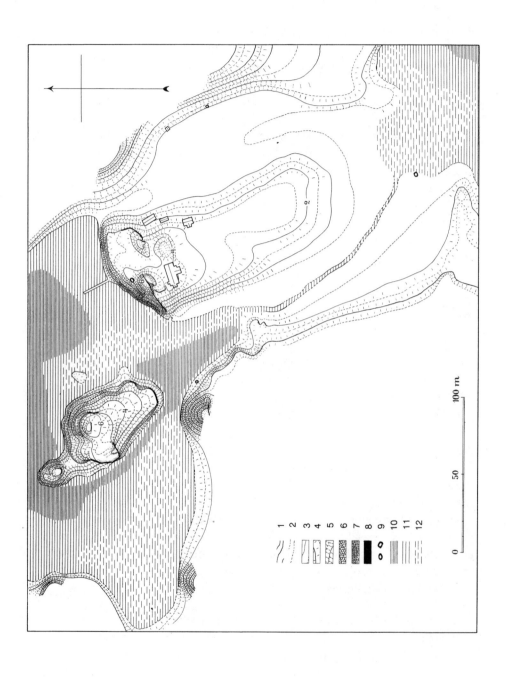

1
2
3
4
5
6
7
8
9
10
11
12

0   50   100 m

the relief, and second, they can easily be examined in the framework of independent features of the relief if they are regarded as forms or form complexes of the earth's surface. This is not to deny the significance of these formations for landscape science, however.

The changeability of the forms of water means that they are not as valuable for landscape definition as the forms of some other materials. We attach critical value to them only if they are approximately constant and permanent.

Even the layman uses a size classification to some extent when talking about the forms of water. Without any attempt to expand this classification to apply to the whole hydromorphographic system, the most common terms used in everyday language to denote the sizes of forms of water are included in the following system.

3.5.1. *Simple forms*

A. Liquid forms of water
  I. Closed forms: rarely completely closed, but these forms are, nevertheless, always dominant in the landscape.
    1. *Lake.* We distinguish four size categories: *pool,* average diameter less than 10 m; *small lake,* average diameter 10–200 m; *lake,* average diameter 200 m–20 km; and *large lake,* diameter at least 20 km. The term *pond* is used of artificial forms.
      a. *Closed lake.* A form without a source or outlet river in the landscape.
      b. *Source lake, terminal lake.* It may be difficult to distinguish one from the other in the landscape. A stream begins from the former and ends in the latter.
      c. *Flowthrough lake.* A form which has a stream flowing into it and out of it.
  II. Open forms: completely or partially open.
    2. *Open water.* Completely open. The water area of large lakes or seas where the shores cannot be seen.

(Facing page)

Figure 3.7. Valosaari relief.

(Altitudes measured from the surface of Lake Saimaa, i.e., 77 m above sea level). *1* =1-m contour line; *2* = 0.5-m contour line; *3* = gradient <5 degrees; *4* = gradient 5–10 degrees; *5* = gradient 10–20 degrees; *6* = gradient 20–30 degrees; *7* = gradient 30–50 degrees; *8* = gradient <50 degrees; *9* = boulders visible in the landscape; *10* = open water; *11* = water partly covered by vegetation; *12* = water mostly covered by vegetation.

Figure 3.8. Water and vegetation in a mountain landscape.
(The alps of Bish-ijirdú and the Tshuja Valley in inner Altai, photographed by the author in 1915.) A river in flood is seen in the foreground and an alpine glacier in the background; bushes, herb terrain and forests are divided by rocky areas; roughly speaking a forest terrain.

3. *Coastal water.* The parts of large lakes and seas where the coast or shore can be seen. A half-open form.
4. *Storm water.* Water from a rainstorm or rapid melting of snow, flowing in various directions.
5. *Bay.* Open at one end.
   a. *Bight.* Maximum length (distance from the head to the mouth) one fifth of the width.
   b. *Cove.* Length more than one fifth of the width, but less than half.
   c. *Arm.* Length more than half of the width.
   d. *Closed bay.* Mouth of the bay narrower than its head. Length varies. A special form of this is the *lobed* bay, which has a winding shoreline. It is recommended that the above terms a–c be used when determining the form of a closed bay (e.g., closed bight, closed arm).
6. *Sound.* Open at both ends, connecting lakes or seas, or separating islands.
7. *Stream.* Open at one or both ends. Size categories: *rivulet,* average width less than 5 m; *brook* average width 5–20 m; *river,* average

width 20–200 m (Fig. 3.9); and *major river,* average width over 200 m.

    a. *Fork.* A branch of a river.

    b. *Connecting stream.* A short stream connecting lakes.

    c. *Placid stream.* In which the flow is so weak that it cannot be seen on the surface (Fig. 3.9).

    d. *Race.* Whirls on the surface caused by the flow of water, sometimes minor waves in places.

  8. *Rapids.* Part of a stream where a strong flow causes high waves and spray.

    a. *Chute.* Gently sloping rapids with waves and variable amounts of spray.

    b. *Cascade.* A more or less foaming waterfall.

III. Vertical forms.

  9. *Geyser.* Independent, constant, and permanent, or more often an incidentally occurring form.

B. Solid forms of water

  I. General forms, see the system of landforms. The words "snow" or "ice" denoting material may be prefixed to the terms depicting the various types of landform (e.g., snowhump, snow barrow, ice table).

Figure 3.9. Water and vegetation in a flat landscape.

(The Jiro Valley in northern Mongolia, west of the town of Urga [Ulan-Bator], photographed by the author in September 1909.) A smooth river, tree-herb terrain, and willows as individual forms, with a steppe mountain terrain in the background.

II. Special forms.
   1. *Smooth ice.* A solid, smooth cover of ice. Immobility may be empha-
      sized by the term *fast ice.*
   2. *Ice cake.* A low, flat, block of ice. A large ice cake is termed an ice
      floe, and an ice cake with rounded corners *pancake ice.* Floating ice-
      floes form *drift ice.*
   3. *Pack ice.* A rough cover of ice formed of jammed ice cakes. High
      heaps of pack ice formed in front of obstacles and in shallows are
      called *pack ice dams.*
   4. *Iceberg.* An ice elevation occurring in the seas of arctic areas and
      occasionally in other places. Its form can be specified using the sys-
      tem of landforms.
   5. *Alpine glacier.* A form occurring in mountain depressions. Its lower-
      most part, which melts and slides slowly down the valley, forms the
      beginning of a glacial stream.
   6. *Marginal glacier.* A form projecting from the edge of a continental
      ice sheet (see form complexes, sec. 3.5.4), often terminating in the sea.

When assessing the value of the above forms in nature it is reasonable to
check the extent to which their influence on the landscape is dependent on
color. The significance of features of the relief often depends to a great extent
on the color of the formations of the earth's crust or of their cover (usually
the vegetation) deviating from their environment. The value of colors is far
greater in the system of the forms of water, which is dominated by nonindependent forms located in depressions and determined only by the landforms
that delimit them.

3.5.2. *Formal elements*

The types of open water can occur as *formal elements* in the same manner as
landforms if they are small enough and occur together with a larger form.
The following formal elements of liquid water should perhaps be mentioned:

A. Elements in open and closed forms
   1. *Inlet.* Corresponds to bay, varying in form in a similar manner.
   2. *Littoral water.* The water area closest to the shore. It is divided by coves
      if the shoreline is winding and should therefore be taken into account
      as a separate formal element only if the shoreline is straight or curves
      around a closed form (lake) in such a manner that no inlets can be dis-
      tinguished.
   3. *Pelagic water.* The water area surrounded by the littoral water.
   4. *Surf.* Foam-crested waves. Only permanent occurrences are taken into
      account when delimiting regions.

5. *Surge.* Permanent surges are taken into account in regional definitions. A special form is *swell,* in which the waves are smooth and gentle.

6. *Whirlpool.* Only constant whirlpools are taken into account as formal elements.

   a. *Suction whirl.* An open conical form in which the water moves downward in a spiral manner. A large suction whirl is termed a *vortex.*

   b. *Ascending whirl.* The water flows upward.

B. Elements in open forms

7. *River head.* The starting point of a connecting stream or river flowing from a lake (or of a fork in a river).

8. *Neck of rapids.* The point from which a stretch of rapids starts.

9. *Mouth.* Rivers, connecting streams and river forks have one mouth, sounds (in which the water does not flow) have two.

10. *Pool.* A calm point between or beside more rapidly flowing areas in a stream.

11. *Torrent.* The most rapidly flowing point in a stream, provided that it can be distinguished in the landscape.

12. *Bend.* A change of direction in a long and narrow form.

   a. *Serpentine.* A bend of less than 180 degrees in a stream. Where this happens repeatedly, one can speak of a winding river.

   b. *Meander.* A bend of over 180 degrees in a stream. Where this happens repeatedly, the stream is then said to *meander.*

C. Elements in vertical forms

13. *Geyser pool* from which a geyser rises.

14. *Geyser.*

The meandering of streams results in the formation of narrow, curved lakes called *oxbow lakes.*

Of the forms of solid water, only alpine glaciers have characteristic formal elements, that is, expansive firn fields from which *glacial lobes* project downward. Terms obtained from the system of forms of liquid water can also be applied to ice formations on glacier surfaces, so that expressions such as ice rapids and ice cascades can be formed as required.

3.5.3. *Complex forms*

The forms of liquid and solid water differ to the extent that they cannot occur together as complex forms, that is, in combinations that occur as morphographically homogeneous entities in the landscape, although complex liquid water and solid water forms can naturally occur separately. Complex forms of liquid water include river systems, bay systems, and fork systems, for example, while all the types characteristic of landforms are at least possible in the case of water in its solid form, if not characteristic of it.

3.5.4. *Cooccurrence*

The form complexes composed of water vary to a considerable extent. Attention must also be paid to the *parallel occurrence* of forms of liquid and solid water, but the chronological aspect should not be ignored, since the *constancy, duration, periodicity,* or *irregularity* of forms can have a considerable influence on the landscape.

A comparative examination of the combinations of the forms of water generates some very clear types of form complexes.

A. Form complexes composed of liquid water
    1. *Water system.* A form complex that can include all forms of liquid water occurring on land. The various forms of such a complex have water connections.
    a. *Lake system.* A water system characterized by successive lakes with connecting streams.
    b. *Coastal waters.* Forms occurring between or separating the mainland and the sea, that is, coastal rivers and lakes, bays, sounds, and the like.
    c. *Inland waterway system.* Form complexes occurring beyond the sphere of influence of the sea.
    d. *Island waters.* Water areas divided by islands.
    2. *Sea, large lake,* with open water, coastal waters, and bays.
B. Complex forms of solid water
    3. *Snow flat.* A winter form complex in the subarctic zone and a permanent form complex in polar areas and at high altitudes. Forms typical of a flat dominate to the extent that the forms of other materials covered by the snow allow this.
    4. *Ice plain.* Occurs in a more or less permanent form in lake and sea areas where the winters are cold and dry.
C. Complex forms of liquid and solid water
    5. *Alpine glacier system,* with its firns, alpine glaciers, meltwater streams, and lakes (Fig. 3.8).
    6. *Continental ice sheet,* with ice and snow plains, crevasses, meltwater streams, marginal glaciers, and ice lakes.
    7. *Ice sea, ice lake.* Apart from forms characteristic of seas and large lakes, these possess a number of more or less permanent solid water forms such as ice cakes, fields of pack ice and smooth ice, or icebergs.

Special codes representing the combinations of the forms of water can be used for definitions in landscape science and for cartographic purposes in the same manner as with landform complexes. In addition to the above complex forms, however, attention should also be paid to simple forms such as *open waters,* which are more significant than any other form or complex form in terms of distribution, and to *rivers* and *lakes*. If we use Roman numerals for the landform complexes, as suggested above, we could use *italicized Arabic numerals* for the forms of water, so that all the inorganic forms and form complexes of the landscape then obtain a numerical index.

The forms and form complexes of water may be numbered in the following manner for the purposes of delimiting regions, in which not only the form but also its frequency of occurrence should be taken into account:

1–open water, *2*–rivers, *3*–lakes, *4*–lake systems, *5*–coastal and island waters, *6*–alpine glacier systems, *7*–continental ice sheet, *8*–ice sea, *9*–snow flat, *10*–ice plain, and *11*–region with very few forms of water.

3.5.5. *Cartographic Representation*

The cartographic representation of the forms of water should not usually cause any problems, since ordinary geographical maps provide practicable data on the forms of liquid water for landscape purposes. It is important, however, to see that the degree of generalization of the source map meets the needs of landscape science and that the permanence of the forms of water and changes in the landscape caused by alterations in water level are taken into account in an appropriate manner in the source map. The significance of aquatic plants and the varying prominence of shorelines should also be considered (see Fig. 3.7).

As far as the purely morphographic aspect is concerned, the facts pertaining to the mapping of the forms of the earth's surface also apply to mapping of the forms of solid water (see sec. 3.4.5).

3.6. Coasts

Although, as mentioned above, liquid water forms and form complexes are nonindependent in the sense that they are dependent on the relief, we have defined the various types only with respect to water forms.

Apart from the above land and water forms and form complexes, there are also simple forms and form complexes consisting of both these materials, where both have to be considered in the definitions. The simple forms include fjords and rias, and the latter island groups and coasts, which merit a more detailed examination since they will be discussed in connection with the definition of geographical regions.

A zone surrounding a sea or a large lake is termed a *coast*, the width of which is determined by the distance of the horizon from the environment closest to the point of convergence of land and water, and in which *coastal land* and *coastal water* are elements of equal significance. The point of contact between the land and water is termed the *shoreline*, which moves from time to time, depending on variations in water levels, tides, and so on. The area within which the shoreline moves back and forth is called *the shore*. This zone, which varies in width and is sometimes dry and sometimes covered with water, separates the permanent coastal water from the permanent dry land.

We may distinguish four coastal types (cf. Passarge 202, I, p. 95):

1. *Flat coast*. Shore and coastal land are flat.

2. *Cliff coast*. A flat shore followed inland by a steep *cliff* belonging to the coastal land.

3. *Steep coast*. Shore and coastal land rise up steeply.

4. *Platform coast*. Steep shore, flat coastal land.

A coast without islands is referred to as an *open coast*, one with islands as a *sheltered coast*, and one with large numbers of islands as an *archipelago coast*. Coasts can also be classified according to the form of their bays (bight coast, arm coast, fjord coast, ria coast, etc.)

3.7. Forms of Vegetation

Plants exhibit various *growth forms:* trees, shrubs, dwarf shrubs, herbs, grasses, mosses, lichens, fungi, and algae. Only the largest of these forms, that is, trees and bushes, various succulents and some large herbs, can act as *individual forms* in the landscape, that is, *simple* forms, namely, when isolated or standing out in their environment (Fig. 3.9). In other cases they act only in groups, or *group forms*, like all other forms of the plant kingdom (Figs. 3.9 and 3.10). These forms are also simple in landscape terms and differ sharply from the land and water *form groups*, which consist of simple forms that can be distinguished from each other in the landscape.

The individual and group forms of the vegetation thus differ in the sense that the former consist of only one plant while the latter consist of more than one. Both are equally uniform entities in the landscape, however, and should be examined as such in landscape science, with no need to describe the special features of the various individual plants within the group forms.

The individual and group forms combine into various complex forms, which are further grouped into *vegetation zones* extending across the world or into *altitudinal vegetation zones* in mountainous regions.

It is clear that only large plants possess formal elements or parts which are visible in the landscape, but these deserve attention provided they are common enough and can be defined reliably. This applies to parts of both individual and group forms.

Trees, as an example of individual forms, have clear formal elements (Fig. 3.11): the *trunk, branches* or *leaves*, and the *crown*, the latter being synonymous with the leaves in the case of palms, for instance. Group forms do not have such permanent, characteristic components.

Figure 3.10. Coniferous forest in hill terrain.

(Lake Sadra and its environment in NE Altai, photographed by the author in June 1914.) A forest of pine (*Pinus cembra*) with individual aspens and birches in places.

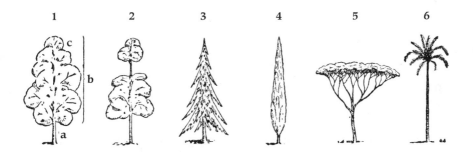

Figure 3.11. Tree forms.

1 = Elliptical crown; *1a* = trunk; *1b* = branches; *1c* = top; *2* = layered crown; *3* = conical crown; *4* = spindle crown; *5* = umbrella (or corymb) crown; *6* = tuft crown.

Both a size classification and a system of forms should be considered for the analysis of vegetation in landscape science, since it is difficult to distinguish between the two in practice. It should also be kept in mind that the value of outlines or profiles is not as great as in the case of landforms. The morphography of the surface of a vegetation form, or the overall morphographic influence of that surface (especially the manner in which the individual plants occur in their groups), is often of crucial significance. The difference between coniferous and broad-leafed forests, for instance, is based on this phenomenon and emphasized by their coloring.

When examining the vegetation or other living aspects of nature in terms of landscape science, it is necessary to employ the taxonomies of the natural sciences, which are to a great extent based on features of appearance. This facilitates the definition and examination of forms and form complexes of living things in some respects and renders it briefer and more accurate than that of the inanimate world.

3.7.1. *Individual and Group Forms*

A. Individual forms

    I. *Trees.* These are divided into two subgroups: *coniferous trees* and *broad-leafed trees,* the latter also including palms and tree ferns. Types may be distinguished within these subgroups by reference to the form of their branches or leaves (Fig. 3.11; cf. Passarge 202, I, pp. 112–13.)

        1. *Elliptical crown*

        2. *Layered crown.*

        3. *Conical crown.*

        4. *Spindle crown.*

        5. *Umbrella (or corymb) crown.*

        6. *Tuft crown.*

    II. *Shrubs.* Two subgroups: *coniferous shrubs* and *broad-leafed shrubs.*

    III. *Cactaceous plants.* These include certain types of succulents, for example, the genera *Opuntia* and *Euphorbia* as well as the cacti of dry regions.

B. Group forms

    I. *Forest.*

        1. *Coniferous forest.* Various subtypes, which can be most conveniently determined on the basis of their tree species (spruce, pine, larch, cedar, etc.; Figs. 3.10 and 3.12)

        2. *Broad-leafed forest.* Various subtypes (birch, oak, beech, palm, etc.)

        3. *Mixed forest.* Coniferous and broad-leafed trees in approximately equal proportions in the landscape. Various combinations possible.

Figure 3.12. Forest terrain in mountains.

(The Valley of Yeloman in the Katun area in Inner Altai, photographed by the author in August 1915.) Larch forests predominate, with rocks and herb terrain in places (a field in the foreground, with a Telengite yurt, fences and a hayrick behind).

 II. *Thicket.*
  1. *Coniferous thicket.* This consists of groups of small, young coniferous trees making up low, forestlike formations in the landscape.
  2. *Broad-leafed thicket* or *jungle.* This may be composed of willows or of young deciduous trees, such as birch, lime, or alder.
  3. *Dwarf shrubs.* For example, heaths.
 III. *Succulents.* A group form characteristic of dry areas, consisting of cacti, opuntias, euphorbias, and the like.
 IV. *Herbs.* Consists of herbs, grasses and sedges. A narrower concept is *grassland,* that is, a group form of grasses and sedges, which can hardly be distinguished from other herb-rich areas in the landscape in terms of its formal features. *Meadow* is a similar concept, which refers to herb-rich land suitable for pasture or mowing, as distinct from a *field,* which supports grain or other cultivated plants.
 V. *Mosses.*
 VI. *Lichens.*
 VII. *Algae.* A group form growing in water, which is morphographically significant in the landscape only in exceptional cases.

3.7.2. *Cooccurrence*

There are numerous vegetation form complexes that can be defined by means of the plant community terms used by phytogeographers, but this should only be done when these are justified in landscape terms. Therefore forests, thickets, and herbs, for instance, are complex forms and not group forms only when their unity in the landscape is broken up by some other form or forms, even though possibly of secondary significance, occurring beside them in the complex.

The determining group form must naturally be taken into account above all in the system of form complex types. We thus obtain six type groups, mainly named after the most familiar or characteristic form or complex:

I. *Forest terrain.* Dominated by forest. This group includes spruce swamps, park woodlands, gallery forests, and the like (Figs. 3.8, 3.10, and 3.12).

II. *Bush terrain.* Bushes dominate, often with a high incidence of dwarf shrubs. Includes maquis (scrubs, chaparrals), subalpine birch scrubs, dwarf shrub heath, bush and dwarf shrub bogs (treeless dwarf birch bogs, etc.).

III. *Succulent terrain.* Dominated by cacti, euphorbias, or other succulents, which occasionally occur as individual forms as well.

IV. *Herb terrain.* Includes steppes (prairies, pampas, alvars), savannas (llanos, campos), tree-herb terrains (individual trees scattered over herb terrain), bush-herb terrains (individual bushes scattered over herb terrain, herb-rich mires (most treeless bogs and fens) (Fig. 3.10).

V. *Moss terrain.* Dominated by mosses: moss-rich mires (e.g., *Sphagnum* bogs), moss tundras, moss-covered rocks.

VI. *Lichen terrain.* Lichen heaths, lichen tundras, lichen-covered rocks and boulder fields.

If shorter symbols are needed for these vegetation form complexes, *italicized capital letters* may be used for this purpose: *A*–forest terrain, *B*–bush terrain, *C*–succulent terrain, *D*–herb terrain, *E*–moss terrain, *F*–lichen terrain, *G*–minimal vegetation. The vegetation forms of Finland and Estonia, like those of the northern coniferous forest zone in general, can be categorized more conveniently in another manner, however, which concentrates on the role of trees in the types of complex forms. We thus obtain the following categorization: *A*–forest terrain, *B*–bush terrain, *C*–spruce mire terrain, *D*–pine bog terrain, *E*–herb terrain, *F*–lichen terrain (mainly on rocks and boulder fields), *G*–minimal vegetation.

An area which has little or no vegetation and may be variable in its relief is termed a *desert.* We speak of a *desert plain* to refer to a plain which is either desert or covered by a low vegetation (dwarf shrubs, herbs, etc.).

Important as vegetation may be as a factor in the complex of materials making up the landscape, its form complexes do not merit so much attention in the establishment of geographical regions as do those of land and water, since many of its forms last only a limited time and are so low that they are entirely covered by snow in winter in areas where the forms of water change. Various forms of vegetation change regularly in a conspicuous manner, as indicated by the expressions *deciduous, green during the rainy season,* and *evergreen,* not to mention the changes occurring as a result of growth, blooming, fruiting, and withering, even within short periods of time.

It is common knowledge that the human impact on the vegetation in civilized countries in particular has often been considerable, sometimes destroying the original forms and sometimes creating forms foreign to the area by sowing and planting. A purely morphographic examination naturally need not concentrate very much on this question, but as we start to examine the genesis of forms, this may perhaps be the first aspect to be considered.

3.7.3. *Cartographic Representation*

Assessment of the significance of vegetation in terms of landscape science is possible only once the forms of the vegetation have been defined and their distribution represented cartographically. If these prerequisities exist, the researcher can start to define regions in terms of vegetation forms, that is, the vegetation must be examined within the framework of landscape science alone in the same manner as land and water. This task of phytogeography is quite as essential and significant for the investigation of geographical entities as the above preliminary work in geomorphography and hydrography, quite apart from the fact that more detailed investigations into regional geography and phytogeography also require such a general view.

Whether the work is carried out in the field or on the basis of maps depends on the extent of the area being investigated. The vegetation maps of Estonia and Valosaari (Figs. 3.13 and 3.14), drawn to the same scale as the corresponding topographical maps, illustrate the nature of the task.

The forms and form complexes of the vegetation of Estonia are known as far as their general features are concerned, but their significance in terms of landscape science has not been examined. No general maps exist of the distribution of the various forms and form complexes, and therefore a map had to be drawn up specifically for this purpose on the principles of botanical landscape science but based on the topographic map (Fig. 3.13).

The classification of the forms of vegetation on our map thus cannot be expected to meet our requirements in every respect, since it can only include the features indicated on the topographical map. Different signs and hatchings are used to distinguish between alvar and sand vegetations, and the various herb areas, mires, and forests.

Of these group forms and form complexes, the areas of forests, fields (cultivated herb terrain), and pine bogs are delimited in a fairly detailed manner on the topographic maps, whereas the definition of meadows, tree meadows, and fens was more difficult, and consequently our map is less reliable in this respect.

The areas characterized by aquatic plants are usually so small that it is not possible to mark them on maps for technical reasons. This is a disadvantage, since they are of considerable significance in the landscape in places..

The map of Valosaari (Fig. 3.14), which represents not only the vegetation but also artificial forms, is based on an actual survey. The large scale of the map permits a very detailed examination of individual forms as well. Attempts have been made to illustrate variations in vegetation in as correct a manner as possible down to the details of the landscape by using various symbols depicting the physiognomy of different vegetation forms and form complexes. Let us take as an example the manner of representing deciduous trees and forest, individual spruces and pines and pine forest, or herbs and aquatic plants. Size has also been taken into account in that larger vertical dimensions are represented by darker symbols (cf. the symbols for lichens, mosses, herbs, and forest).

3.8. Forms of Fauna

Animals have an influence on the landscape as individual and group forms in a similar manner to plants, although their significance is far smaller, especially in the defining of regions, since they mcve from one landscape to another and, with the exception of domestic animals, tend to escape out of sight.

It is possible for the fauna to affect the landscape only where other phenomena do not conceal them, that is, in wasteland areas and on coasts. The wild animals on savannas and steppes, as studied by Waibel (282, 283) in particular, cattle roaming in open areas and the bird cliffs in the Arctic Ocean are of principal interest here. In these cases the animals concerned mostly occur in group forms and only the largest animal species act as individual forms in the complex.

(Facing page)

Figure 3.13. Vegetation in Estonia.
1 = Alvar, vegetation of sandy soils; *2* = natural herb terrain (mainly peatland meadow); *3* = tree and bush herb terrain (mainly damp); *4* = forest; *5* = bog (pine bogs, spruce swamps, fens); *6* = cultivated herbs (field); *7* = city, town, village, church; *8* = border.

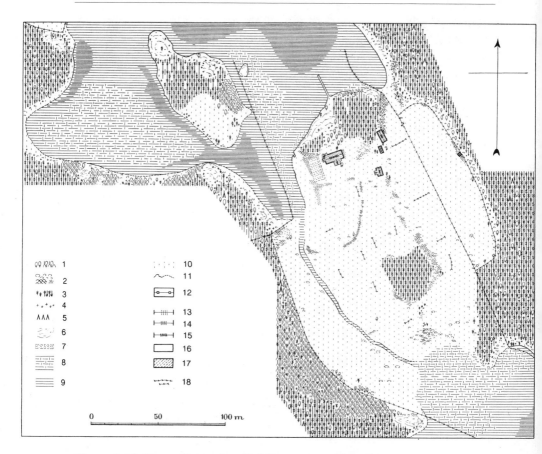

Figure 3.14. Vegetation and artificial matter at Valosaari.

1 = Broad-leaved trees/forest; *2* = broad-leaved bushes, jungle, brushwood; *3* = pines, pinewood; *4* = small pines, junipers; *5* = spruces; *6* = lichen and moss-covered rock faces; *7* = kitchen garden; *8* = dense reed, rush, or sedge stands in water; *9* = sparse aquatic vegetation; *10* = grassland; *11* = distinct and indistinct shoreline.; *12* = building with a pitched roof and chimneys; *13* = roof inclination 10–20 degrees; *14* = roof inclination 20–30 degrees; *15* = roof inclination 30–50 degrees; *16* = building more than 2 m in height; *17* = single-story building less than 2 m in height; *18* = fence, hayrick.

The significance of flying members of the animals kingdom in landscape physiognomy and the role of the fauna as a part of the mobile sphere will be discussed below (see sec. 3.11.2).

3.9. Human Presence in the Landscape

People differ from animals as a factor in the landscape in that their wide variety of clothing introduces considerable variation, although this is manifested more frequently in terms of color than of form. Sometimes the people present can be so numerous that we can speak of a human landscape, for example, in the business centers of large cities, at fairs, in busy market places, at religious gatherings and other mass meetings, and during the movements of military troops and large groups of people at times of war.

If people are constantly moving in the same area, they must be considered part of the mobile form complex (see sec. 3.11), regardless of the fact that the individual people change.

3.10. Artificial Forms

Artificial forms, like artificial matter, are those generated by human or animal agency. The nests or dens and paths made by the latter are, nevertheless, so insignificant and so rare in the landscape, except for termitaria, tracks frequented by large animals, and comparable cases that it is unnecessary to discuss them here. We will therefore concentrate on *artificial forms of human origin.*

In terms of landscape science, *buildings* are three-dimensional forms of substantial size made of artificial material. If the forms are positive, that is, elevations, they are usually made entirely of artificial material, whereas negative forms, that is, depressions, are mainly only lined with artificial material from the inside.

Structures are artificial forms that have a maximum of two dimensions in the landscape (e.g., fences or roads) and which usually contain such small amounts of artificial material that it would be difficult to think of them as forms on the basis of their material alone, for example, a road across a steppe (Fig. 3.3). In this case they will have been created in one way or another on the surface of natural forms and can be distinguished better by virtue of their color than their form.

Artificial forms are so numerous that it may seem presumptuous to start systematizing them. They are also perhaps thought to depend on the arbitrariness and whims of individual people to such an extent that a purely morphographic examination is unnecessary.

A fact that nobody is likely to deny is that buildings occur as the dominant characteristics over vast areas of landscape, often being more significant than any landforms, whose smallest, hardly visible features we are used to observing and examining with commendable accuracy. Artificial forms are particularly significant in those areas where towns and cities are becoming increasingly large and numerous in our day. This fact obliges the landscape scientist to pay serious attention to such artificial forms, and this can be done if he has a system at his disposal for the purpose. Various geographers have in fact worked for the creation of such a system (Schlüter 244, Brunhes 27, Passarge 202, Geisler 67, Kant 135, Martiny 165, etc.).

The above assumption regarding the crucial influence of arbitrary human decisions is valid only to a restricted extent, since human actions are usually so conservative and dependent on practical considerations and prevailing tastes that the variations in artificial forms are actually smaller than might be expected. The most marked variations occur in modern urban societies, although the most significant forms and formal elements are always easy to recognize and can be defined within the framework of the system.

The question is such an extensive one, however, that it cannot be discussed here from all aspects. We shall therefore concentrate on *residential buildings, outbuildings,* and *roads,* and some matters concerned with the classification of these.

Residential buildings can be classified according to height, that is, on the basis of the number of storeys. This unit is quite satisfactory, since the height of one storey varies within fairly narrow limits, while more or less round figures must be used for the other dimensions.

3.10.1. *Forms and Formal Elements*

Since the terminology of geometry is the most suitable for determining the general features of a form, we should attempt here to define the plan view, cross section, longitudinal section and other features relevant to each general form. A simple form is then an entity occurring as a building unit regardless of the number of storeys, and a complex form one in which several such units have been built together in such a manner that they have at least one entire wall in common. It is often very hard to decide, however, whether a building belongs among the simple or complex forms.

Residential buildings and outbuildings have two necessary formal elements, the *roof* and the *walls.* The *floor* constitutes a feature of the landscape only if the building is above the surface of the ground or water, on piles or in a tree. A *canopy* is a roof resting on not more than three walls or only on pillars.

Apart from size and plan view, *roof forms* are of particular interest. It is most expedient to base the system of forms for describing residential and some other buildings on the relations between their plan view, height, and width and on the form of the roof. A series of major groups can easily be obtained on the basis of the plan view, while the examination of the relations between height and width and the roof forms provides a more detailed division into types.[5] With the exception of their formal elements, walls are usually vertical, thus conforming with the plan view, while a description of the roof provides a statement of the morphology of the highest part of the form under discussion, which is often also the most conspicuous part in the landscape.

5. Kant presents a detailed system along these lines in his methodologically significant research into the city of Tartu (135, p. 230).

Ignoring for the moment the stone buildings of cities, manors, and monasteries, which present a fairly wide variety of forms in this respect, we can easily systematize roof forms by means of the following scheme (Fig. 3.15):

I. *Flat roof.* A horizontal surface.

II. *Dome roof.* The roof merges directly with the walls. The plan view of the building is round or oval.

III. *Arched roof.* Curves down on both sides to produce a convex form. The building is often a semicylinder in form.

IV. *Conical roof.* This may either end in vertical walls or continue to the ground, in which case one can speak of a tepee form.

V. *Pitched roofs.*

1. *Double pitched roof.* The slopes of the roof are straight.
2. *Sagging pitched roof.* The slopes, and often also the ridge, are concave.
3. *Lean-to roof.* Slopes to one side only.
4. *Hip roof.* The roof consists of four planes inclined in different directions. A steep, high roof without a crest is called a *pavilion roof.*
5. *Gabled roof.* The slopes at the gables are shorter than the other two.

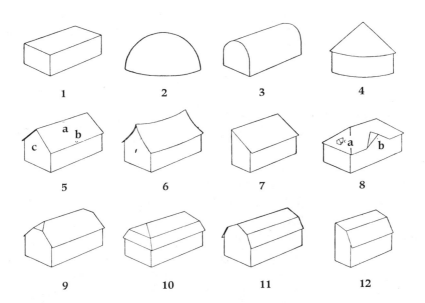

Figure 3.15. Common roof forms.

1 = Flat roof; *2* = domed roof; *3* = arched roof; *4* = conical roof; *5* = double pitched roof; *5a* = ridge; *5b* = eaves; *5c* = gable; *6* = sagging pitched roof; *7* = lean-to roof; *8* = hip roof; *8a* = dormer window; *8b* = front gable; *9* = gabled roof; *10* = mansard roof; *11* = gambrel roof; *12* = lean-to gambrel roof.

6. *Mansard roof.* Each slope consists of two parts at different angles.
7. *Gambrel roof.* The roof consists of two folded surfaces.
8. *Lean-to gambrel roof.* A folded surface inclined in a single direction.

General formal elements of inclined roofs include not only the *ridge* (Fig. 3.15, feature 5a) and *eaves* (5b), but also *dormer windows* (8a) and *front gables* (8b). The upper parts of the latter are usually lower than the main ridge, although they may sometimes be at the same level, and the wall of the front gable is flush with the main wall. If it is not, that is, if there is an extension with a separate roof, this is called a *transverse gable* or *longitudinal gable* depending on its relation to the main ridge of the building. If a transverse gable is as high as or higher than the main roof and covers an extension or *wing* of the building, it is referred to as a *transverse roof.*

Walls are usually planes, which rarely have *projections* or *depressions,* that is, they are rarely curved or bend inward or outward. One should also pay attention to the form and number of windows and to any *balconies* and *porches.* A special formal element of double-pitched roofs is the *gable end,* delimited at the sides and from above by the roof itself (5c).

3.10.2. *Form Groups and Complexes*

A residential building and its outhouses make up a form group, a *dwelling,* which can occur either alone as an *individual dwelling* (Figs. 3.12 and 3.16), in small *hamlets* of just a few dwellings, or in larger complexes of varying density known as *villages, towns,* and *cities.* All these terms are also used for the corresponding form complexes and landscape complexes. In the former case they include not only the residential houses with their outbuildings and other buildings but also structures such as fences, wells, street lamps, and statues, and above all yards and roads. In the latter case they include the forms of the various materials, colors, and sources of light in the area. No matter which of these meanings is considered, the most significant factor in the definition is the grouping of the buildings and their relation to the yards and roads. We therefore use the term *open yard dwelling* or *open dwelling* to denote a form group that has an approximately open yard, in that either it is surrounded only by a few buildings or it surrounds the buildings, and a *closed yard dwelling* or *closed dwelling* for a group in which the yard is surrounded by buildings or by a high, wall-like fence. Similarly, we can distinguish a group of village types on the basis of a classification of artificial forms and their relations:

1. *Loose village.* Dwellings dispersed, perhaps at considerable distances from one another.
   a. *Clustered settlement.* Scattered dwellings in an approximately circular area or situated around a road junction or beside a waterway. Such

Figure 3.16. An individual dwelling in a closed landscape.
(A Japanese spa in the Hakone Mountains.).

   clusters occur in the Finnish archipelago, for instance, where navigation and fishing are significant sources of livelihood, and at
   crossroads and close to railway stations.
   b. *Ribbon settlement.* Scattered dwellings forming an elongated chain,
      mostly along rivers or roads. These are common along the rivers of
      the coastal expanses in Finland, for instance.
   c. *Branch settlement.* Dwellings or small groups of dwellings on one or
      both sides of the road, but at some distance from it and connected
      to it by means of smaller roads. This form occurs in some places in
      Estonia, for instance.
2. *Cluster village.* Dwellings close to one another without any systematic
   arrangement, along a network of roads winding and branching off in various directions. The village is more often roundish than elongated in
   form. Often occurs in similar places to clustered settlements.
3. *Ring village.* Dwellings arranged close to one another in a circle around
   the village square.
4. *Street village.* Dwellings arranged close to one another in rows, beside one
   or more long main village streets. The plan of the village is elongated, often long and narrow (Fig. 3.17).

Figure 3.17. A street village in the mountains.
(Koton-karagay in SW Altai, photographed by the author in June 1909).

There are various transitional forms between these types, with a continuum leading from the loose village forms, for instance, to cluster and street
villages. The borderline between individual dwellings, hamlets, and loose
villages is also fairly vague.

When defining towns and cities, attention is paid not only to size but also
to the planning and density of the street network and the width of the streets
themselves, the number and size of the parks and squares, the height of the
buildings, and the distribution of various types of buildings (cf. Geisler 67,
Martiny 165 and especially Kant 135).

The following types of towns and cities can be distinguished on the basis
of their street network:

1. *Clustered town.* Streets wind and branch in an irregular manner. The
buildings are usually close to one another.

2. *Circular town.* Streets either radiate from the center or surround it con-
centrically.

3. *Grid town.* Streets intersect one another at right-angles.

4. *Rib town.* Short side-streets branch off from a long main street.

The term *road network* refers to the complex of roads on dry land. Waterways (canals, etc.) can be more conveniently discussed in connection with the forms of water, to which they belong as far as landscape science is concerned. The examination of roads running on land does not require its own system of forms, since the generally employed classification based mainly on variations in width and the substrate from which they are made is quite sufficient for our purposes. The main thoroughfares in village types with dense settlement and the roadways in towns and cities are referred to as *streets*.

Various codes, for example, *small letters,* can be used to represent the form complexes of artificial matter in the same manner as above. Again the ordering is determined by relative size: *a*–towns, cities, *b*–street villages, *c*–cluster villages, *d*–ring villages, *e*–ribbon settlements, *f*–clustered settlements, *g*–branch settlements, *h*–hamlets, *i*–individual dwellings, *k*–structures alone (mainly roads), *l*–artificial forms rare. The following classification corresponds to Finnish conditions: *a*–ribbon settlements, *b*–clustered settlements, *c*–individual dwellings, *d*–artificial forms rare.

3.10.3. *Cartographic Representation*

Our discussion above has concerned only *immobile* artificial forms, which are indeed the most significant factors for the determination of geographical regions on land and those that the geographer most often has to represent on maps. The opposite is true of the description of water areas, since the artificial forms visible in open water landscapes belong almost without exception to the mobile phenomena. An open sea, which lies outside the territories affected by human activities, will differ in terms of landscape from an expanse of water that is crowded with shipping. Each ship as such is naturally only a temporary phenomenon in the landscape, but the ships as a complex occupying a sea area of this kind form a constant, characteristic feature, which is also highly distinctive in that the number of salient characteristics in the area is otherwise fairly small.

In the case of broad generalizations, when defining geographical provinces or larger entities, for example, we consider primarily the number and grouping of buildings and dwellings and the density of the road network, while a more detailed examination requires concentration on the various forms and formal elements making up the buildings.

When drawing up the map of Estonia below (Fig. 3.18), only the main features of the artificial form complexes were considered. The forms and formal elements of the buildings differ so little from one part of Estonia to another that the variations do not have any effect on the general nature of the largest geographical entities in the country.

Since the size, plan view, and distribution of the dwellings and the network of roads are represented in sufficient detail on the Topographical Map

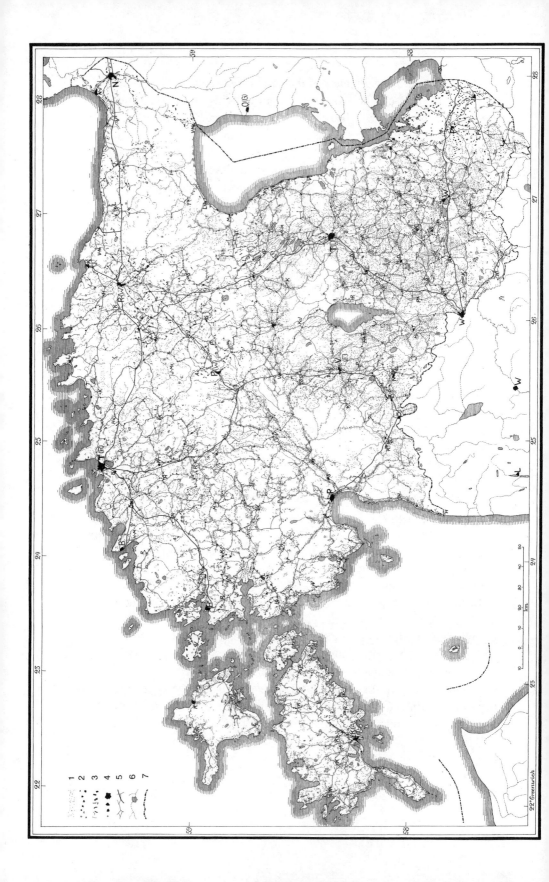

of Estonia, the areas characterized by the various artificial forms can also be represented on the basis of the material provided by it. Although this is to some extent dated, and although the forms included on the final map are exaggerated in relation to the scale, the result of the generalization is entirely serviceable, since the various areas have not altered greatly in terms of settlement and traffic in the past few years and the exaggeration of certain features for technical reasons is similar in all parts of the map, thus promoting rather than hindering the creation of a general impression.

The map of Valosaari (Fig. 3.14) provides a more detailed examination of artificial forms, since it includes the plan views and heights (hatchings and symbols) of the various buildings, chimneys, and roofs with their forms and inclinations and also indicates structures, that is, fences and hayricks. The plan view of the building complex at Valosaari, representing the proximate field of vision, in which even the smallest artificial features visible in the landscape are included (Fig. 4.5), is also worth mentioning in this connection.

3.11. Mobile Forms

The significance of the *mobile form complex,* that is, the entity composed of mobile forms, is small compared with the *immobile form complex* in the part of the landscape where all the above-mentioned complexes are situated, where land and water form the substrate and of which we use the general term "earth" in everyday language (see sec. 1.7), but in the second major part of the landscape, that situated above the horizon, that is, the "sky," it is the mobile element that dominates.

3.11.1. *Forms in the Sky*

The forms we can point to in terms of landscape science as either occurring in the air or existing in the sky represent a variety of materials and belong to two essentially different groups, in that some exist as local forms within the boundaries of the landscape, and others, which are undoubtedly more distinctive, participate from greater distances. The latter group includes a series of formations that could as well be classified as belonging to the forms of either the sky or the air.

(Facing page)

Figure 3.18. Artificial forms and form complexes in Estonia.

1 = Individual dwellings; *2* = clusters of dwellings (estates, etc.) and cluster villages; *3* = ribbon settlements and street villages; *4* = church, village, town and city; *5* = roads, railways; *6* = rivers, brooks, lake; *7* = border.

Since our task here is restricted to the examination of form, we will not discuss alterations in color and light in the sky. The aurora borealis, lightning, zodiacal light, and other such phenomena are not tied to any element of the landscape any more than are the changing colors of the sky. But the celestial bodies are also primarily lights for the landscape scientist rather than forms. It is more difficult, however, to decide where mirages should be classified. They are undoubtedly worth attention, since they call forth visual sensations that resemble those directly caused by the form complexes of a landscape, but nevertheless they do not integrally belong to the objects of that landscape but are only indirectly dependent on reality and correspond to it to a restricted extent. The fact that a mirage is to some extent realistic, although a picture of a geographical complex in a false location and thus misleading, should justify its inclusion in the system of landscape forms at some point.

The short duration of most of the forms occurring in the sky, their isolation from the other forms in the landscape and their occurrence even at high levels above and outside the territories in which human beings live and act were the reasons for classifying them in the following by their material composition regardless of any contradictions that may arise.

I. *Mirage.*

II. *Smoke, ash, dust* and *sand clouds* or *storms.* Mainly local forms.

III. *Mist.* A thick mist may be designated separately as *fog.* A local form.

IV. *Clouds.* Mainly distant forms. Defined according to the meteorologists' accepted classification of clouds, which can be considered a pure representative of landscape morphography.

V. *Precipitation.* Almost without exception a local form. Occurs in the form of *rain, snow,* and *hail.* Special forms of rain may be distinguished: *drizzle, shower,* and *downpour.* Among the forms of snow one could mention *blizzard. Sleet* is an intermediate form between rain and snow.

VI. *Flying animals* (birds, bats, grasshoppers, etc.)

VII. *Artificial forms moving in the air* (airships and aeroplanes).

Many of these may occur in various ways in combinatory forms and form complexes. Illustrative in this sense are the various combinations of clouds and formations caused by volcanic eruptions. Many forms also occur frequently or always at such a low altitude that they could just as well be counted as properties of the land.

3.11.2. *Cartographic Representation of Mobile Forms*

It is appropriate to represent mobile forms on maps when they occur often or permanently in the same places in the landscape to the extent that they come to be of considerable importance.

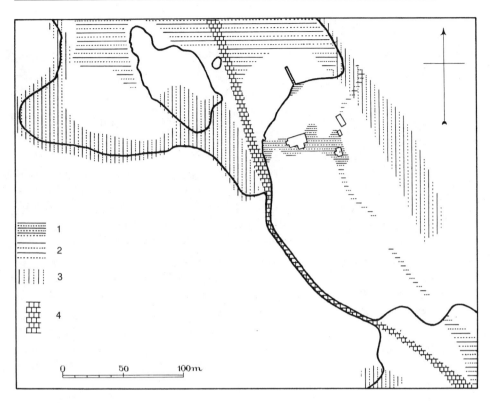

Figure 3.19. Mobile form complex of Valosaari.

1 = People (on foot) frequently in summer; *2* = people (on foot or by boat) sometimes in summer; *3* = cattle (sometimes horses or sheep) often in summer; *4* = people and vehicles at all times of the year, especially in winter (boating route in summer, ice road in winter).

It was considered necessary to pay attention to mobile forms in the above-mentioned mapping of Valosaari (Fig. 3.19). Cattle are grazed in the meadow of this small area and on the grass near the shore, people are to be seen around the buildings and on the paths winding through the grass, and boats on the water. There are no roads, and thus no traffic in summer. In winter, on the other hand, the cattle have been taken away and the buildings are uninhabited, since the house is used by a family from the town as a summer cottage, but a major ice road runs along the narrow sound of Kuivasalmi and on to Mikkeli. The areas of mobile forms in the different seasons are indicated on the map, but only to the extent that these forms are visible in the landscape. The mobile forms in the forest belong to the proximity and will be discussed in connection with it.

3.12. Variable Forms

The category of variable elements includes all those that change during the year as seen from the point of view of descriptive landscape science (see sec. 1.8), and correspondingly variable forms are those that change in form on this time-scale.

The forms of a landscape change approximately in the same manner every year, which results in a *morphographic rhythm* perceivable in time and often connected with a clear sequential alteration in color.

The various materials that make up a landscape are represented in different ways in the variable form complex. The earth's surface is mainly an invariable element within the scope of one year, as also are artificial forms. The forms of the vegetation exhibit growth everywhere but the consequences of this are not of any great significance in our landscapes within the short term. Thus, the coniferous forests that are dominant everywhere in the north are elements of the invariable form complex despite their growth, while a morphographically more significant feature of the variable form complex is the periodic occurrence of leaves in deciduous forests.

The most significant element of the variable form complex is water when occurring in the solid state during the cold season, represented in particular forms and form complexes characteristic of winter landscapes, so that entire zones of the earth change into almost continuous areas of snow and ice. The varying amount of liquid water in the landscape in different seasons is also worth considering. The floods in lowlands and the streams and lakes that evaporate and vanish in dry areas are extreme cases in that they disappear entirely at times.

3.13. Colors

Ostwald writes in the introduction to his *Die Farbenlehre* (Theory of colors, 193, I, pp. 4–5):

> The activity of the eye is called *seeing* and it should thus first be considered whether we see anything else other than colors. The answer is probably obvious for most people in the sense that apart from colors we see *forms,* which we tend to regard as being of primary significance and most often perceived. A deeper examination of the matter soon indicates, however, that what we actually see first and most commonly is color. If we look at the contents of what we see quite spontaneously, without considering its "meaning," we see that it is a multicolored surface composed of patches of color . . . What we call *form* arises only from the interaction of those patches; that is, form is only a result of the existence of colors and their spatial arrangements, apart from which the of-

ten highly complex experience of the affinity between certain patches of colors should be considered.

If the object of geographical description were only the perceived environment as a mere combination of phenomena, we could conveniently have started with the discussion of colors. The experience of the affinity between various patches of colors mentioned by Ostwald and certain important practical considerations have, nevertheless, led us first to forms and to objects, the most significant and essential phenomena regarding which are their forms, on account of the immobility and invariability of these.

The fact that colors vary to a great extent in the landscape should not lead us to underestimate their significance, however. A description in terms of landscape science that concentrated only on forms would naturally be biased. Information should thus also be provided on colors to the extent the area is characterized by them, not only on *specific colors,* which we perceive when looking at objects from close range in white daylight, but also on subjective colors, which are dependent both on the specific colors of the objects concerned and on the properties of the air, lighting, relief, and the like. Therefore, the alternation of shadows and light areas is quite different in the tropics, where the sun rises and sets perpendicularly, from that experienced in arctic areas, where the sun travels on a nearly horizontal path close to the horizon for weeks. Similarly, the coloring of distant ridges and forests looming from behind a thick layer of air in an open landscape is different from that of similar formations in a closed landscape, where they are much closer and therefore separated from the observer by a far thinner layer of air.

The specific colors of the earth's surface are invariable but are mainly visible only in deserts, while the colors of the vegetation and the white colors of snow at times in places that are cold in winter are dominant elsewhere on land. The colors of the vegetation are for the most part invariable (in evergreen forests), although variation also occurs (in deciduous forests or forests and grasslands that are green during the rainy season). Artificial forms are also mainly invariable in color.

There are thus a relatively large number of permanent colorations in the landscape, but often they cannot truly be perceived since we mostly see them through a screen of subjective colors. Variable distances and lighting conditions cause repeated changes, apart from which the sky as a whole, which can be vast in area in an open landscape, is variable in color (Heim 108), and this combination of variable colors is further reflected to our eyes from the surface of water.[6]

6. Ostwald has created a system of colors (193) that could be used for chromatological examination of the landscape. A less detailed and accurate classification of colors is perhaps sufficient in most cases, however.

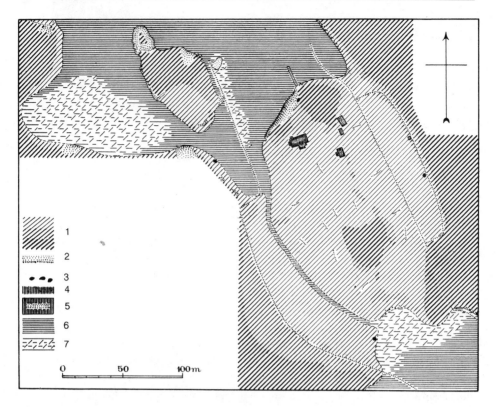

Figure 3.20. Colors of the summer landscape in Valosaari.

1 = Green (*thin hatching* = green of grass; *medium hatching* = green of deciduous forest; *thick hatching* = green of coniferous forest); *2* = grey (rocks, roofs, walls, fences, hayricks); *3* = boulder grey; *4* = red (roofs); *5* = building (*center* indicates roof color, *edges* wall color); *6* = water (reflecting various colors); *7* = green of aquatic plants. The map represents the characteristic colors of the elements in the landscape, except for water, the characteristic color of which is less significant than the fact that it reflects the colors of the sky and the environment.

3.13.1. *Cartographic Representation*

It is mainly the colors that are characteristic of a landscape that should be represented cartographically. The necessity for doing so depends on the existence of features characterizing the area to a significant extent in terms of their distribution or seasonal rhythm. The distributions of colors should not be ignored even when defining vast, morphographically monotonous open sea areas, but a map of the colors of the landscape is particularly necessary when defining small land areas or sublocalities that are uniform as regards landscape. Such maps are probably less often needed when defining districts or provinces, since as generalization increases the colors are either grouped in a similar manner all over the landscape or, more often, are grouped in a manner indicated by the vegetation map.

Figures 3.20–3.22 represent the colors of the landscape at Valosaari, which are partly variable and partly invariable. The green color of the vegetation in its various hues is dominant in summer (Fig. 3.20), and the white of the snow in winter (Fig. 3.21). The invariable colors are the dark green of the pine forests (Fig. 3.22) and, as a secondary factor, the red or time-worn silver-grey of the walls, and the grey of fences, hayricks, and bedrock outcrops. The maps usually represent the specific colors; only unfrozen water is indicated with the color of subjective observations, that is, the constantly changing color of its reflections.

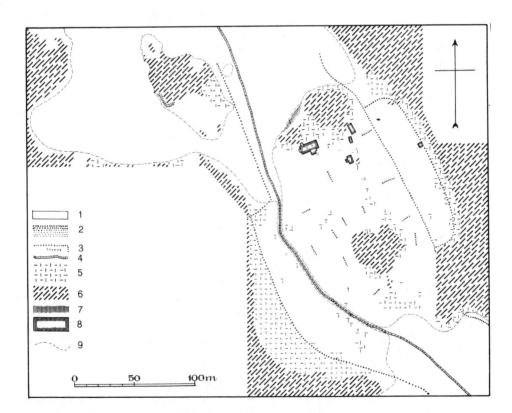

Figure 3.21. Colors of the winter landscape in Valosaari.

1 = White (snow flat); *2* = grey (rock faces, walls); *3* = grey fences; *4* = light grey ice road; *5* = deciduous forest and bushes (grey, brown); *6* = dark green coniferous forest; *7* = red (walls); *8* = building (roof covered by snow, red walls); *9* = shoreline (to facilitate orientation).

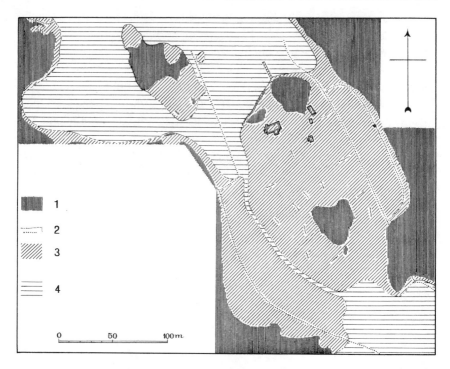

Figure 3.22. Invariable and variable colors at Valosaari.

1 = Permanent color (coniferous forest, rock faces, walls); *2* = secondary permanent color (fences, hayricks); *3* = color changing twice a year (vegetation covered by snow, deciduous forest, roofs); *4* = color changing more often (water reflecting surroundings and covered by vegetation at times).

3.14. Lights

While in physical terms light denotes everything that is perceived with the sense of sight, *in a geographical field of vision light is everything that shines.* If such a light illuminates its environment, it is a *source of light.*

The boundary between light and color is an indeterminate one. Apart from illuminating celestial bodies, artificial lights used for various purposes, and organisms that shine in the dark, all of which can be referred to without hesitation as lights, there are an abundance of reflections and glows in the landscape of which we cannot be sure. We took the changing colors of the surface of the water into account in the color maps of Valosaari, but perhaps it would be more correct to regard such a surface as light. We could also regard the sky, the variations in the color of which were also discussed above, as a vast source of light. The point here is to decide whether a certain phenomenon should be examined as a color or as a light. What is regarded as a color in one environment may just as well be a light in another. Generally speaking, the sky is primarily the sphere of light and earth that of color.

Lights are often divided into two main classes, warm and cold lights. The former include flames and glows, and the latter fluorescence and reflections. This system is inadequate for the needs of landscape science, however, the following classification being a more suitable one:

I. *Landscape illuminators.* Illuminate the whole landscape.
  1. *The sun.*
  2. *The moon.*
II. *Landscape lights.* Shine, but can illuminate only limited areas in the landscape.
  3. *Shining lights.* Shine and illuminate in an even manner (electric and gas lights, paraffin lamps, candles, etc.).
  4. *Flares.* Flaming and illuminating in a restless manner (light from volcanic eruptions, fires, campfires, and bonfires, torches, aurora borealis, ignis fatuus, etc.).
  5. *Gleaming lights.* Shine evenly (clear sky, surface of water, ice, and snow, rainbow, smooth, polished artificial surfaces, etc.).
  6. *Glittering lights.* Glitter in an irregular manner (sun or moonlight reflected in water, ice, or snow, gilded towers, windows, etc.).
  7. *Flashing lights.* Sudden flashes (lightning, explosions, etc.).
  8. *Twinkling lights.* Shining restlessly but hardly illuminating at all (stars, etc.).
  9. *Glows.* Small lights shining peacefully (certain insects, especially in the tropics, etc.).

Some of these are distant lights and others local lights occurring within the boundaries of the landscape, the nature of the latter being greatly influenced by the intervening distance, a fact that must be mentioned particularly because it is in general difficult to estimate the distance of a light shining in the dark. Shining lights thus become glows as distance increases, and flares twinkling lights.

The photology of a landscape could be of use for the purposes of cartographic representation in two cases in particular: for the examination of the largest light regions and areas on the earth and for describing the distribution and number of artificial lights.

3.15. Evaluation in Terms of Landscape Science

Our classification of phenomena in the landscape focuses attention separately on forms, colors, and lights and presents a system of types that meets the requirements of *descriptive* landscape science and the definition of regions. This system has been drawn up very much by a process of broad generalization, since an entity such as landscape is difficult to deal with on a more detailed basis. The smaller the number of types in the various systems of forms, colors, and lights, the smaller, naturally, will be the number of possible combinations of types, that is, types of landscape.

If the types of the various phenomena in the landscape are determined on the basis of certain significant characteristic features, as above, a description or division into regions in terms of landscape science based on such a system is for this very reason inevitably evaluative.

A mere analytical evaluation, which manifests itself in the use of a logical system and an accurate terminology, is not enough, however. We must also carry out a synthetic evaluation to identify the determinant phenomena in the *complex,* no matter whether our object of examination is an anthropocentric landscape or a regional entity that is uniform in its landscapes.

3.15.1. *Characteristics*

When defining characteristics we turn our attention to spatial quantity and intensity and temporal immobility and invariability. These aspects must be examined from two viewpoints. We must find out which determinant features occur in the region in the same manner, creating *unity,* that is, *uniting* its various parts, and examine the extent to which the features are *distinguishing* characteristics of this region as compared with surrounding ones. Actually we mainly come across the same phenomena all the time, taking them to be *typical* of the region in the former case and to emphasize the *individuality* of the region in the latter.

The quantity and quality of the unity perceivable in a landscape or region can be briefly expressed in a symbolic landscape code, which can also be used in cartographic representation, while the distinctive characteristics can be represented on a map using various hatchings or "individuality symbols."

3.15.2. *The Landscape Code*

The form complex types for various materials can be briefly characterized by numbers and letters if necessary. It was suggested above that Roman numerals should be used for landforms and Arabic numerals for forms of water, capital letters for vegetation types and small letters for artificial elements. By placing the numbers and letters representing the characteristics of a landscape or region in sequence, we obtain the *landscape code* for the entity in question, representing its main characteristics in a nutshell (cf. Granö 94, 95). Such a formula naturally varies in length depending on the number of elements in the complex and the number of complexes representing the same element.

It is in the nature of our system of landscape analysis that the vertical dimension is crucial in the definition of landforms, and also of vegetation types to some extent, whereas the horizontal dimension is of primary interest in the classification of water and artificial elements. This method is fully justified from the point of view of evaluation and is also the only possible one as far as the forms of liquid water are concerned.

The various characteristic features of the distribution and grouping of form complexes could be marked with lines situated above or below the figures and letters in the codes. Thus underlining of these figures or letters could indicate parallelism between corresponding forms, for example, a more or less clear striation in the landscape.

This may be illustrated by means of some examples of landscape codes:

1 = open water area, that is, only a shoreless water surface visible (except for the sky, of course, the variability and mobility of which is not revealed in the formula).

IV = mound terrain, an area so dry and bare that it can be characterized only in terms of a landform complex, that is, a complete desert.

II 5 = desert mountains and coastal waters.

VI 2 A = forested plain divided by rivers.

I VII 4 6 B F 1 = high mountains and tables partly covered by glaciers, lake systems, bushes, and lichens (a rock-face vegetation), with some artificial forms in places. The forms of the land, water, and vegetation are oriented in the same direction, so that the landscape may be deemed striated.

3.15.3. *Individual Features of the Landscape and the Individuality Symbol*

The individuality of a landscape, or of a region corresponding to a landscape, is greater the more distinctly the entity stands out from its surroundings in terms of the phenomena it contains. In other words, the degree of individuality of a region depends on the extent to which the form complexes change at its boundaries and on the number of elements with complexes that change at the boundary. The landscape formula does not provide any information on this, but it can easily be represented on a map by means of *hatching.*

A certain direction of lines can be taken to indicate a certain material. Thus, vertical lines can represent landforms, horizontal lines water, lines running NW-SE vegetation and lines running NE-SW artificial matter. Only the element(s) whose forms change at the boundaries of the area being examined are marked on the map, and the clearer this boundary is, the thicker the lines. The greater the distance between the form complexes to be compared is in our type catalogues, as indicated by the numbers and letters, the more distinct the boundary will be in nature.

Thus, a thick vertical hatching and a weak hatching running NE-SW, for instance, would indicate that the landforms of the region concerned differ very markedly from those of the surrounding regions and the artificial forms less markedly, while a thick horizontal hatching would mean a distinct change in the forms of water at the boundary of the region, and so forth. Such a map becomes even more illustrative if different colors are used to represent the various materials.[7]

A suitable means of illustrating the degree of individuality on a map is an *individuality symbol* (Granö 95), in which short lines of the same length intersecting each other at their midpoints represent different materials, particularly those whose forms change in a distinct manner at the boundary of the region, that is, as in the map with hatchings described above. A vertical line in the sign or star, which in its complete form is similar to an eightpoint compass rose, thus refers to landforms, a horizontal line to water, a NW-SE line to vegetation and a NE-SW line to artificial forms.

3.15.4. *Landscape Profile*

The horizontal extent of forms has too often been regarded as decisive in comparative analysis, for it should be kept in mind that we usually see the landscape surrounding us in profile, from the side. The various form complexes should thus also be compared in terms of their vertical extent, since this enables us to avoid various misconceptions that would otherwise lead to false assessments. Many contemporary geographers are probably apt to overestimate the significance of landforms in the landscape and to regard artificial forms and even vegetation as less significant than they really are.

The synthetic assessment discussed here can be considerably facilitated by a *landscape profile* in which immobile forms can be represented and also, if necessary, mobile forms that occur regularly in certain places. When using a large scale, the vertical extent of elements can be represented in the correct proportions, that is, the same scales can be used for height and length. Exaggeration of the vertical dimension must be used for profiles on smaller scales, however, even though the picture obtained will be distorted to some extent, as it will mean that the forms of the various elements will become more distinct and easier to compare. A slight vertical exaggeration in a small-scale profile does not even seem unnatural, but perhaps even more natural than a profile with the correct proportions. The smaller the horizontal scale, the more we can proportionally increase the vertical one without distortion. This is probably because larger objects further away in the landscape (hills, towers, tall trees, etc.) seem to be of "real size" even at relatively great dis-

---

7. I have drawn up a map representing the geographical regions of Finland for the recently published *Atlas of Finland* (94) in which brown vertical lines indicate landforms, blue horizontal lines the forms of water, green NW-SE lines vegetation and orange NE-SW lines artificial forms.

tances (see sec. 4.2), while smaller objects seem to be smaller than in reality or disappear from sight even when close at hand. Hence, we tend to magnify variations in the distant field of vision in the vertical direction; that is, we see a slightly "distorted" landscape profile in reality. We see mountains that loom blue far away in the horizon as higher and steeper than they are in reality.

The enclosed landscape profiles of Valosaari (Fig. 3.23) are sufficiently large in scale, thus in a way representing the parts of the landscape closest to the observer, that no increase in scale was necessary. The sketch map in the lower left-hand corner of the diagram shows the directions of the profiles, and the dashed lines on the profiles representing altitudes at 10-meter intervals above the lake level indicate the vertical dimensions of the various forms and form complexes.

3.16. The Physiology and Genesis of Landscape

The life functions of a geographical complex can be dealt with in two essentially different ways. First, the natural and cultural forces operating in the area can be examined, once the area itself has been defined and described, and the entity and its features can be studied as an arena for interaction between these forces. This is the commonest procedure if physiological questions of landscape are to be examined. Spethmann (260) has gone so far as to emphasize the physiological viewpoint at the expense of description and examines areas only as the fields of operation of given forces, that is, as dynamic complexes. Seen from this point of view, it would be unnecessary to speak separately of the physiology of a landscape, since landscape and proximity should be discussed together.

From the second point of view, the main task of geographical physiology is to examine the significance of complexes and their various objects and phenomena as *agents* and *objects* in interaction (see sec. 1.9), and not, as in the previous case, to examine the results of the various forces and energies present in the area studied. The physiological significance of the sun, gravity, and so on cannot be neglected even in this case, but principal attention will be focused on the functions of the various factors in the complex and on the physiological functions of the whole area in a larger entity. We are then not primarily interested in the forces that keep the machinery running, which are highly significant as such, but in the functions of the various parts of the machinery, that is, forms of phenomena dependent on the local conditions of the operating forces.

In the latter case both the landscape and the proximity require their own physiological examination, despite the fact that the same forces operate in both, since the factors of the landscape are only partially involved in the proximity, that is, the agents and objects present in the landscape occur only

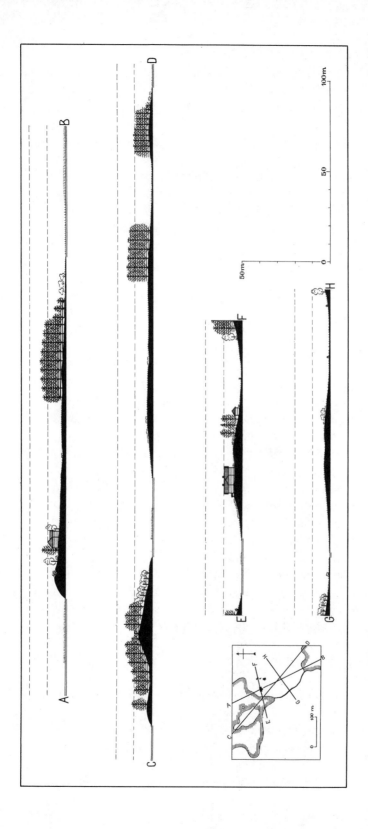

to some extent in the proximity. If the objects of study of geography are defined as above, the latter method should be regarded as the more correct one.

When examining the *genesis* of a landscape, we can safely attach only secondary value to things and phenomena and turn our attention to the forces
operating in the area and to the manners of operation of these forces, which
are dependent on local conditions. We should thus find out the extent to
which the area contains disharmonic and foreign elements and what interaction periods have left their traces in it (see sec. 1.10). Evidence of earlier
stages in development can primarily be found in the immobile forms, mainly
in complex landforms and artificial forms and in the structures of these, while
the living kingdom, which adapts to its physiological environment in a relatively short time, provides less developmental evidence which is visible in
the landscape.

(Facing page)

Figure 3.23. Landscape profiles across Valosaari.
Distance and altitude are on the same scale. The profiles represent both a cross-section
of the landforms *(black)* and also buildings and forms of vegetation drawn to scale:
pines and individual coniferous trees *(dense hatching),* birches *(in profiles A–B, E–F, and
G–H),* smaller alders *(in profiles C–D and G–H),* and willow bushes *(in profile A–B).*

4

PROXIMITY

4.1. Proximics: The Proximity and Its Main Parts

The proximity is that part of the environment that is perceivable with all the senses and is situated between the observer and the landscape. The landscape is composed of phenomena of the field of vision alone, and of these only the phenomena that occur in the distant field of vision, while the proximity includes the nearest part of the environment, that perceived by the senses as a whole.

The proximity may be divided into three main parts in terms of qualitative phenomena (see sec. 1.7):

1. The complex of visible phenomena and objects in the proximity: *proximate field of vision.*

2. The tactile, auditory, and olfactory phenomena of the surrounding or adjacent elements: *medium.*

3. Tactile phenomena of the ground: *substrate.*

As objects of study, proximities are just as significant as landscapes, and we thus assign proximics, the branch of geography dealing with them, an equal status beside landscape science.

The task of proximics is to examine, describe, and interpret the proximities and types of proximities of the earth's surface, and areas and regions that are uniform in terms of their proximities.

We will discuss in the following the various parts of the proximity and the cartographic methods related to the study of proximities, the latter being illustrated by means of maps and plans depicting the proximic features of Valosaari. Since a considerable number of the points mentioned above regarding methods of research and presentation in landscape science also apply to work in the field of proximics, we shall focus our attention only on methodological issues pertaining particularly to the proximity.

4.2. Boundaries and Size of the Proximity

Although the medium and substrate are proximate complexes (see sec. 1.7), their spatial location is indefinite. Their identification in the proximity therefore occurs mainly in the field of vision and by means of visual phenomena (see Giessler 73, p. 282).

When defining the outer limit of a proximity we are thus forced to keep to phenomena that are dependent on increasing distance in the field of vision; in other words, the outer boundary of the proximate field of vision is at the same time the outer boundary of the proximity.

It is relevant here to discuss the grounds on which the proximate field of vision can be distinguished from the distant field of vision, or landscape, for it is in this way that we can best explain the issues which must be taken into account when defining this outer boundary.

1. Our conception of the extent of objects on the dimension of the radius of the field of vision becomes clearer the closer to us they are, since our eyes can see them more distinctly from various angles from a short distance. Stereoscopic vision leads to a plastic perception of a three-dimensional object if the angle between the axes of vision, that is, the visual angle or binocular parallax, is greater than a certain minimum. Beyond a certain limit, which is dependent on the size and shape of the object, we no longer see the object as three-dimensional. It is only the part of the proximity close to us that we can perceive with all its elements as a combination of objects possessing a certain "depth."

2. The substrate on which we move, and on which or in which the objects in the field of vision seem to be located, is visible in our proximate environment as a distinct surface with a considerable extent in the direction of the

radius of the field of vision. Some way from us this surface turns into a narrow streak from which the objects project like the scenery in a theater. If we divide the distance from ourselves to the horizon of a completely open landscape, such as an open sea, into two parts which are *seemingly* equal in size, the boundary between these will be only 20 m from us if our eyes are at the height of 1.5 m, as is usually the case with adults. Two concentric circles can thus be distinguished in the field of vision, of which the radius of the outer one, that is, the horizon, is twice as long as that of the inner one as observed visually, and of which the inner one delimits an area in which the substrate is considerably more distinctly visible than in the outer one. This follows not only from the principle of binocular parallax but also from the fact that we see the substrate closer to us from above at a highly oblique angle, so that the altitude of the eyes is of crucial significance as well. It is therefore obvious that the field of vision of a child is quite different in its dimensions from that of an adult (see also Fig. 4.1, taken at an altitude of approximately 4 m above the lake). The critical altitude that must be considered here is 1.5 m, however, or the average height of the eyes of an adult standing on a horizontal surface, the corresponding inner circle being at a distance of approximately 20 m and the horizon at 4.7 km (see sec. 3.2).

3. The objects in our most immediate environment are appreciated in terms of their *real* size, while those located farther away seem to be smaller than they actually are; that is, they have a certain, *ostensible* size. It is necessary to differentiate between mathematical and physiological perspective (Grabke 76, Gellhorn 69, etc.). Every object in our field of vision has a definite distance limit, or "critical limit" (Filehne 51–54), dependent on its size, within which its size is real in our opinion. The human face, the diameter of which is approximately 20 cm, can be seen in its real size up to a distance of about 20 m, while the human body seems smaller than it really is when seen from a distance of 50–100 m. In our proximate environment, where objects are visible in a plastic manner and where the substrate can be distinguished as a surface, the whole field of vision is seen in its real size and independent of the mathematical perspective (Gellhorn 69).

4. The color and cloudiness of the air, "air perspective," causes objects to seem bluish, yellowish, or reddish and more indistinct in outline in the more distant parts of the field of vision. "The blue haze of the air is distinctly visible in bright sunlight even at a distance of 100 m. A tree standing at this distance is more bluish green than one viewed from 50 m. The blue sky exists not only above us but everywhere; it consists of air illuminated by the sun. A distant mountain seems blue since a patch of blue sky lies between it and us" (Heim 108, p. 34).

Figure 4.1. Transitional zone between a proximate view and a distant view, or landscape.

(View northwards from a rock at Valosaari almost 4 m above the lake surface.) The mathematical perspective is decisive in the picture; that is, all the objects have an "apparent size," sometimes larger, sometimes smaller, depending on distance. A person standing beside the photographic apparatus would see the boat at a distance of 50 m and the people in it at their "real size."

All these factors make it necessary to distinguish between the proximate view, the proximity, and the distant field of vision, the landscape. The *boundary* between these main parts of the environment cannot be accurately determined, since it is rather a *transitional zone* situated at a distance of 20–100 m from the observer. If one wants to refer to it as a boundary, however, the best equivalent is a circle at a distance of 20 m, since it is there that the radius of the open field of vision divides into two halves of ostensibly equal length and since all the suggested properties of the proximate view characterize the entity that lies within this boundary. The additional observations that we also see other people at their real size within this boundary and that communication between people takes place in this small area are not insignificant matters in terms of landscape science.

By virtue of this definition, the area of a distinct open proximity, that is, one extending to 20 m, is thus almost 1500 m, while that of a distinct landscape is approximately 3 hectares, as its inner boundary lies at a minimum distance of 100 m. It is thus possible to define the minimum size of a *vicinity* (see sec. 1.11) at the same time.

4.3. Proximate Field of Vision

Although the proximate field of vision differs from the distant field of vision in many respects, it is methodologically roughly similar to a landscape as an object of study. It merely requires a different kind of evaluation, a different scale. Since sight cannot encompass the major forms and form complexes of the landscape in the proximate field of vision, they are not of any direct significance for proximics. Mountains and valleys, forests and lakes, villages and towns are not objects of study, whereas many features that are perhaps quite insignificant in the landscape may be highly dominant in the proximate field of vision, just as there are a great number of formations that are of no value at all in terms of landscape science. When we turn our attention from the landscape to the proximity, we see an entirely new world of forms and colors,

Figure 4.2. A proximate view in autumn.

(A tent in the forest region of Katun in Central Altai, photographed by the author in September 1915.) High umbelliferous plants constitute individual forms in the right and left foreground, with bushes and trees rising from beneath the first snow of autumn in the background. A mountain dweller in winter clothes is in front of the tent in the foreground.

Figure 4.3. A proximate view in summer.

(Furrow valley of a mountain brook in the Irtysh area of SW Altai, photographed by the author in August 1905.) Apart from the brook and its waterfall, the proximate view is characterized by a rock face and boulders covered by lichen, high herbs, and some bushes and trees.

which are an integral part of the perceived environment, the examination of which cannot therefore be ignored.

This distinction between the main parts of the field of vision can be perceived even in an open natural environment. No matter how monotonous an expanse the landscape may be, the proximate field of vision may, nevertheless, contain a highly variable combination of stones and boulders, grass and tufts, lichen-covered rock faces, paths, pools, brooks, and the like. But the difference between the landscape and the proximate field of vision becomes even more distinct when we move into interior proximities, whether it be the dim shelter of a forest, a thick jungle, or a human dwelling. *These interior fields of vision lie entirely beyond the subject matter of landscape science.* One of the factors of special significance in terms of proximics that deserves special mention concerns *people,* whose anthropological features and clothing may even be the decisive characteristics of proximities.

Despite these differences, the description of the proximate field of vision does not require any special morphographic system or nomenclature developed for this purpose alone because most objects in the proximate field of vision have their familiar, accurate names in everyday language, which is natural in that we are concerned with that part of the field of vision in which we operate and where all the objects are within our reach and subject to our constant attention. The terms of landscape science, however, are not associated with any size category and can also be used to describe the proximate field of vision.

Since the various objects in the proximate field of vision arouse the geographer's interest only if they are dominant or characteristic in a visible complex and since the perception of this also requires a certain minimum distance in the case of the proximate field of vision, very small, insignificant objects or features are not interesting in terms of proximics. The average height of the eyes, or approximately 1.5 m, can be regarded as the suitable minimum distance, since we are used to viewing the part of the proximate field of vision in which we move from at least this distance. If we take an object in our hand in order to scrutinize it more closely, we are not making a proximic observation, no matter how significant our observations may be indirectly, since we do not see the complex to which the object belongs, or in other words, the background against which it must be examined. In this sense geography really is, as Penck has remarked (213), a macroscopic (or megascopic) branch of science.

The plan of a part of Valosaari (Fig. 4.5) may perhaps indicate the elements that should be marked on a proximic map and the kinds of elements that may occur in a Finnish proximate field of vision, for instance (Figs. 4.14 and 4.15). Proximate profiles drawn up on a proportional scale (Fig. 4.6) provide data on the vertical dimension of the same field of vision. Some features of the medium and the substrate are also included in both the plan and the profiles. In order to avoid misunderstandings it should be mentioned, however, that proximic plan views and profiles are necessary for geographical investigations only if they are needed to illustrate the *typical* features of the area examined (see sec. 2.3) and that diagrams depicting proximities have been drawn up only with respect to the methodological aspect of our investigations. The proximities of Valosaari, in which artificial forms in particular are dominant, include features that are not characteristic of this part of Finland but rather are foreign to it.

Of the elements of the natural environment, the vegetation in particular is subjected to a more detailed examination in proximics than in landscape science. But even so the proximics of the vegetation must not turn into floristics or phytogeography. We distinguish individual and group forms and complex forms in the proximate field of vision in the same manner as in the landscape, although the dimensions are naturally different. Apart from forms, the colors of the vegetation are important, for example, the colors of flowers and fruit, which can be perceived relatively rarely in the Finnish landscape, are significant characteristics of a number of proximities. Figures 4.7 and 4.8 indicate that apart from green, the white, yellow, red, and violet of flowers were represented in the proximity of Valosaari in July and August 1923.

There are considerable differences in illumination even within small areas in the proximate field of vision. Interior proximities in particular vary to a great extent in this respect. Some have a lot of daylight, others hardly any, some are entirely dark (e.g., caves) and others always or sometimes lit by artificial light. Figure 4.13 illustrates the lighting conditions at Valosaari, although only in broad outline.

Mobile forms are usually of greater significance in the proximity than in the landscape, and the mobile form complex of Valosaari (Fig. 4.9) also includes a variety of elements that deserve our attention.

4.4. Medium

The medium consists of auditory, olfactory, and certain tactile phenomena. In its function as a medium, the sense of touch resembles that of sight in that it

Figure 4.4. Interior proximate view of a dwelling.

(A Japanese dwelling. In the background, the "room of ten carpets," with opened paper doors on its right-hand wall. On the back wall is a platform, "tokonoma," for valuable objects and flowers. On the left, a corridor.)

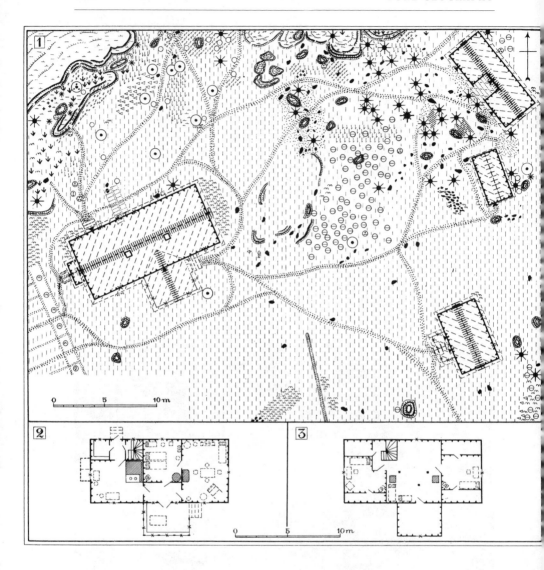

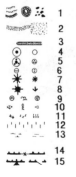

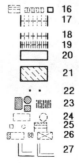

conveys information on the topological features of the environment, although only in the environment closest to the observer. It is difficult to say in some cases whether certain topological observations are based on visual or tactile phenomena. When we see a wall in front of us, it also acts as a distinct *obstacle* in our medium, since we know that we cannot get to the other side of it without going around it or opening a door in it, or, if these possibilities do not exist, without climbing over it or even making an opening in it. And when we see a building surrounded by walls and covered by a roof, we also know that the walls and roof, as *isolators,* surround a closed medium.

4.4.1. *Degree of Openness or Obstructiveness*

The information concerning tactile phenomena in the medium conveyed by the sense of sight in the respect mentioned above is so certain that the degree of openness of the medium outward and its degree of obstructiveness inward can be determined and represented cartographically, as in Figures 4.10 and 4.11.

The degrees of openness in the Valosaari medium are represented in Figure 4.10, in which a *closed medium* (see sec. 1.6) is an area surrounded by walls and a roof, a *semi-open* one a pine forest forming a row of pillars in front

(Facing page)

Figure 4.5. Proximate field of vision of Valosaari.

Plan 1 = External proximate field of vision comprising the building complex; *Plan 2* = internal field of vision on the ground floor of the dwelling house; *Plan 3* = internal field of vision on the upper floor of the dwelling house. Significant pieces of furniture are marked with *dashed lines.*

1 = Slope, threshold, boulder, rocks; *2* = path, track, bare land (covered by soil or sand); *3* = ditch; *4* = birches (of various sizes); *5* = rowans (of various sizes); *6* = alder bush, small aspen; *7* = pines (of various sizes); *8* = spruce, juniper; *9* = *Ribes* bush, raspberry bush, rhubarb; *10* = *Artemisia, Verbascum, Pteris* group; *11* = heather, cowberry, bilberry; *12* = grasses and herbs; *13* = moss, lichen; *14* = isolator: opaque (wall) and transparent (window); *15* = same: penetrable (door in Plan 1), open (door in Plan 1), or openable (door in Plans 2 and 3); *16* = outside steps, ladder, chimney; *17* = double-pitched roof, inclination 10–20 degrees; *18* = double-pitched roof, inclination 20–30 degrees; *19* = double-pitched roof, inclination 30–50 degrees; *20* = building <2.5 m in height; *21* = >2.5 m in height, single-storeyed or with an attic; *22* = roof structures; *23* = stove, chimney, pile of firewood; *24* = tables; *25* = chairs, rocking chair; *26* = bed, washstand, cupboard; *27* = wall shelf, wall seat.

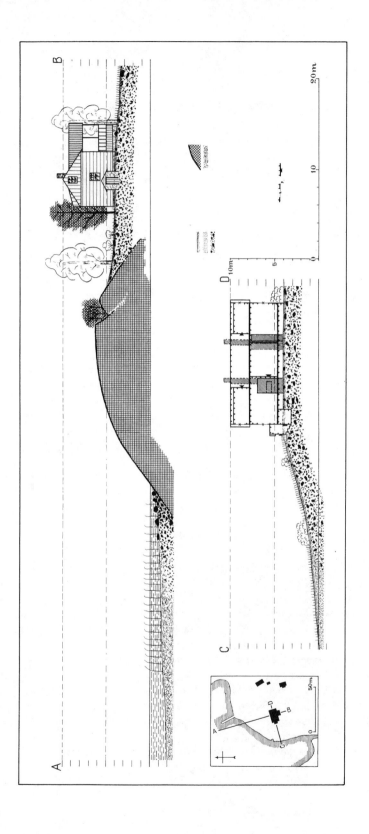

(Facing page) **Figure 4.6.** Proximate profiles across Valosaari.

Length and altitude on the same scale. *Profile A–B* provides both a cross-section of the substrate (bedrock, humus, stone soil, mud further out in the lake) and littoral water and also the external form of the main building, and *profile C–D* the longitudinal cross-section of this building, so that the isolated internal proximities are visible. Vegetation is presented in the same manner as in the landscape profiles of Figure 3.23 and isolators in the same manner as in Figure 4.5.

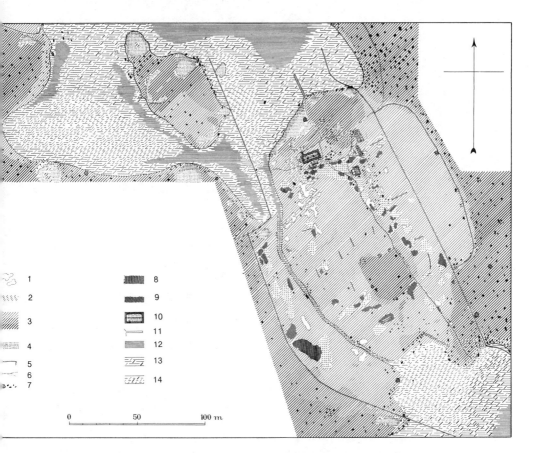

Figure 4.7. Proximate colors at Valosaari, 10–12 July 1923.

1 = White (*Chrysanthemum, Trifolium repens, Aegopodium, Achillea, Galium, Eriophorum, Nymphaea*); *2 =* yellow (*Ranunculus*); *3 =* green (the *thin hatching* indicates the lightest green, i.e., that of grass; *medium hatching* that of deciduous forest, and the *dark hatching* that of coniferous forest); *4 =* grey (lichen-covered rock faces and roofs); *5 =* grey fences and hayricks; *6 =* dark grey paths; *7 =* grey rocks and boulders; *8 =* red (*Cirsium, Trifol. pratense, Pedicularis palustris*); *9 =* purple, blue (*Campanula patula, Vicia cracca*); *10 =* building (the center indicates the color of the roof, the edges that of the walls); *11 =* jetty (grey); *12 =* water (reflects various colors); *13 =* sparse aquatic plants (light and dark green); *14 =* dense populations of aquatic plants.

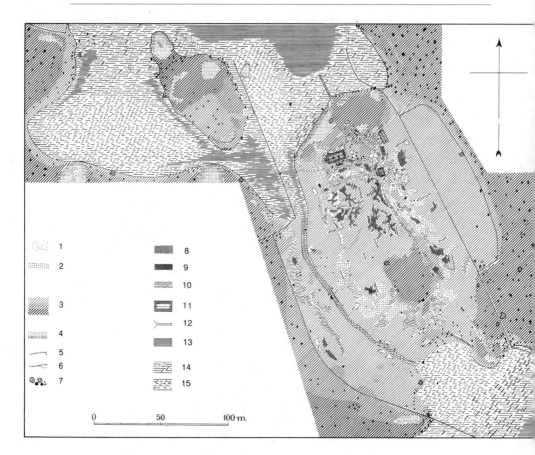

Figure 4.8. Proximate colors at Valosaari, 7–9 August 1923.

1 = White (*Chrysanthemum, Carum, Achillea, Ulmaria, Trifolium repens, Eriophorum*); *2* = yellow (*Leontodon, Hypericum, Ranunculus, Potentilla, Lysimachia vulgaris, Nuphar*); *3* = green (the *thin hatching* indicates the lightest green, i.e., that of grass, *medium hatching* that of deciduous forest, and the *dark hatching* that of coniferous forest); *4* = grey (lichen-covered rock faces and roofs, greyish areas of dried *Rhinanthus*); *5* = grey fences and hayricks; *6* = dark grey paths; *7* = grey rocks and boulders; *8* = red (*Cirsium, Trifol. pratense*); *9* = purple, blue (*Epilobium angustifolium, Vicia cracca*); *10* = dark purple tinge (*Agrostis canina*); *11* = building (the center indicates the color of the roof, the edges that of the walls); *12* = jetty (grey); *13* = water (reflects various colors); *14* = sparse aquatic plants (light and dark green); *15* = dense populations of aquatic plants.

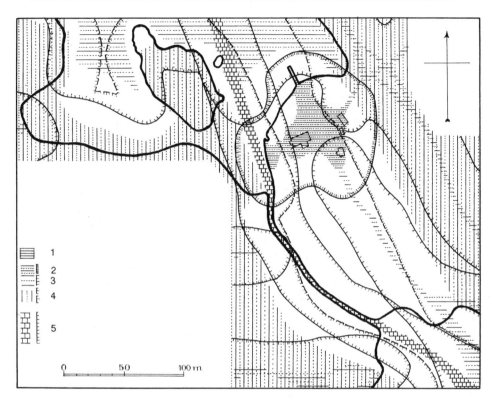

Figure 4.9. Proximities of mobile elements in Valosaari.

1 = People constantly in summer; *2* = people frequently in summer; *3* = people sometimes in summer; *4* = cattle in summer; *5* = people, vehicles, and horses frequently in winter. The areas of occurrence of mobile elements are *hatched,* the phenomenal spaces (see sec. 1.4) have phenomenal isopleths at 25 m, except for the internal proximities, where the walls serve as phenomenal boundaries.

of the observer, a *semi-closed* one an almost impenetrable coniferous thicket and an *open* one an area of grass or water. A deciduous forest (e.g., a clump of alders at Valosaari) is chronologically speaking a *mixed medium,* whose degree of openness varies with the seasons. Apart from the walls that occur as isolators, fences are also characterized in the diagram as opaque surmountable obstacles, while the edges of the forest (as a complex) are transparent, penetrable obstacles.[1] The fields of vision in Figures 5.15–5.17 and 5.21–5.23 can also be examined in terms of the degree of openness of the medium.

The degrees of obstructiveness to be found in the same area can be seen in Figure 4.11. Apart from the above-mentioned isolators and obstacles, this il-

1. Obstructiveness attributable to high grass, deep snow or water will be discussed in connection with the substrate.

lustration includes rock faces, which are represented as opaque and thus impenetrable obstacles, and hayricks, which are avoidable or surmountable transparent obstacles. Three types of medium have also been distinguished in terms of obstructiveness: a medium without obstacles (an area of water or grass, the interior of a building), a medium with few obstacles (a pine forest for the most part), and a medium with numerous obstacles (a thick coniferous forest, a clump of alders, a willow thicket). The difference in the manner of representation between the two diagrams can best be perceived from the manner in which the buildings have been described, in that they are marked with a dense crosshatching as closed media in Figure 4.10, but have no hatching in Figure 4.11, since there are no obstacles hampering movement in the rooms.

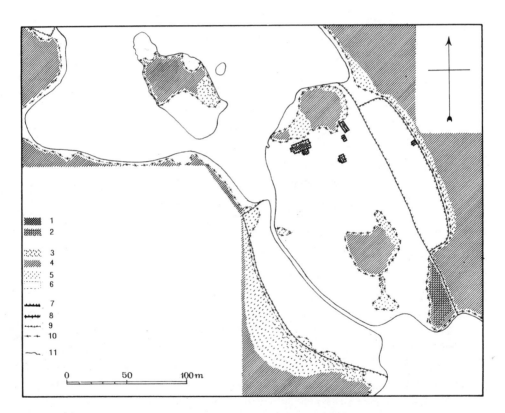

Figure 4.10. Degree of openness of the medium in Valosaari.

1 = Closed medium; *2* = almost closed medium; *3* = medium closed to some extent in summer; *4* = semi-open medium; *5* = semi-open medium in summer, almost open in winter; *6* = open medium (white); *7* = isolator, opaque; *8* = isolator, partly transparent; *9* = obstacle, opaque, surmountable; *10* = obstacle, transparent, penetrable; *11* = shoreline (main boundary for the substrate).

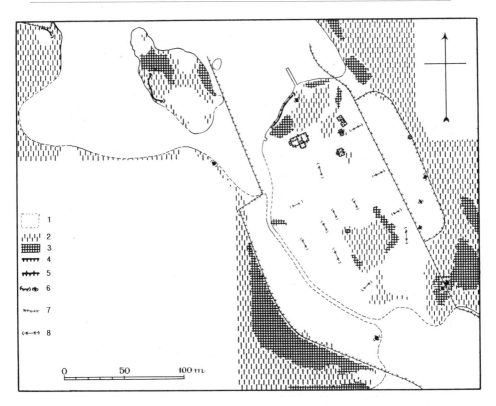

Figure 4.11. Obstructiveness of the medium in Valosaari.

1 = Medium without obstacles *(white)*; *2* = medium with some obstacles; *3* = medium with many obstacles; *4* = opaque isolator; *5* = partly transparent isolator; *6* = opaque isolator, avoidable; *7* = opaque isolator, surmountable; *8* = transparent isolator, avoidable or surmountable.

4.4.2. *Tactile Phenomena*

Apart from the phenomena of the medium, which are essentially related to the field of vision, certain proximic properties of the air are significant as actual tactile phenomena, including temperature and movements, humidity and dampness (rain or snowfall), composition and electrical properties. These significant phenomena are studied by meteorology and climatology, so that there is no need to go into them any further here.

Proximics is mainly interested in the "microclimate," the local climate of the smallest areas, and the features shared by the local climates of various areas. The task is so comprehensive that it also includes the examination of interior media, which is not normally regarded as belonging to the sphere of actual climatology. The objects of study are naturally the *phenomena* of proximate climate. The psychological and physiological influences of this climate, as examined by Hellpach (109) in particular, merit our attention only if they lead to observable consequences in the geographical environment.

Series of observations made at meteorological stations contain a large amount of material suitable for our purposes, but it is obvious that they are nowhere near sufficient.

Some features of the proximate climate are very clearly dependent on our classification of the materials of the landscape and its objects and the form and size of the latter. This dependence becomes obvious from Figures 4.12 and 4.13. The interior media of a residential building are entirely protected from winds and are also *isothermal,* that is, they have a constant temperature in summer and winter, if they are inhabited throughout the year, whereas the thickets in a forest are *heterothermal,* that is, their temperature varies according to the seasons and times of the day, even though the area may again be more or less protected from winds. Open grass terrains and water areas are

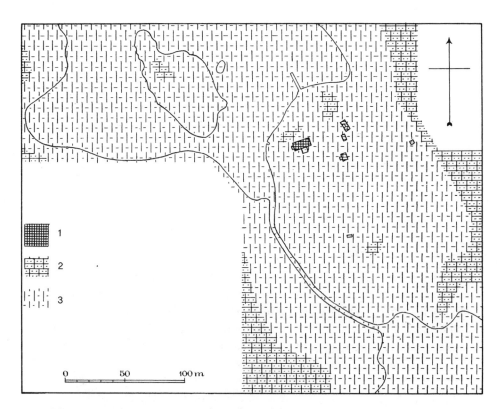

Figure 4.12. Temperature and wind conditions at Valosaari.

1 = Isothermal, protected from winds; *1* = heterothermal, mainly protected from winds; *3* = heterothermal, open to winds. Temperature conditions of the medium are marked with *vertical hatching* and wind conditions with *horizontal hatching.*

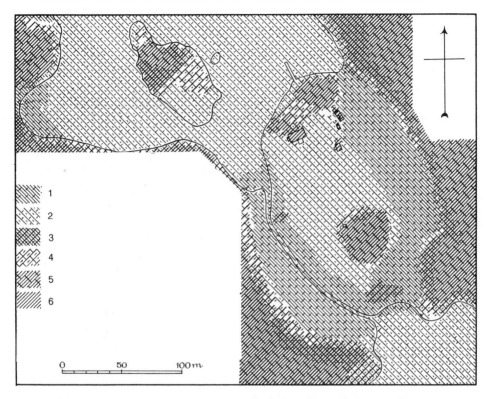

Figure 4.13. Lighting and humidity conditions of the medium in Valosaari.

1 = Susceptible to sunshine and rain, often rainy; *2* = as above, but seldom foggy; *3* = partly shady, susceptible to rain; *4* = partly shady, partly protected from rain and fog; *5* = very shady, partly protected from rain and fog; *6* = very shady, entirely protected from rain and fog; lighting conditions of the proximate view are indicated by *SW-NE hatching* and humidity by *NW-SE hatching*. The denser the hatching, the more shady or humid the place is.

both heterothermal and susceptible to winds, and are also more heavily affected by rain (Fig. 4.13). The low-lying shores of Kuivasalmi are frequently affected by mist.[2]

4.4.3. *Auditory Phenomena*

Auditory phenomena are highly relevant factors in a proximity, even though they do not necessarily occur in all cases, since completely silent environments do exist. Auditory phenomena are nevertheless so common that their absence, "deathly silence," is perceived to be awkward if not unnatural.

2. Illumination conditions at Valosaari (Fig. 4.13) are discussed above in connection with proximate fields of vision (see sec. 4.3).

The common auditory phenomena characterizing natural proximities include the roar of waves, cascades, or rapids, the sough of the wind in the forest and the singing of birds, while the "field of hearing" of artificial proximities is characterized by human voices and the noise of traffic and industry.

As mentioned above, auditory phenomena can be localized only to some extent, in that we can estimate the direction in which the source of a sound is situated binaurally, but our ears do not provide much information on its distance. Hearing provides more temporal information than the other senses, however, and therefore it has been referred to as the *sense of time.* Things that occur are of a greater significance in the auditory complex, or *field of hearing,* than things that exist, for everything that is heard is an occurrence: tones, sounds, noises, harmonies, and discords.

More information on the auditory phenomena of Valosaari, not only the quality and frequency of occurrence of phenomena but also the most audible locations of the various sounds, is provided in Figure 4.14. Since the sources of noise include people, cattle, and birds, and since their locations are known, it is easy to add the appropriate hatchings along the isopleth at a distance of 25 m from the locations and leave the more distant areas, where the sounds are less audible, unhatched. The unhatched areas are thus the most silent parts of Valosaari, except for the closed media, in which the damping effect of the isolators must be considered and where sounds from the exterior proximity will not be very loud. Auditory phenomena caused by the wind, which may be very prominent in the forest and on the shores, are not included in the diagram.

4.4.4. *Olfactory Phenomena*

The opinion may not be entirely foreign in geographical circles that olfactory phenomena do not merit examination at all. This can be argued from the viewpoint of both the highly justified claim that the sense of smell varies to a great extent from one individual to another and the less justified claim that difficulties will arise at least *in practice* if such "less sophisticated" phenomena, which are "at a lower stage of development" are considered. It is especially the latter opinion, which reflects insufficient knowledge and a rather naïve point of view, to which people readily resort.

Many geographers, however, regard these phenomena as belonging to the landscape and as fairly characteristic features of it. According to Sapper (241, pp. 3–5), a geographer need not restrict himself, as an artist does, to "what the eyes see, but he can also include in his descriptions the things that he observes by means of the other senses, especially by the senses of hearing, smell, and touch . . . ; he may even go so far as to mention the associations related to these sensations, unless they are highly eccentric. Such a scientific association often arouses interest in the picture examined and enhances un-

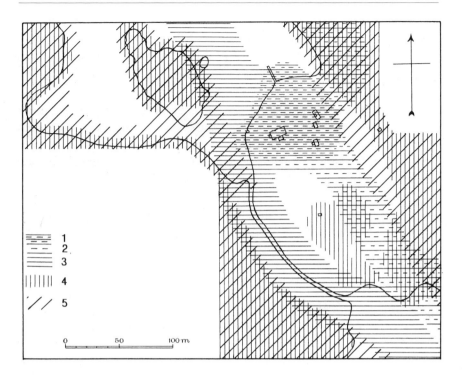

Figure 4.14. Auditory phenomena of the Valosaari medium.

Sounds and noises: *1* = Produced by people always in summer; *2* = produced by people sometimes in summer; *3* = produced by people frequently at all times of the year (boating route, ice road); *4* = bird song in spring and summer; *5* = clanging of cow bells (less often mooing of cattle or bleating of sheep) in summer. The hatched area for each auditory phenomenon terminates at the 25-m phenomenal curve.

derstanding of its nature." And further "Apart from auditory phenomena, olfactory phenomena are often typical: the smell of hay on the meadows in summer, the odor of manure emanating from the fields in late autumn, the smell of soil on the newly plowed fields in the cultural landscape, the simultaneous occurrence of the peculiar smell of decay and the sweet scent of orchids in various low-lying forest areas in Central America, the stench of fish in coastal areas in Iceland, the sulfurous fumes from hot springs or volcanic eruptions occurring in a few places; all these characterize certain landscapes to such an extent that when we perceive even remotely similar smells or scents we can immediately recall amazingly vividly the images of those landscapes in which we observed such olfactory phenomena previously." Gradmann suggests the same (80, pp. 7–8) and adds: "Anyone who scorns these factors deprives himself of one of the most significant possibilities for the description of landscapes."

If smells belong to a geographical complex, be it a landscape or a proximity, they must be studied and their value assessed. It would also be odd if we could not utilize the evidence provided by *all* our senses in the same manner as other branches of natural science do.

The sense of smell is undoubtedly less of an environmental sense than those of sight, touch, and hearing. On the other hand, it is just as significant in connection with the acquisition of food as is taste, and, as Sapper claims with justification, it often conveys information to us on quite essential properties of the environment. It remains for the geographer making the evaluation to decide when olfactory phenomena should be taken into consideration. The areas of distribution and times of occurrence of significant smells are often highly limited, and there are vast areas in which no special characteristic smells occur.

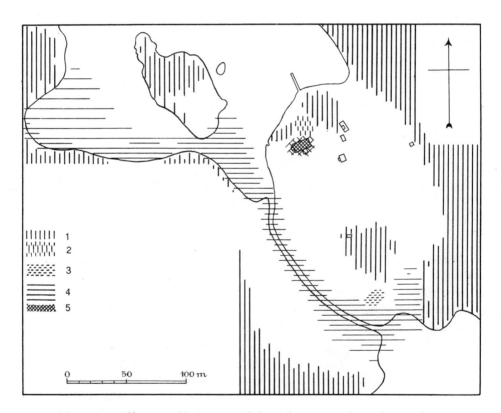

Figure 4.15. Olfactory phenomena of the Valosaari medium during the warmer part of the year.

1 = Smell of coniferous trees; *2* = smell of birch; *3* = smell of bog myrtle (*Myrica gale*); *4* = smell of mud; *5* = variable. Areas with no significant smells are left unhatched.

A less significant practical matter is the fact that the systematization of smells is not yet complete, since when studying the proximity we can manage with concepts and names that are familiar from everyday language. Something has been achieved in this sector, however, for as early as 1759 Linné published a system of smells that is still in use in supplemented form in physiological and psychological investigations. Henning (110) presented a "prism of smells" some ten years ago, which brings to mind Ostwald's famous system of colors, in which the six main smells are located at the corners of a three-sided prism.[3]

Olfactory phenomena are absent in the proximities of Valosaari for the majority of the year, but are observable, although weakly, in some places during the hottest part of the summer (Fig. 4.15).

4.5. Substrate

The substrate is a combination of tactile phenomena alone. It resembles the part of the medium that provides tactile information and whose special features include obstructiveness. The substrate could be regarded as a part of the medium if it were not that our relation to the material beneath us is quite a special one, in that gravity in a way binds and connects us to it, so that we are dependent on its phenomena no matter whether we are standing still or moving.

The sense of touch is thus a localizing sense, but only if we are concerned with the part of the environment closest to us, so that we can touch the objects in it. This naturally applies to the substrate as well. We can, of course, also use visual phenomena based on our experience to obtain information on phenomena in the substrate situated at a greater distance, which are manifest as distinguishable and interpretable formal features in the field of vision.

The most significant phenomena of the substrate are:

1. *Gradient.* An even slope with an inclination of less than 5 degrees does not deviate from a horizontal surface to any significant extent in its capacity as a *substrate.* A slope with an inclination of 5–10 degrees is very easy to climb, 10–20 degrees is still relatively easy, 20–30 degrees is difficult, 30–50 degrees highly difficult, and an even slope with an inclination of more than 50 degrees is impossible to climb (Figs. 4.16 and 3.7).

2. *Microrelief.* This involves the degree of evenness or roughness and the number of hummocks, holes, grooves, stones, etc. (Figs. 4.17 and 5.16).

---

3. Henning places the following main smells at one end of the prism: floral (violet), decayed (hydrogen sulfide), and fruity (lemon), and at the other end spicy (nutmeg), burned (tar), and resinous (incense).

3. *Bearing capacity.* Soil, moss, and rock substrates, and also wooden floors, all differ in this respect, in spite of the fact that all of them may have an even surface. A hard substrate should be distinguished from a soft, boggy, or fragile one (e.g., thin ice!) (Fig. 4.17).

4. *Obstructiveness.* The number of obstacles that rise from the substrate or are situated deeper on a more solid base and either give way under the feet of a moving person or can be moved away. Such obstacles include water, snow, loose soil, plants, etc. (Fig. 4.18).

5. *Wetness.* Humidity, moisture, depth of water (Figs. 4.17 and 4.18).

6. *Temperature.* Hot, warm, mild, cold, freezing.

7. *Mobility.* The degree and manner of movement of the substrate, in earthquakes, landslides, etc.

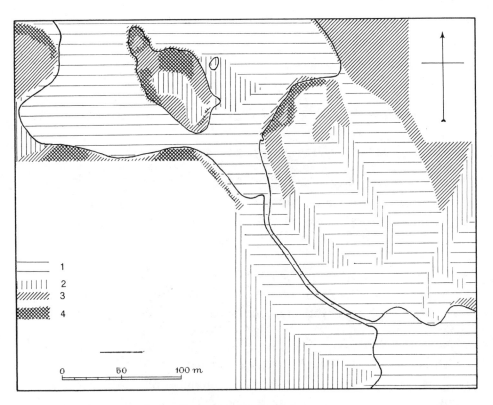

Figure 4.16. Gradient of the substrate in Valosaari.

1 = < 5 degrees (substrate horizontal or sloping in a hardly noticeable manner); *2* = 5–10 degrees (very easy to climb); *3* = 10–20 degrees (fairly difficult to climb); *4* = > 20 degrees (difficult, very difficult, or impossible to climb in places).

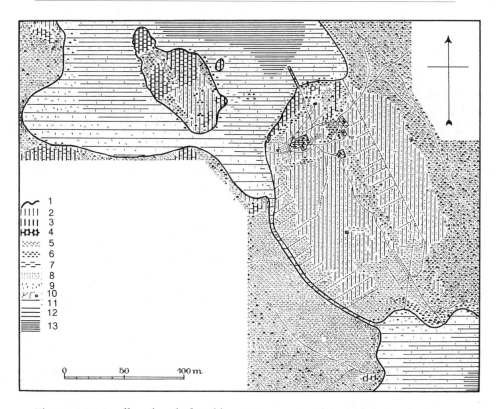

Figure 4.17. Small-scale relief and bearing capacity of the substrate of Valosaari in summer.

1 = Main boundary of the substrate (shoreline); *2* = flat soil or vegetation substrate; *3* = flat bedrock substrate; *4* = flat wooden substrate (floor); *5* = tussocky substrate; *6* = stony substrate; *7* = hard substrate; *8* = soft substrate; *9* = boggy substrate; *10* = path, ditch, well; *11* = water, depth < 50 cm; *12* = water, depth 50–150 cm; *13* = water, depth > 150 cm. Boundary values of 50 and 150 cm were selected for water depth since the former roughly corresponds to water extending up to one's knees and the latter up to one's neck.

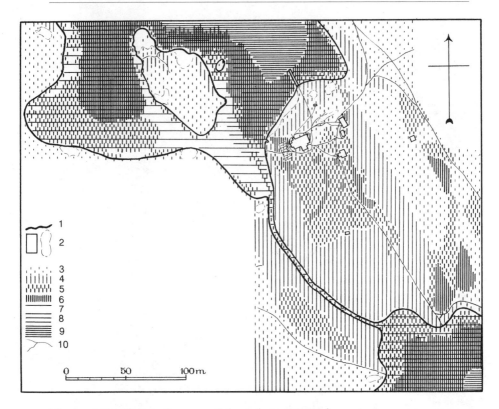

Figure 4.18. Obstructiveness of the substrate in Valosaari.

1 = Main boundary of the substrate (shoreline); *2* = substrate without obstacles (floor, rock with a thin cover of moss or lichen); *3* = thickness of vegetation 1–20 cm; *4* = thickness of vegetation 20–50 cm; *5* = thickness of vegetation 50–100 cm; *6* = thickness of vegetation >100 cm; *7* = depth of water < 50 cm; *8* = depth of water 50–150 cm; *9* = depth of water >150 cm; *10* = path. The average heights of the dominant plant species in the vegetation at Valosaari are as follows: < 20 cm: mosses, lichen, cowberry; 20–50 cm: *Pteris,* bilberry, grasses, and herbs in natural meadows; 50–100 cm: shore sedges, sown timothy, and clover, *Pteris* in places; > 100 cm: raspberry, alder coppice, reeds, and various other aquatic plants.

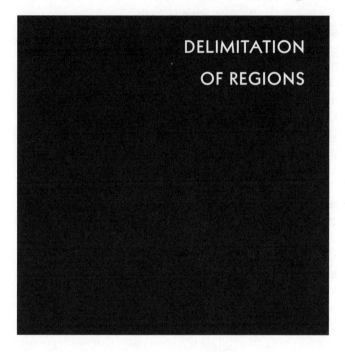

5

DELIMITATION
OF REGIONS

5.1. Formation of Geographical Entities

Geography is a science that forms entities (sec. 2.1), a synthetic task that requires a deliberate analysis of the properties of the area to be studied. It must be determined what the features in question are, how specific they are and how widespread they are, in order to establish the characteristics of a region (see sec. 1.5) that can be combined to form an entity, albeit a greatly simplified one, abstracted from the reality studied. This entity, a geographical region or area, is uniform as a complex in a certain sense, but also stands out from its environment in some specific way.

The formation of geographical entities naturally always leads to the definition of boundaries and transitional zones. To combine in one place is to separate in another. The formation of entities is at the same time the division of a larger area into regions. *When a uniform geographical entity is formed, a representative of a certain geographical type is obtained. When a delimiting boundary is drawn around this entity, a distinction is made between a geographical individual and its environment.*

The formation of entities or the division of areas into regions is an absolutely essential, although neglected part of geographical research. It was the
division of Africa into "natural landscapes" by Passarge in 1908 (197) that
marked the first purposeful attempt at doing this. Passarge discusses the factors that in his opinion determine the geographical nature of this continent
in the analytical part of his investigation, compares the significance of these
factors with each other, assesses them, selects the most important, those that
constitute characteristics, and delimits areas that are uniform in terms of
these, that is, "natural landscapes." It is, nevertheless, questionable whether
the regions thus obtained were geographical entities, and it is true that the
synthetic part of his investigation was indeterminate and arbitrary. Generally
speaking, however, it was his work that paved the way for a technique of delimiting regions. The method can be used not only to define geographical
units of various sizes, but also to form geographical complex types.[1]

5.1.1. *Cartographic Method*

The larger the area to be studied, the more necessary a map is as an instrument in the delimitation of its regions and the more clearly the formation of
entities becomes a purely cartographic procedure. In the work described
above, Passarge first presents analytical maps illustrating the distribution of
certain factors, which he compares. He then produces a synthetic map of regions in which the "natural landscapes" are more or less uniform in terms of
their most significant elements. The synthetic part was later altered and supplemented (Granö 88) so that all the boundaries or transitional zones that appear on the analytical maps are marked on the same map; that is, the analytical maps are in a way superimposed one upon another and the assessment
carried out after that but only in terms of the transitional zones, parts of
which are then appended to one or other of the adjacent, completely uniform
regions as is most reasonable.

The following should be kept in mind when using the cartographic
method of delimiting regions:

1. "Absolute" maps representing the real size, form or intensity, distribution, grouping, and number of the various elements in the area studied, such
as topographical maps or the landscape and proximity maps and plans mentioned above, are suitable as analytical maps for defining regions only if the
scale is very large and the grouping of the elements in question very rough
and in a way generalizable in terms of the regions themselves. These absolute
maps often have to be used to draw up special analytical regional maps,

1. The significance of landscape types is especially emphasized by Gradmann (79),
while Rosberg (234) has examined the landscape types of Finland (see also Granö 94
and 95)

which show the areas of occurrence of the various elements as entities. A relief map (see Fig. 3.5) or a map of rivers is thus not suitable for this purpose, nor a map that represents dwellings and roads (Fig. 3.18), but special maps must be drawn up representing the areas characterized by a flat, a mountain terrain, a system of valleys and a table terrain, brooks, major rivers, lake systems, cluster villages and dense road networks, single dwellings, a loose road network, and so forth.

2. When drawing up analytical regional maps, it is primarily uniform regions and areas that must be looked for and not maximally distinct or sharp boundaries, since the latter are rare in reality and transitional zones of varying width are considerably more common. It is therefore reasonable to avoid excess emphasis on boundaries in cartographic representation and to take the indeterminate nature of geographical entities in this respect into consideration wherever possible (Granö 88).

3. The same type of region, such as a mountain terrain, a plain, or an area of cluster villages, can naturally occur in various parts of the area studied, as isolated regions standing out prominently from their environment. But these different regions naturally cannot belong to the same regional entity or geographical individual. No matter how obvious this may seem to be, those who draw up systems of regions do not seem to be conscious of it. Regions that represent the same type are instances of the same individual only if, being situated close to one another and small in size, they can be combined via the intermediary areas into an entity that is a mixed region in nature.

4. The same amount of generalization and equal assessment must be used throughout the analysis, but the features on the various maps must not be compared at this stage. The more detailed the analysis, the tighter the boundaries within which the assessment must take place. If the areas of the forms of the various elements in the landscape are marked on analytical maps, for instance, the comparative assessment must concentrate only on the forms of one element at a time.

5. Evaluation should be avoided at least at the beginning of cartographic synthesis. Attention should be concentrated only on the degree of uniformity and the nature of the individuality (i.e., degree of individuality, see sec. 3.15.3). A geographical complex contains a number of elements, the order of precedence of which is difficult, if not impossible, to determine. When are artificial forms more significant than the forms of water in a landscape that contains both, for instance, or when are the landforms more significant than the colors of the vegetation? If we are only concerned with the forms of the various elements, it is possible that evaluation will succeed in the synthesis as well, since only one series of phenomena in the field of vision is to be studied, apart from which the person carrying out the investigation also has a map

and the landscape profile to work with (see sec. 3.15.4 and Fig. 3.23). Evaluation is hardly necessary when forming vicinities, nor in the case of systems of regions based on a wide variety of features of the nonmaterial environment.

5.1.2. *Factors to Be Considered*

The question of what factors should be taken into consideration when defining uniformity is of crucial significance in the delimitation of regions. The nature and number of these factors will again depend on the concept of geography and its purposes held by the person responsible for the delimitation. Differences of opinion on this major question are unfortunately reflected all too distinctly in the work that is done. The following list illustrates this fact:

Passarge (1908); region: Africa; factors considered: geology, orographymorphology, gradients and river systems, climate, precipitation, vegetation, weathering and soil formation, the animal kingdom.

Schultz (1920); region: Turkestan in Russia; factors: orography, climate, genetic morphology, hydrography, dynamic morphology, pedology, vegetation, the animal kingdom, ethnography, settlement, economic geography, and the geography of communications.

Granö (1922 and 1929); regions: Estonia and Finland; factors: form complexes of landforms, water, vegetation, and artificial matter.

De Geer (1925); region: Sweden; factors: landforms, cultivated areas, distribution of industry, and population.

Stoltenberg (1927); region: Paraguay; factors: orography, petrographic tectonics and pedology, climate, hydrography, phytogeography, and geomorphology.

Niemeyer (1927); region: the steppe area of southeastern Spain; factors: geological structure, geomorphology, and nature of the coasts, the vertical dimension, precipitation, water systems, vegetation, culture.

Frenzel (1927); region: western Lombardy; factors: landforms, vegetation, and towns.

De Geer (1928); region: Northern Europe; factors: the bedrock area of Fennoscandia, the peninsulas of Northern Europe, Fennoscandia and its marginal region characterized by till topography, the land uplift areas of Fennoscandia, the core area of the northern race, both Fennoscandian language areas, diffusion of Protestantism, the present countries, and the maximum extent of the two 1000-year-old realms that have existed in the area in modern times.[2]

2. The boundary between the Finnish and Swedish languages is nevertheless disregarded in the synthesis, being of secondary importance in De Geer's opinion, in that no other boundaries discussed in the analysis exist at that point.

Provided that we regard landscape, proximity, and regions and areas that are uniform in terms of their landscapes and proximities as the objects of study in geography, the nature and quantity of the factors to be considered when defining regions can be accurately determined. When looking for regions that are homogeneous in terms of their landscapes, that is, provinces, districts, localities, and sublocalities, only visual phenomena can be considered, while in the case of entities that are homogeneous in terms of proximics, that is, vicinities and larger areas, all phenomena can be considered but nothing else, since the purpose is to examine the *actual objects of study* of geography. When examining the physiology and stages of development of these entities, factors other than those affecting the division into regions must naturally be taken into consideration, which means that it is undoubtedly useful to form complexes of other kinds, both individuals and types.

5.1.3. *Division of Estonia and Valosaari into Regions*

Three systems of regions constructed in terms of the degree of homogeneity of the landscape and proximity and carried out on different scales are presented below as examples of our concept of the formation of geographical entities, that is, the definition of the localities of Estonia and the sublocalities and vicinities of Valosaari. These divisions into regions are based on the absolute maps and plans discussed above in connection with landscapes and proximities.

Attention will be paid only to methodological considerations, and features of local geography and nomenclature will be employed only where necessary. The localities of Estonia have been discussed in greater detail earlier (88) and the sublocalities and vicinities of Valosaari are significant only to the extent that they represent widespread types of landscapes and proximities.

Since approximately the same factors must be taken into consideration in the formation of both localities and sublocalities, and the same points of view are decisive, these systems of regions are presented in parallel, in the order of their elements, so as to make the significance of different scales and degrees of generalization clearer.

5.2. Definition of Localities and Sublocalities

5.2.1. *Form Regions and Areas of the Earth's Crust*

Since localities and sublocalities are homogeneous regions or areas in terms of their landscape features, the various phenomena of the distant field of vision must be dealt with analytically by means of maps when forming them. For the reasons discussed above, the world of forms, or mainly the complex forms of immobile and invariable elements, will deserve our primary attention, although mobile form complexes and colors cannot be neglected when examining individual cases. The landform complexes of the earth's crust will be discussed first. The form regions of Estonia and the form areas of Valosaari are listed in the legends to the relevant maps, which also include the codes representing the above units (Roman numerals, see sec. 3.4.4).

The definition of the form regions of Estonia is based on the map in Figure 3.5. The glacial formations marked on it are not significant on account of being of a certain structure and created in a certain manner, however, for the first thing to be examined is not the structure or the origin of the topography, nor its absolute altitude, but the relief and relative variations in altitude.

Looked at from this perspective, the majority of the eskers and drumlins in Estonia are insignificant. It is only where they occur at such a density that the ground is undulating or striped that they must be taken into consideration as characteristic elements.

Generally speaking, the northwestern and to a great extent also the central part of Estonia is dominated by a plain, while the southeastern parts are dominated by various types of elevations that are roundish or elongated in plan view. When examining the features of the relief in further detail, it can also be observed that the areas that seem to be even are nevertheless fairly variable. Small humps, ridges and crests, and groups of these rise from the plain, and valley systems exist on the cliff coast of the Gulf of Finland in particular.

The landform regions in Estonia are presented in Figure 5.1. The following aspects were regarded as decisive when drawing up the map:

1. The orographic division into regions should be based solely on features of the relief that characterize it in terms of landscape.

2. All features of the topography (elevations, depressions, plains) should be taken into account. The decisive ones are those that characterize the landscape regardless of their position in the morphographic system.

3. When considering the features characterizing the relief, one should define first the clearly distinguishable features and then the less clearly distinguishable ones. With the form regions defined in this manner, various indefinite boundary areas and transitional zones of varying width will emerge as well.

The small form regions of Valosaari (Fig. 5.2) contain only simple forms: a dome, a hump, or terrace, so that we cannot use the Roman numerals referring to complex forms. Variations in altitude are small. As can be seen from the map in Figure 3.7, the highest point (on the island) is only 7 m above the level of Lake Saimaa, so that all the elevations must be either humps or domes (see sec. 3.4.1).

The fact that slopes as formal elements are both parts of a certain elevation and parts of the depression delimiting this elevation caused problems when defining the form areas of Valosaari. If, according to the definitions of the areas, the slope characterizes only one of them, the other being charac-

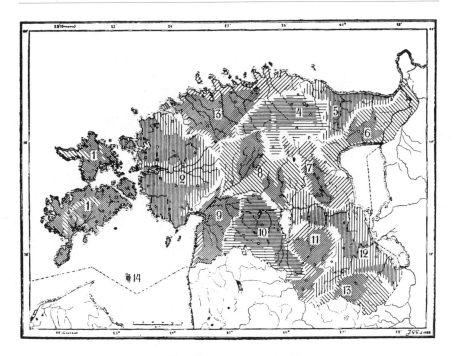

Figure 5.1. Form regions of landforms in Estonia.

(Typical areas are *densely hatched* and transitional zones left *blank*. Hatchings are drawn in different directions to aid recognition of the regions.) *1* = Plain region on the islands (*VI,* see sec. 3.4.4); *2* = region with small humps, ridges and plains in western Estonia (*V, VI*); *3* = tableland of NW Estonia (*V VII*); *4* = Rakvere-Pandivere region of ridges and major humps (*III IV*); *5* = tableland of NE Estonia (*VI VII*); *6* = Alutaguse region of small ridges and plains (*V VI*); *7* = Tartumaa region of major barrows and domes (*III*); *8* = The Türi-Põltsamaa region with small barrows and plains (*V VI*); *9* = Pärnu plain (*VI*); *10* = Viljandi-Helme region of dish valleys, barrows and major humps (*III IX*); *11* = Otepää-Karula region of major domes (*III II*); *12* = SE Estonia region of dish valleys, barrows and major humps (*VI IX*); *13* = Haanja region of major domes (*III II*); *14* = Ruhnu hump region (*IV*).

terized by a plain (the summit plain of an elevation or the bottom plain of a valley), the boundary will naturally run along the upper or lower edge of the slope, but if one of the areas was defined as an elevation and the other as a depression, the whole slope is actually a kind of transitional zone. Alternatively, this area held in common can be divided in two when expedient, in which case the boundary will run along the middle of the slope.

5.2.2. *Form Regions and Areas of Water*

The summer landscape, which is here used to refer to a landscape in which water occurs in its liquid state, is more suitable as a basis for delimiting re-

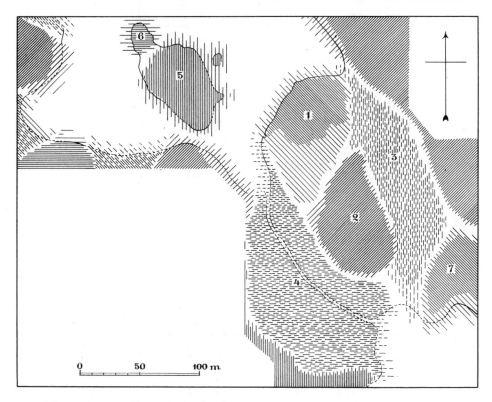

Figure 5.2. Landform areas of Valosaari.

1 = Northern dome; *2* = central hump; *3* = Tiusanen's plain; *4* = Puuskansaari plain; *5* = central dome of island; *6* = northwestern dome of island; *7* = southeastern table. Elevations are marked with *lines,* valleys with *half-dashed lines,* and plains with *dashed lines.* Distinct areas are marked with *dense hatching,* while transitional zones and water are left *blank.* The *sparse hatching* along the shoreline indicates that the phenomenal space rising on the shore continues into the space of another element (water in this case).

gions than the winter landscape, in that the distinctions between water and other elements are more clearly visible.

The *extent of the water surface* is of primary significance, and therefore seas should be mentioned before other features. A sea of which the opposite shores cannot be seen is termed an open sea (see sec. 3.5.1). The size, plan view, and structure of an open sea area is dependent on the shoreline of the surrounding mainland. Large gulfs in the sea with relatively narrow mouths, for example, the Gulf of Riga or Gulf of Livonia, have their own open sea areas. An open sea is surrounded by coastal water (see sec. 3.5.1), which is delimited by the islands and coastal land visible in the landscape. The width of this coastal water depends on the height of the relief and the translucence of the air, that is, on factors that influence the range of vision in a decisive manner. Apart from coastal water, the coastal zone includes coastal land, in which water is a significant element of the landscape. This is nevertheless narrower than the coastal water, since the view is usually more open on the sea than on the land.

Of the forms of inland water, rivers and lakes should be taken into account, whereas bogs as features of the landscape are a type of vegetation rather than water. Major lakes such as Lake Ladoga, Lake Baikal, or the Great Lakes of North America resemble seas, having large open water areas, while smaller lakes are often combined into groups, lake regions, which are defined on the basis of plan view, grouping, size of the various lakes and extent of the intervening land areas. The dimensions and characteristics involved thus depend mainly on the landforms.

The significance of rivers in a landscape depends mainly on the extent to which they are obscured by landforms and vegetation. A brook winding in an open valley on a steppe is more significant for the landscape than a body of water flowing in a gorge or within a jungle, which would be hardly visible. Larger rivers are naturally less dependent on their immediate environment.

The *manner of flow* is also worth considering and should be taken into account when delimiting regions if it leads to the formation of rapids, while the hydrographic identity between various parts of the same river system is of secondary significance and must not prevent the division of that system into form regions if the considerations mentioned above support this. The indefinite watersheds found in gently sloping areas are also less significant in this respect, as is the question of where the river discharges, or its general direction of flow. The differences between the upper course of a river, with narrow brooks, and the lower parts, with wider stretches, and those between stretches of rapids and the slowly flowing parts of a river system are frequently of considerable significance, just as it is often expedient to combine sets of rapids on various rivers into one form region and the placid stretches into another, despite the fact that this tends to dismember the river systems, which are in themselves hydrographic entities. The degree of meandering and the size of the bends is also a relevant feature from the point of view of landscape science.

Water occurs in the landscapes of Estonia in different forms at various times of the year, and therefore a distinction must be made between summer and winter form regions and the topographical significance of each defined and assessed, since snow and ice are of greater significance in the eastern and southeastern parts of Estonia, where the winter lasts longer.

Since the whole land area, the coastal sea area and most of the open water areas in Estonia are covered with snow and ice in winter, the winter landscape is *distinctly a water landscape*. And since ice and snow cover all the other elements on the land, *the form regions of water in winter are the same as the geographical winter localities.*

The areas in which the sea is dominant are most significant in summer, that is, the open sea and coasts, which are divided by islands, groups of islands, capes, and peninsulas into more or less clearly distinguishable regions. These are characterized by either the total absence of landforms in the same manner as the open sea areas, or the variable shape of the shoreline in the

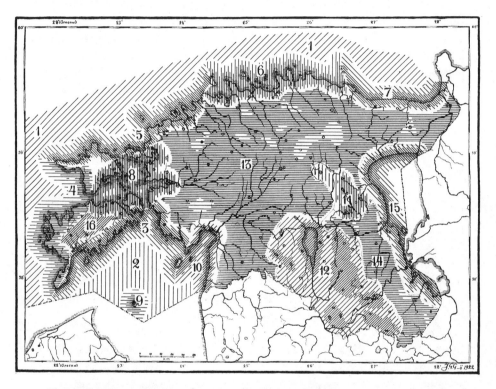

Figure 5.3. Form regions of water in Estonia in summer.

(Typical areas are *densely hatched* and transitional zones left *blank*. Hatchings are drawn in different directions to aid recognition of the regions.) *1* = Open water of the Gulf of Finland and Baltic Sea (*1;* see sec. 3.5.4); *2* = open water of the Gulf of Riga (*1*); *3* = Kuresaare-Töstamaa arm coast with islands (*5*); *4* = Cove and arm coast of the western part of the islands (*5*); *5* = Hiiumaa-Paldiski cove and island coast (*5*); *6* = Tallinn-Loksa cove and island coast (*5*); *7* = Open straight coast of Virumaa (*5*); *8* = Estonian archipelago (*5*); *9* = Ruhnu open coast (*5*); *10* = Pärnu open coast (*5*); *11* = Tartu region of parallel lakes (*3*); *12* = Southern Estonian region of scattered lakes and rivers (*32*); *13* = major region of winding rivers in northern and southwestern Estonia (*2*); *14* = winding river region of southeastern Estonia (*2*); *15* = Lake Peipsijärv cove and arm coast (*5*); *16* = brook region of Saaremaa (*11*).

coastal zone, and often also the nature of the lower course of the rivers flowing into the sea. Thus, the decisive element in the hydrographic division into regions is the plan view of the water area and not the relief of the mainland surrounding it, the significance of the latter being only indirect, so that it should not be underlined in the nomenclature of water areas. It is true that the system of regions would not change even if landforms were considered, but their inclusion would be a methodological error. Such names as the cliff coast of Northern Estonia or the flat coast of Pärnu are suitable designations for geographical complexes but not for water areas, whereas if we talk about the open cove coast of Northern Estonia, we are emphasizing the fact that water is the dominant factor in the definition of this region and are aware that this entity includes a certain land area.

The relief of the coast of Estonia is so flat that the maximum width of the coastal zone, including the islands and bays, is hardly greater than 45 km. The average width is 30–40 km, of which 15–20 km is the characteristic coastal zone and the same amount again somewhat less typical. Approximately two-thirds of the whole zone is composed of water. On account of the openness of the view, the coastal region is widest in Northern Estonia, where high cliffs rise abruptly from the sea.

The main lake in Estonia, Lake Peipsijärv, resembles a gulf of the sea in terms of landscape, in that it has a clearly distinguishable littoral area, while Lake Virtsjärv is a quite typical inland lake. The other lakes are very much smaller and constitute form regions only where they occur in groups.

The rivers of Estonia flow either into the sea or into Lake Peipsijärv, which is connected to the sea by the River Narva. Since the shore of the lake on the Estonian side runs approximately parallel to the sea coast, that is, toward the west, southwest, and south, and the main watershed runs in the same direction, the rivers and lakes flow radially outward to the sea, branching in a fanlike manner, but radially inward into Lake Peipsijärv. This categorization is mentioned only because it manifests the influence of *absolute altitude*.

With few exceptions, the rivers of Estonia are insignificant and monotonous in landscape terms. The water form regions of Estonia in summer are presented in Figure 5.3. The above aspects were also decisive for defining the water regions of Valosaari in summer (Fig. 5.4). The only new element is a "waterless area," which could have been left without hatching had it not been regarded as necessary to distinguish between it and the surrounding transitional zone (in white) on the map.

5.2.3. *Form Regions and Areas of Vegetation*

The vegetation map of Estonia (Fig. 3.13) indicates that alvar grasslands are dominant on the islands and in the NW, where they occur in the same manner as on Öland and Gotland. Apart from these sparse herb terrains char-

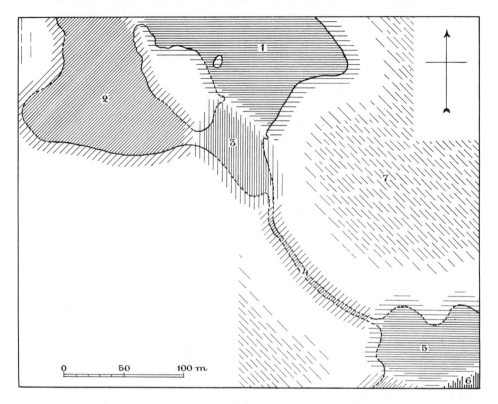

Figure 5.4. Form areas of water at Valosaari in summer.

1 = Main bay; *2* = "small lake"; *3* = head of bay; *4* = Kuivasalmi sound; *5* = southeastern bay; *6* = Marjaniemi open water; *7* = dry area. Open water is hatched with *thicker lines* and dry areas with *dashed lines*. The edges with *sparse hatching* and the *blank areas* indicate the indefinite nature of transitional zones and the extension of phenomenal spaces beyond the area of occurrence of water.

acteristic of calcareous soils, there are a great number of tree-herb terrains, that is, wooded meadows, mainly with birches, and a zone of forests and bogs further to the southeast which surrounds the Bay of Pärnu and extends up to the sea coast in the north. This zone is widest (70 km) in the southwest, near Mihkli and Kõpu. The third major vegetation region consists of cultivated and tree-herb terrains and is situated in mid-Estonia, extending to the sea in the north and to the border in places in the south. The southeastern part of Estonia also belongs to this region, whereas the northeastern part constitutes the fourth major region in vegetational landscape terms, being characterized by bogs and forests.

The criteria on which the vegetation regions of Estonia (see Fig. 5.5) were defined included variations in those group forms that are covered with snow in winter and thus do not characterize the landscape for several months in the year. The same principle was followed when drawing up the map of Valo-saari (Fig. 5.6), in that a distinction is drawn between lichen terrain and herb terrain, and relatively low bushes are also recognized. Even when operating on a very large scale, it is reasonable to determine the extent to which the forms and form complexes of the vegetation remain the same in appearance in the field of vision throughout the year (e.g., coniferous forests) or change

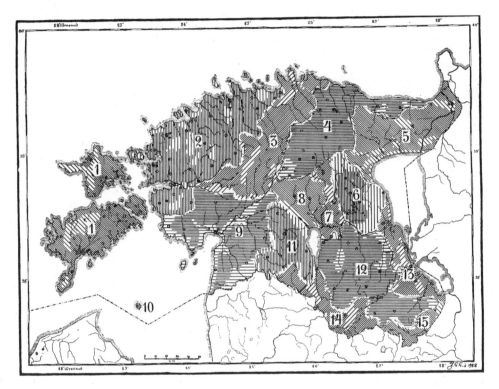

Figure 5.5. Form regions of vegetation in Estonia.

(Typical areas are *densely hatched* and transitional zones left *blank*. Hatchings are drawn in different directions to aid recognition of the regions.).

1 = Island region of alvar vegetation and tree-herb terrain (*EA;* see sec. 3.7.2); *2* = major alvar and tree-herb terrain region of NW Estonia (*EA*); *3* = Lelle-Aegviidu region of large forests and bogs (*AD*); *4* = Rakvere-Peetri region of large fields and cultural wood-lands (*EA*); *5* = Alutaguse region of large forests and pine bogs (*AD*); *6* = Tartu striated region of fields and meadows (*EA*); *7* = Kursi forest and bog region (*ACD*); *8* = Põltsa-maa-Võhma region of tree-herb terrain and fields (*EA*); *9* = Pärnu region of major pine bogs and forests (*DA*); *10* = Ruhnu mixed region (*AE*); *11* = Viljandi field and strip meadow region (*EA*); *12* = Otepää-Võru mixed region of small fields, meadows and woods (*EA*); *13* = Alatskivi-Lobodka region of large meadows and forests (*EAC*); *14* = Valga-Hargla region of forests and scattered fields (*AEC*); *15* = Irboska-Laura region of forests, tree-herb terrain and fields (*AED*).

(e.g., deciduous forests) and to what extent they are covered by snow (or floodwater) at certain times (Fig. 5.7).

5.2.4. *Form Regions and Areas of Artificial Elements*

As indicated in the map in Figure 3.18, the distributions of dwellings and roads in Estonia reflect requirements of human life and action that are dependent on the complex forms of other materials. Large, totally or partially uninhabited areas characterized by vast bogs and forests occur close to the Bay of Pärnu and Lake Peipsijärv. There are four main concentrations of pop-

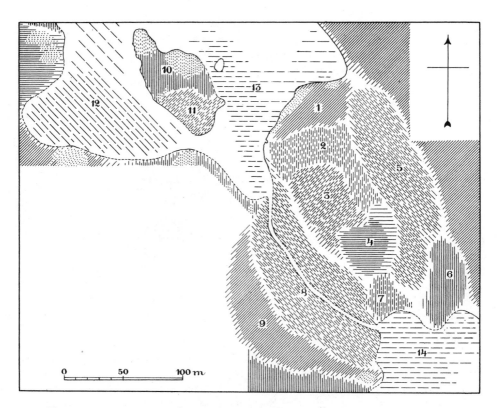

Figure 5.6. Form areas of vegetation at Valosaari in summer.

1 = Northern woods and lichen terrain; *2* = northern mixed region of grassland and small bushes; *3* = central grassland; *4* = central pine wood; *5* = Tiusanen's meadow; *6* = southeastern pine thicket; *7* = southern bush and tree meadow; *8* = Kuivasalmi meadow; *9* = southwestern clump of alders; *10* = woods and lichen terrain on the island; *11* = tree meadow on the island; *12* = sedge area in the "small lake"; *13* = reeds of the main bay; *14* = reeds and rushes of the southeastern bay. Trees are marked with *lines,* grasses and herbs with *dashed lines,* and less distinctive parts of the land areas and aquatic plants with a *sparse hatching.*

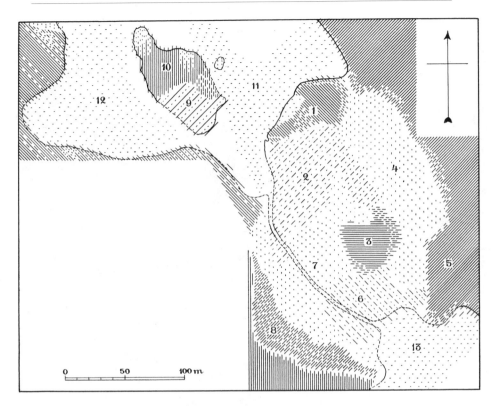

Figure 5.7. Form areas of vegetation at Valosaari.

1 = Northern woods; *2* = northern bush meadow; *3* = central pine wood; *4* = Tiusanen's meadow; *5* = southeastern pine wood; *6* = southern bush and tree meadow; *7* = Kuiva-salmi meadow; *8* = southwestern clump of alders; *9* = tree meadow on the island; *10* = pine wood on the island; *11* = reeds in the main bay; *12* = sedges in the "Small lake"; *13* = reeds and rushes in the southeastern bay. Permanent, invariable vegetation (coniferous forests) is marked with *lines,* permanent, variable vegetation (deciduous forests, bushes) with *dashed lines,* and vegetation occurring in the snowless times of the year (herbs, etc.) with *dots.*

ulation: the western part of Harjumaa, the eastern half of Järvamaa together with the western part of Virumaa, a large portion of Tartumaa together with the adjacent Võrumaa and the southern part of Viljandimaa.

The influence of historical factors is also manifest in the grouping of settled areas. The northeastern part and the Petseri district, where the influence of a Slavic population and a different kind of government have left their traces, are characterized by large villages, each centred around a clearly defined main street, which stand out so obviously on our map that their distribution could easily be used to define the position of the former border between the government of Pskov and Livonia.

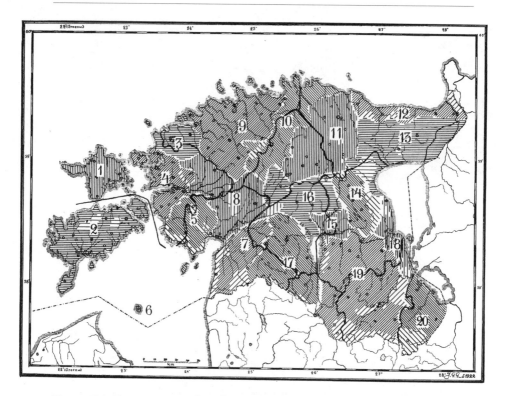

Figure 5.8. Form regions of artificial matter in Estonia.

(Typical areas are *densely hatched* and transitional zones left *blank*. Hatchings are drawn in different directions to aid recognition of the regions. Boundary lines indicate province boundaries.)

1 = Hiiumaa region of coastal settlement (*icf;* see sec. 3.10.2); *2* = Saaremaa estate and cluster village region (*fci*); *3* = Risti region of individual dwellings with a sparse road network (*il*); *4* = Haapsalu-Lihula mixed region of small settled areas and ribbon settlement (*ieb*); *5* = Mihkli-Tõstamaa mixed region of individual dwellings and ribbon settlement (*iel*); *6* = cluster village of Ruhnu (*c*); *7* = Pärnu region of individual dwellings, ribbon settlements and a sparse road network (*leb*); *8* = Vändra-Pärnu ribbon settlement region (*ie*); *9* = Tallinn-Rapla region of cluster villages with a dense road network (*fce*); *10* = Loksa-Aegviidu region of individual dwellings with a sparse road network (*il*); *11* = Rakvere-Tapa region of major villages, estates and a dense road network (*cbf*); *12* = Jõhvi-Narva region of individual cluster and street villages (*cb*); *13* = Alutaguse region of individual dwellings, street villages and a sparse road network (*ib*); *14* = Tartu region of parallel ribbon settlements and estates (*ef*); *15* = Laeväküla-Kavilda region of individual dwellings and sparse road network (*li*); *16* = the Türi-Põltsamaa region of clustered settlements with a dense road network (*fc*); *17* = Viljandi-Helme region of large major farms with a dense road network (*fi*); *18* = street village region on the shore of Lake Peipsijärv (*bl*); *19* = Otepää-Haanja region of small farms and estates with a dense road network (*if*); *20* = Petseri street village region (*b*).

The dependence of administrative borders on factors associated with land-scape science and human geography is manifested only in some places here, for example, along the southern and southeastern borders of Harjumaa and the southwestern border of Virumaa, which are marked by sparsely populated areas.

The division of Estonia into form regions of artificial elements (Fig. 5.8) is nevertheless independent of these genetic considerations and is based directly on the data shown in Figure 3.18. The following aspects were regarded as decisive:

1. The system of regions should be based on the grouping and distribution of dwellings and the density and quality of the road network.

2. An area in which the distribution, plan view and size of the dwellings, and the road network are similar everywhere may be is considered to comprise a form region of artificial elements.

3. Relatively narrow areas in which the characteristic features change may be regarded as transitional or boundary zones. The definition of these should be based in particular on the existence of uninhabited areas and areas not traversed by roads.

Valosaari is a special area in the sense that it has no roads (see Fig. 3.14). Traffic moves only along the waterways, as elsewhere in the lake region of Finland. The narrow paths in the yards and grasslands are not visible in the landscape. Fences, which also occur in the littoral water in places, and hayricks are the only representatives of structures on our analytical map (Fig. 5.19).

5.2.5. *Color Regions*

If a map of the color regions of Estonia were to be drawn up, it would approximate the map of form regions for the vegetation (Fig. 5.5). Only the color regions near the sea and Lake Peipsijärv, where water abounds, would be delimited roughly in the same manner as the form regions for water (Fig. 5.3). The colors of the Estonian landscape will thus be taken into consideration in the synthesis even without any separate color map, but indirectly, for the colors of the earth's crust and the artificial landscape elements do not have any particularly great effect on the definition of regions, although it must be admitted that the bedrock of the Silurian calcareous areas of northern Estonia in particular differs markedly in this respect from the Devonian bedrock that predominates in the southern parts of the country.

Colors are more significant in a detailed system of regions, where the colors of artificial elements in particular add a variety to the field of vision, which is apt to be overlooked when forming larger regional entities. Thus, the colors of the vegetation and artificial elements are decisive at Valosaari (Fig.

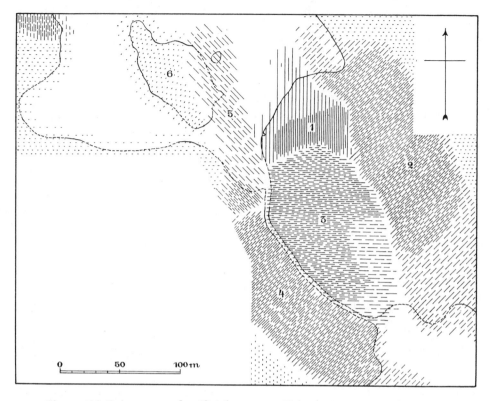

Figure 5.9. Form areas of artificial matter at Valosaari.

1 = Building complex; *2* = eastern fenced area; *3* = central hayrick area; *4* = southwestern fenced area; *5* = fenced area at head of bay; *6* = area of the island in a natural state. The building complex is marked with *solid lines,* areas with fences and hayricks with *dashed lines,* and areas in a natural state with *dots.* Less distinct areas are indicated with *sparser hatching.*

5.10), even though our color map does not add any new information to the synthetic definition of boundaries already achieved by the maps of form regions.

5.2.6. *Synthesis: Localities and Sublocalities*

5.2.6.1. The Localities of Estonia. The permanent form complexes of Estonia were discussed above and the form regions based on the various elements in the landscape defined and presented cartographically. We have now come to the stage in our inductive method at which we can address the synthetic part of our task, the definition and delimitation of geographical regions. We must first determine the extent to which the various form complexes occur together and whether there are zones in which the form complexes of more than one element change within a limited area.

In order to obtain such a generalized view, a map was drawn up on which
the form regions of all four elements were marked (Fig. 5.11). This time, however, the regions are not bounded by transitional zones but by the center
lines of these zones, which, wherever two or more such lines occur side by
side, serve to mark the boundaries of the resulting complexes, the *landscape
boundary zone.* The maximum width of such a zone may be taken to be 10
km, corresponding to the width of an open landscape. If we mark zones in
which three or four boundary lines coincide in black, since they constitute
three or four-element boundary zones, and *two-element boundary zones* with
dots, our map will indicate in a distinctive manner the extent to which regions as *geographical individuals* stand out from their environment and how

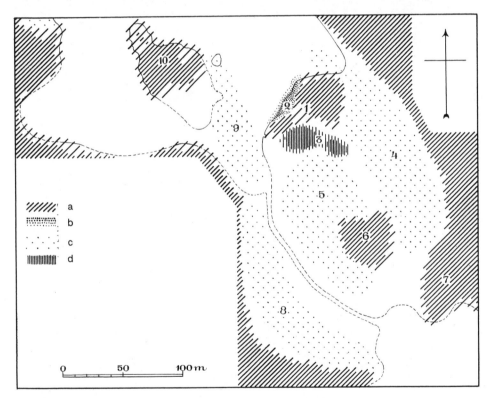

Figure 5.10. Color areas of Valosaari.

a = Dark green; *b* = grey; *c* = blotchy grey; *d* = red. The areas were defined with respect
to the above colors, which remain unchanged throughout the year.

1 = Dark green northern pine wood; *2* = grey northern rocks; *3* = red building complex;
4 = greyish eastern area with fences and hayricks; *5* = grey central area with hayricks;
6 = dark green central pine wood; *7* = dark green southeastern pine wood; *8* = greyish
southwestern fenced area; *9* = greyish fenced area at head of bay; *10* = dark green pine
wood on the island.

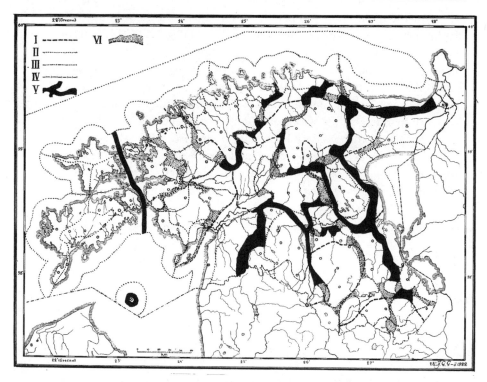

Figure 5.11. Boundaries of the form regions and transitional zones of the geographical localities of Estonia.

I = Landform region boundary; *II* = water form region boundary; *III* = vegetation form region boundary; *IV* = boundary of form region of artificial matter; *V* = three or four-element boundary zone; *VI* = two-element boundary zone.

these individuals are combined into larger groups. If the intervening area is wider than 10 km, it may be termed a *transitional landscape zone.* Our map thus presents not only boundary zones and their distinctive features but also regions and their degrees of homogeneity. If all the elements that are relevant to the definition of a set of regions in terms of landscape science, that is, landforms, water, vegetation, and artificial matter, occur in these regional entities we can refer to them as *four-element localities,* or localities distinguished in terms of four-form regions.[3]

If the border of one form region occurs within the boundaries of the geographical entity, this naturally interferes with the unity of the whole complex, which will then be homogeneous only with respect to three elements, and we

3. An open sea area is naturally also a distinct geographical entity, although it consists of only one form region and is dominated by one element. The various phenomena of the sky are not considered when defining regions, for the reasons stated above. Ships are of minor significance in the open sea off Estonia.

will have a *three-element locality,* which comprises all or part of five-form regions, since the element whose border violates the unity of the locality is represented by two-form regions in this case. Even less distinct geographical entities are *two-element localities,* the landscape of which is more variable and is represented by six-form regions.

Theoretically, the best definition of a set of regions is naturally one that results in entities that are uniform with respect to all the landscape elements, *four-element localities* in this case, but such a method is not always the most expedient, as localities are often surrounded by broad transitional zones which themselves require attention. It is therefore often most sensible to be satisfied with a lower degree of homogeneity, since the boundary and transitional zones then become narrower and the number of localities smaller. Especially when a large area of land has to be divided into geographical individuals, it is more expedient to understand geographical homogeneity in a broader sense.

Regions of three and four elements (the latter with either exclusively dense or exclusively open hatching) are presented in Figure 5.12.

Regions defined in terms of two elements are quite sufficient for everyday purposes and for school geography (Fig. 5.13), but it is then the main characteristics selected that should be taken as decisive and an effort should be made to keep the transitional and boundary zones suitably narrow. Since it is quite possible that two-element regions may be introduced for general use in Estonia, I have selected short, easily memorizable names for them. It is probably not entirely a coincidence that some of the old historical regions correspond to these geographical entities as defined here, and the use of the old names would seem justified in this connection insofar as they can be regionally substantiated.

As indicated in Figures 5.12 and 5.13, the above geographical regions could be replaced fairly well with groups of local government districts, in statistical surveys, for example. These districts are so large in Estonia, however, that it is difficult to use their boundaries instead of geographical boundary zones.

5.2.6.2. The Sublocalities of Valosaari. As mentioned in the analytical treatment of regional divisions, not only forms but also colors may be considered when defining the sublocalities of Valosaari. The synthesis is thus based on five analytical maps (Figs. 5.2, 5.4, 5.7, 5.9, and 5.10).

The map of the sublocalities of Valosaari (Fig. 5.14) differs from the synthetic maps of Estonia in two respects. First, the boundaries of the forms representing various materials are sometimes shown by thick lines and sometimes by thin lines depending on the sharpness of the boundary, so that the degrees of individuality of the sublocations are clearly visible. Second, the sublocalities are marked by hatching or symbols denoting the element, form, or color that particularly characterizes it as an individual.

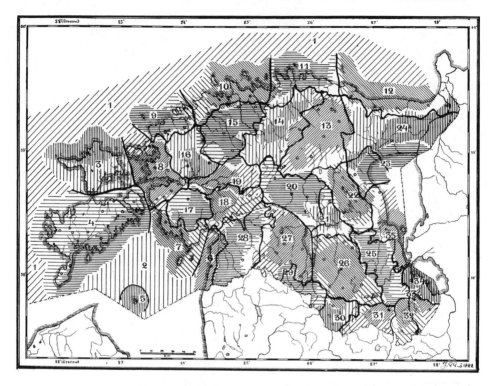

Figure 5.12. Geographical localities of Estonia defined by three or four elements and groups of communes corresponding to these.

(A change in the configuration of the form complex of the fourth element within the boundaries of a locality is marked with sparse parallel lines. Boundary and transitional zones are left *blank*. *Hatchings* are drawn in different directions to aid recognition of the areas. Boundaries of groups of communes are marked with *thick solid lines*.)

The numbered localities defined by *three elements* are: *1* = Open water of the Gulf of Finland-Baltic Sea (*1*); *2* = open water of the Gulf of Riga (*1*); *3* = Hiiumaa (alvar and tree-herb terrains, sparse settlement and cluster villages; *VI EA fc*); *4* = Saaremaa (plain, alvar and tree-herb terrains, estates, cluster villages; *VI EA fc*); *5* = Ruhnu (humps, coastal water, cluster village; *IV 5 c*); *6* = Pärnu (barrows, ridges, coastal waters, rivers, ribbon settlements, *IV 52 eb*); *7* = Tõstamaa (minor humps and plain, coastal waters, in-dividual dwellings and ribbon settlements; *VI V 5 ie*); *8* = Haapsalu (minor humps and plain, coastal waters and rivers, individual dwellings and ribbon settlements; *V VI 52 ie*); *9* = Risti (ridges and plain, major alvars, sparse settlement and loose road network; *V VI E i*); *10* = Tallinn (tableland, coastal waters and rivers, alvar and tree-herb terrain; *V VII 52 E*); *11* = Loksa (tableland, forests and scattered herb terrain, sparse settlement and loose road network; *V VII AE i*); *12* = Narva (tableland, coastal waters, individual cluster and street villages; *VI VII 5 cb*); *13* = Pandivere (winding brooks, large fields and cultural forests, major villages and estates, dense road network; *2 EA cb*); *14* = Aegvi-idu (winding brooks, small lakes, large forests and bogs, sparse settlement and loose road network; *23 AD il*); *15* = Hageri (winding brooks, alvar and tree-herb terrains, cluster villages, dense road network; *2 EA fc*); *16* = Kullamaa (minor humps, ridges, plain, winding brooks, tree-herb terrains; *V VI 2 EA*); *17* = Jõpre (plain, minor humps and ridges, forests and bogs, individual dwellings and street villages; *VI V DA ie*); *18* = Vändra (winding rivers, bogs and forests, ribbon settlements; *2 DA e*); *19* = Lelle (winding rivers, forests and bogs, ribbon settlements; *2 AD e*); *20* = Türi-Põltsamaa (minor barrows and plain, winding rivers, cluster villages and a dense road network; *V VI 2 fc*); *21* = Kursi (plain, forests and bogs, individual dwellings and a sparse road network; *VI AC li*); *22* = Palamuse (major barrows, parallel strip fields and meadows, parallel ribbon settlements and estates; *III EA ef*); *23* = Lohusoo (minor ridges and plain, forests and tree-herb terrains, individual farms and street villages; *V VI AE bi*); *24* = Alutaguse (winding rivers, large forests and bogs, individual farms, street villages and a sparse road network; *2 AD ib*); *25* = Põlva (plain, dish valley, winding rivers, small farms, dense road network; *VI IX 2 if*); *26* = Otepää (scattered lakes, small fields, meadows and forests, small farms, estates and dense road network; *32 EA if*); *27* = Viljandi (major humps, barrows and dish valleys, fields and strip meadows, large farms and dense road network, *III IX EA fi*); *28* = Kilingi (winding rivers, large bogs and forests, individual farms and a sparse road network; *2 DA li*); *29* = Valga (barrows, humps and dish valleys, scattered lakes, forests and scattered fields; *III IX 3 AE*); *30* = Karula (scattered lakes, forests and scattered fields, small farms; *32 AE i*); *31* = Haanja (major domes, scattered lakes, individual dwellings, dense road network; *III II 32 if*); *32* = Laura (domes, winding rivers, individual dwellings and street villages; *III 2 ib*); *33* = Petseri (plain, tables and dish valleys, winding rivers, street villages; *VI IX 2 b*); *34* = Lobodka (plain, dish valleys, coastal waters, winding rivers, street villages; *VI IX 52 b*); *35* = shore of Lake Peipsi-järv (coastal waters, large meadows and forests, street villages; *5 EA b*).

The largest and most distinct localities with *four defining elements* are the following (numbers refer to the densely hatched areas above): *13* = Pandivere (ridges and major humps, winding rivers, large fields and cultural forests, large villages, estates and a dense road network; *III IV 2 EA cb*); *15* = Hageri (flat, winding rivers, alvar and tree meadows, cluster villages and a dense road network; *V 2 EA fc*); *20* = Põltsamaa (minor barrows and a plain, winding rivers, tree meadows and fields, cluster villages and a dense road network; *V VI 2 EA fc*); *22* = Palamuse (major barrows, parallel lakes, strip fields and meadows, parallel ribbon settlements, estates; *III 32 EA ef*); *26* = Otepää (major domes, scattered lakes, small fields and meadows, forests, small farms, estates and dense road network; *III II 32 EA if*); *27* = Viljandi (major humps, barrows and dish valleys, scattered lakes and brooks, fields and strip meadows, large farms and dense road network; *III IX 32 EA fi*); *28* = Kilingi (plain, winding rivers, large bogs and forests, individual dwellings and a sparse road network; *VI 2 DA li*)

5.3. Regions Defined in Terms of Proximics: Definition of Vicinities

The cartographic method presented above, consisting of an analytic and a synthetic part, can also be used to define areas that are homogeneous in terms of their proximities, or vicinities. The task is considerably more difficult, however, since a far greater number of phenomena must be taken into consideration than in the formation of regions as homogeneous landscape areas. But we are not as dependent on the definition of regions in proximics

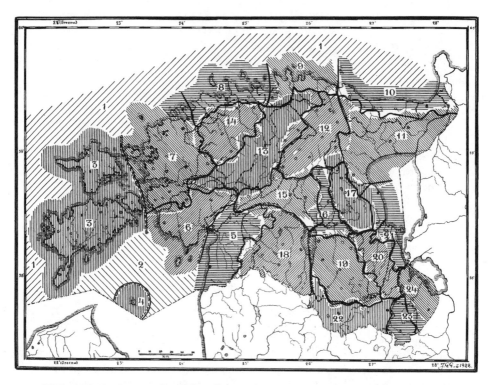

Figure 5.13. Geographical localities of Estonia with two defining elements and the groups of communes and parishes corresponding to these.

(Boundary and transitional zones are left *blank. Unbroken lines* indicate the boundaries of commune groups and *dashed lines* those of parish groups. *Hatchings* are drawn in different directions to aid recognition of the areas.)

1 = Gulf of Finland-Baltic Sea (*1*); *2* = Gulf of Riga (*1*); *3* = Western islands (plain, alvar and tree-herb terrain; *VI E*); *4* = Ruhnu (humps, coastal waters; *IV 5*); *5* = Soomaa (plain, large bogs and forests; *IV DA*); *6* = Sootaguse (plain and minor humps, forests and bogs; *VI V AD*); *7* = Rotala (plain, minor humps and ridges, alvar and tree-herb terrains; *VI V EA*); *8* = Tallinnamaa (tableland, alvar and tree-herb terrains; *V VII EA*); *9* = Lahemaa (tableland, forests and scattered fields; *V VII AE*); *10* = Lavamaa (tableland, individual cluster and street villages; *VII cb*); *11* = Alutaguse (major forests and bogs, street villages; *AD ib*); *12* = Suurkülamaa (large fields and cultural forests, large villages and estates; *EA cb*); *13* = Vahemaa (winding rivers, small lakes, forests and bogs; *23 AD*); *14* = Hagerimaa (alvar and tree-herb terrains, cluster villages; *EA fc*); *15* = Põltsamaa (minor barrows and a plain, winding rivers; *V VI 2*); *16* = Jõetaguse (forests and bogs, individual farms; *AC i*); *17* = Vooremaa (major barrows, parallel strip fields and meadows; *III EA*); *18* = Sakala (barrows, major domes and dish valleys, major dwellings; *III IX fi*); *19* = Ugala (scattered lakes, minor fields and meadows, forests; *3 EA*); *20* = Põlvamaa (plain, dish valleys, large farms; *VI IX if*); *21* = Peipsimaa (large meadows, forests, street villages; *EA b*); *22* = Haanjamaa (scattered lakes, large farms; *3 if*); *23* = Lauramaa (domes, individual dwellings, street villages; *III ib*); *24* = Palumaa (plain, dish valleys, street villages; *VI IX b*).

as we are in landscape science, for it is necessary only if accurate data are required on *proximity types* that would otherwise be difficult to examine. Vicinities, like sublocalities, are insignificant in their role as geographical individuals, even in detailed regional investigations.

It is, neverthess, worth considering the division of Valosaari into regions in terms of proximics to the extent that is necessary in order to understand the

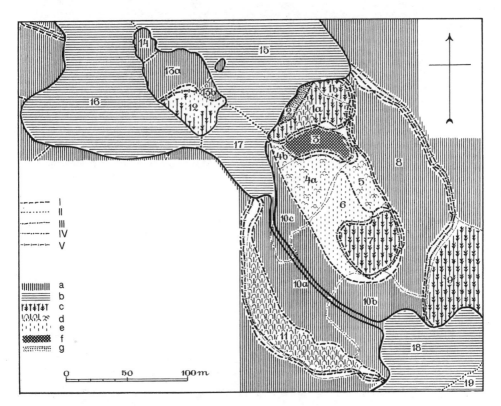

Figure 5.14. Sublocalities of Valosaari.

I = Boundary of form area of landforms; *II* = boundary of form area of water; *III* = boundary of form area of vegetation; *IV* = boundary of form area of artificial matter; *V* = boundary of form area of color. Determining features: *a* = landform complex; *b* = water; *c* = coniferous forest; *d* = deciduous forest, shrubs; *e* = grass; *f* = buildings; *g* = grey color. Decisive boundaries are marked with *thick lines,* secondary ones with *thinner dashed or dotted lines.*

Sublocalities: *1* = Northern forest; *2* = northern rock; *3* = building complex; *4* = northern bush meadow; *5* = bush meadow on eastern slope; *6* = central meadow; *7* = central pine wood; *8* = Tiusanen's meadow; *9* = southeastern pine wood; *10* = Kuivasalmi meadow; *11* = Puuskansaari alders; *12* = tree meadow on the island; *13* = central elevation of the island; *14* = northern dome on the island; *15* = main bay; *16* = "small lake"; *17* = head of bay; *18* = southeastern bay; *19* = Marjaniemi open water.

Figure 5.15. Sublocalities recognized in northern Valosaari.

(Photograph taken eastwards from the rock on the edge of the "head of the bay" at the western end of the area in July 1923.) *From the left:* the southernmost littoral water of the "main bay" with reeds (sublocality 15 in Fig. 5.14), the "northern rock" (sublocality 2), the "northern pine wood" (1), the "building complex" (3) and in front of the latter the "northern bush meadow" (4). In the foreground, a part of the "head of the bay" with its reeds and fences, and in the background a pine wood rising behind the mapped area.

Figure 5.16. Sublocalities recognized in southern Valosaari.

(Photograph taken southwards from the "northern bush meadow" in June 1923.) On the left, part of the "central pine wood" (sublocality 7 in Fig. 5.14), in the middle the "Kuivasalmi meadow" (10) and behind it the "Puuskansaari alders" (11). In the foreground, the "northern bush meadow" (4) with its hayricks, and in the background the "southeast bay" (18), the "open water of Marjaniemi" (19) and the shore of Marjaniemi.

methodological details, that is, to a broader degree than an examination of types alone would require. The illustrations of the various phenomena belonging to the proximity of Valosaari presented above in Figures 4.9–4.18 will serve as analytical plans of the area, and the synthesis can most conveniently be performed in two parts by first forming areas that are homogeneous in terms of certain restricted combinations of phenomena and then vicinities, by means of the resulting synthetic maps (in the narrow sense of the word).

5.3.1. *Proximate View, Medium and Substrate Areas of Valosaari*

Figure 5.18, which presents areas homogeneous in terms of permanent forms and colors of the proximity and types of proximate view, does not differ to any appreciable extent from the maps of the sublocalities (Fig. 5.14), on account of the fact that the analytical cartographical material is roughly the same in both cases. The distinction between them is thus more of theoretical than of practical significance. Analysis of a proximate view starts with an examination of the immediate environment of the observer and continues toward the outer boundary of the proximate view, while sublocality analysis begins with the details of the distant view examined from beyond the border, that is, it proceeds in an inward direction. Although the map is drawn on the

Figure 5.17. Sublocalities recognized in NW Valosaari.

(Photographed westwards from the "building complex" in July 1923.) In the background, the "small lake" (sublocality 16 in Fig. 5.14) with its growth of sedges, and in the foreground the "head of the bay" (17; see Fig. 5.15). To the left of the sound in the middle of the picture is the lichen-covered rock forming the edge of the "head of the bay" in the west, and on the right the "island tree meadow" (12).

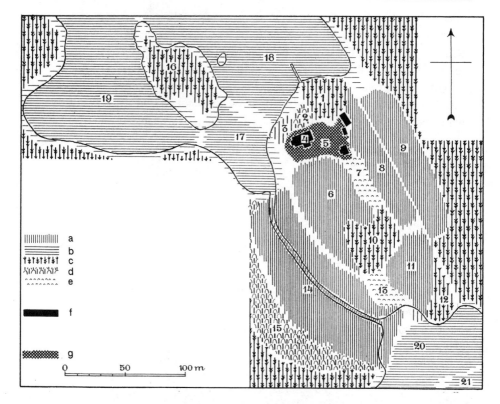

Figure 5.18. Proximate fields of vision in Valosaari.

Types of natural field of vision: a = grassland; b = water; c = pine wood; d = deciduous forest; e = deciduous bushes.

Artificial field of vision: f = interior field of vision of a building.

Mixed, or transitional type: g = yard.

Natural fields of vision change entirely or partly in appearance and color, artificial fields of vision are invariable in both appearance and color, and mixed fields of vision change partly in appearance and color.

Areas of proximate fields of vision: 1 = northern pine wood; 2 = northern birch wood; 3 = northern thicket; 4 = artificial field of vision composed of a group of buildings; 5 = yard; 6 = central grassland; 7 = bushes on the slope; 8 = eastern grassland; 9 = Tiusanen's meadow; 10 = central pine wood; 11 = southeastern grassland; 12 = southeastern pine thicket; 13 = southern bush meadow; 14 = Kuivasalmi meadow; 15 = southwestern clump of alders; 16 = pine wood on the island; 17 = head of bay; 18 = main bay; 19 = "small lake"; 20 = southeastern bay; 21 = Marjaniemi open water.

same scale in both cases, a different manner of examination and a greater degree of generalization are used when forming sublocalities. In order to emphasize this difference in approach, the representations of proximities are
termed *plans* regardless of the fact that maps representing details of a landscape may be drawn on the same scale.

The definition of areas of mobile elements at Valosaari (Fig. 5.19) is based
on Figure 4.9. Since the object locations (see sec. 1.4) of mobile forms are constantly changing, the areas concerned are defined by drawing isopleths
around these locations at a distance of 25 m to indicate the areas in which
the mobile forms are located in the proximate view.

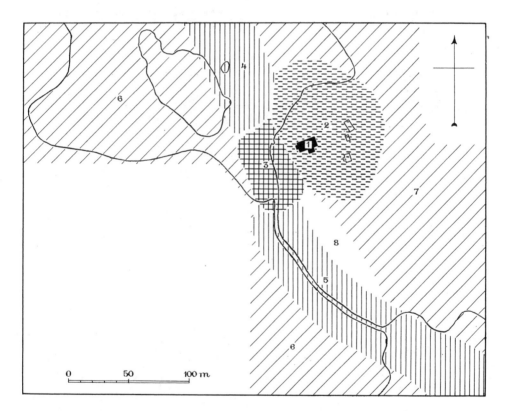

Figure 5.19. Areas of mobile phenomena in the proximate field of vision at
Valosaari.

1 = Interior field of vision of the main building; *2* = yard and neighboring wood; *3* =
anchorage (the "transport center" of Valosaari); *4* = boating route and ice road on the
main bay; *5* = Kuivasalmi boating route and ice road; *6* = west pasture; *7* = east pasture; *8* = "empty slope" of the central hump. The 25-m phenomenal isopleths (see sec.
1.5) serve as the boundaries of the areas of mobile phenomena.

The material presented in Figures 5.18 and 5.19 is taken into consideration in the synthetic plan in Figure 5.20, in that areas which are homogeneous in terms of their immobile forms are marked with hatching, which is interrupted at the boundaries and transitional zones, while the boundaries of the mobile phenomena are marked by dotted lines.

Phenomena associated with the medium are divided into two groups in the synthetic treatment, these being presented on the plan in the same manner as the immobile features of the field of vision, with parallel lines. The obstructiveness of the medium, which varies from place to place to a considerable extent in the various parts of the proximity of Valosaari, is illustrated by distinctive hatching. The second group consists of the other phenomena of the medium, the degree of homogeneity of which was obtained synthetically by means of Figures 4.12–4.15.

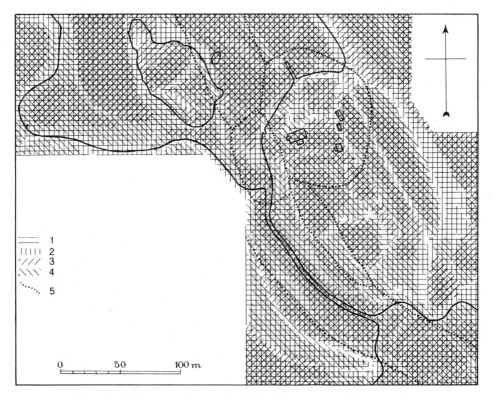

Figure 5.20. Synthetic formation of the vicinities of Valosaari.

1 = Proximate field of vision (forms, colors), homogeneous; *2* = obstructiveness of medium; *3* = other phenomena of medium, homogeneous; *4* = substrate, homogeneous; *5* = 25-m phenomenal isopleth for mobile phenomena.

Figure 5.21. Proximate views in eastern Valosaari.

(Photographed northwestwards from "Tiusanen's meadow" in July 1923.) In the foreground, "Tiusanen's meadow" covered by tussocks and bordered by a fence. Behind the fence is the "eastern grass area," the "yard," all the areas of the "building complex" and the "northern pine wood."

The degree of homogeneity of the substrate at Valosaari was finally obtained by combining the data on gradient, relief, bearing capacity, and the obstructiveness of the substrate in the same plan (Figs. 4.16–4.18). This combination is also marked with special hatching in the synthetic plan, interruptions in which indicate changes in the phenomena of the substrate, that is, a boundary or transitional zone in the substrate area.

5.3.2. *The Vicinities of Valosaari*

The larger the number of continuous hatchings in certain places in Figure 5.20, the more numerous the proximity features in which this area is homogeneous. Areas in which all the hatchings are continuous are thus vicinities. These can be distinguished in the diagram as darker "cells" around which the hatching is sparser or completely absent, depending on the sharpness of the boundaries or transitional zones surrounding the vicinity in each case, that is, depending on the extent to which these small entities stand out as individuals in their environment.

Figure 5.22. Proximate views in northern Valosaari.

(Photographed southeastwards from the southeastern corner of the main house on 15th July 1923.) In the foreground, a couple of representatives of mobile phenomena and a large number of *Ranunculus acris* flowering in front of the "storehouse" in the "yard." In the background are the "bushes on the slope," the "eastern grass area" and the forest marking the boundary of Valosaari.

Figure 5.23. Sublocalities at Valosaari: the pines in the "yard" and the "wood-shed." (Photographed in August 1923.)

The result of the synthesis is shown in Figure 5.24, in which natural vicinities are marked with crosshatching, buildings in black, and transitional
zones in white. The vicinities could naturally be expanded and the boundary
zones between them made narrower by incorporating various parts of the
transitional zones into the completely homogeneous crosshatched areas—at
the cost of the degree of homogeneity, but this is hardly necessary, since we
are chiefly interested here in the types of proximities at Valosaari and not in
vicinities of a certain size or delimited in a certain manner.

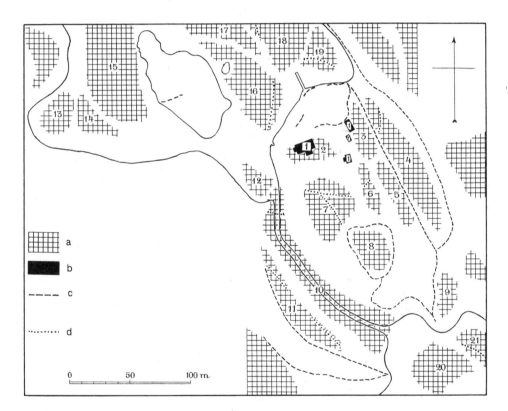

Figure 5.24. Vicinities of Valosaari.

a = Natural vicinity; b = artificial vicinity; c = distinct boundary of a vicinity; d = boundary of the area of mobile phenomena in an otherwise homogeneous vicinity.

1 = Vicinity group of buildings; 2 = yard; 3 = back of shed; 4 = Tiusanen's meadow; 5
= eastern meadow; 6 = eastern slope of bushes; 7 = central meadow; 8 = central pine
wood; 9 = southeastern thicket; 10 = Kuivasalmi meadow; 11 = southwestern meadow;
12 = head of bay; 13 = head of "small lake"; 14 = sedges of the "small lake"; 15 = mouth
of "small lake"; 16 = reeds at head of main bay; 17 = island channel; 18 = Viljankan-
vuori shore water; 19 = southeastern head of main bay; 20 = reeds in southeastern
bay; 21 = rushes in southeastern bay.

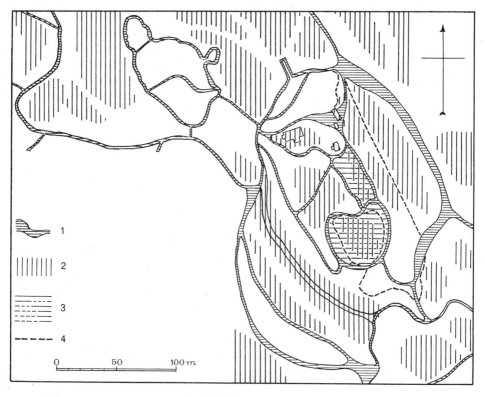

Figure 5.25. Sublocalities and vicinities of Valosaari.

1 = Boundary or boundary zone of a sublocality; *2* = vicinity; *3* = sublocality highly homogeneous in terms of its proximity; *4* = distinct boundary of a vicinity within the boundaries of a sublocality.

The distinguishing proximic characteristics of the various vicinities and the types of proximities at Valosaari can easily be identified by means of the analytic material and the synthetic plans. To take an example representing a common type of proximity in Finland, the *descriptive definition* of vicinity no. 10[4] (Fig. 5.24) would thus be as follows:

The *Kuivasalmi meadow*. The *proximate view* is an open dent area with herb vegetation in summer and covered by snow in winter. This is divided down the middle by the sound of Kuivasalmi, which is 2–3 m in width at times of mean water level but completely covers the meadow in the flood season and almost dries up during rainless periods. A few willow bushes and boulders occur in places. There are occasionally people moving about in the vicinity at all times of the year, sometimes on foot, sometimes by boat along

4. The size of this vicinity roughly corresponds to that of the "Kuivasalmi meadow" pictured in Figure 5.16.

the sound of Kuivasalmi and sometimes by sleigh over the ice. The *medium* is an open, poikilothermic[5] area susceptible to sunshine, winds, and rain. Human voices and noise from boat or sleigh traffic is heard at all times of the year and the mooing of cows and birdsong in summer; the smell of mud can be detected during the hottest period of the summer when the water is low in the sound. The *substrate* in the center of the vicinity is covered by the water of the sound, which is 10–40 cm deep at mean water level, and a growth of sedges 50–100 cm in height during the summer. Elsewhere there are mixed herbaceous plants 20–50 cm in height. The substrate consists of small tussocks of turf or mud and is soft or slightly boggy on the shores and the bottom of the sound. There is a road over the ice in winter.

5.4. Comparison of Sublocalities and Vicinities

Although it is obvious that vicinities and groups of vicinities stand out to some extent even in the distant field of vision through their visual phenomena, a plan of vicinities differs considerably from a map of sublocalities. This is because of the differences between the landscape and proximate field of vision mentioned above (see sec. 4.3) and because not all features of the medium and substrate can be seen as differences in the field of vision.

This is illustrated in Figure 5.25, which contains the boundaries of both sublocalities (Fig. 5.14) and vicinities (Fig. 5.24). Only two of the 19 sublocalities of Valosaaris, the "shrub meadow on the eastern slope" (sublocality 5 in Fig. 5.14 and vicinity 6 in Fig. 5.24) and the "central pine wood" (sublocality 7 in Fig. 5.14 and vicinity 8 in Fig. 5.14), are completely homogeneous in terms of their proximities and correspond to a vicinity of equal size.

5. The opposite of a homeothermic indoor proximity. Annual and daily variations in temperature are approximately the same as in other outdoor vicinities at Valosaari.

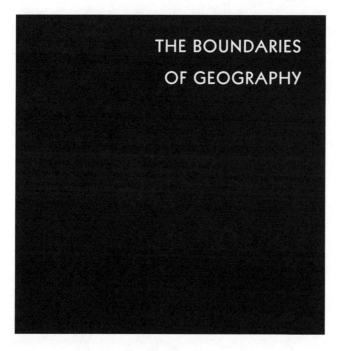

6

THE BOUNDARIES
OF GEOGRAPHY

6.1. Auxiliary Disciplines and School Geography

If we take the stand, as we did above, that *pure geography* is an environmental science, many of the branches of the former general geography will become independent disciplines which are of an auxiliary nature with respect to it. This will be the case with climatology, the achievements of which are of vital importance for proximics, but which we can also promote with our investigations into the media, and it will also apply to oceanography, limnology, potamology, phytogeography, zoogeography, and economic and political geography, although pure geography will remain in close contact with all of these.[1]

The same must also be said of geomorphology, since no matter how important landforms are in many respects, they are not *as such* objects of a science that deals with the perceived environment but only insofar as they can be observed as phenomena in the complex concerned or to the extent that they are of considerable physiological significance in some geographical

1. This chapter is based on an article published earlier in Finnish (Granö 91).

entity. We must not give them priority over other phenomena in geographical description, since it often turns out that the forms of water, vegetation, and artificial matter, for instance, should take precedence over landforms in a geographical evaluation.[2]

It should perhaps be admitted that these branches of science already operate quite independently, setting their own research objectives and developing their own methods. They have been de facto independent disciplines for varying lengths of time, and geography for its part has no just cause or right to refuse to acknowledge them as de jure independent disciplines as well. On the contrary, this independence is the best alternative from our point of view. We may hope that these closest neighbors of ours will soon acquire a permanent representation at universities to promote the interests of science in general and those of geography in particular.

As far as ethnography is concerned, the situation has been resolved and the attitude is unanimous: it is an independent discipline although for the present somewhat obscure in its boundaries. It is as close to geography, and its achievements as significant to geographers, as any of the above disciplines. The level of civilization of a people and its forms of culture, religion, and even language, as examined by various specialized disciplines, act as sources of interesting phenomena in the perceived environment, the study of which requires preliminary scientific education and an intimate knowledge of the subject. But probably nobody would think of incorporating such areas into geography merely by virtue of the requirements placed on the individual scholar or on the discipline.

Of the "losses of territory" that we have defended here, the independence of economic and political geography is probably the hardest to face and the most difficult to accept for both geographers and the patrons and devotees of our discipline. But it has to be kept in mind that the ability to construct purposeful definitions of research tasks and complete freedom of development are significant advantages for all scientific work. A clearly defined, specialized division of labor certainly does not mean neglect of some features or aspects characteristic of the geographical entity in this case, and geography alone must continue to be responsible for ensuring that this does not happen.

It should also be mentioned in this connection that recognition of the independence of political geography does not mean that we consider geographical nomenclature irrelevant or unnecessary. We only have to recall what was mentioned above about artificial elements, or the significance of placenames as designations of geographical individuals.

2. I understood both the tasks of general geography and the geographical complex in a far broader sense in my first methodological publications (Granö 84–87), but I have since become convinced of this need for a greater and more distinct concentration.

It is also relevant to consider *school geography* in this connection. It should be made perfectly clear that not everything that a representative of our discipline is responsible for teaching at the secondary school level is geography, since in view of everyday needs and the division of labor between school subjects, the syllabus that he teaches is a separately defined body of knowledge that includes many other things.

Although a teacher of geography must also venture beyond geography itself by the force of circumstance, he should always remember that his principal task is to present the theories and achievements of *our science* whenever he considers them to be of advantage to an educated person and to the extent the pupils can understand him. In this way the teaching of geography will come to be based on a solid framework, whereas negligence in this respect will lead to disorder and confusion. The classroom should not become a place for recounting whatever happens to come into the teacher's mind concerning countries and peoples.

6.2. Geography and Historical Disciplines

There has been some friction between geography and *geology* for a long time, and there is a whole literature that reflects this prolonged boundary dispute, which has been waged with variable success. A geography that deals with the perceived environment would soon be able to make peace if it were given a chance to speak, since the only bone of contention would perhaps be the question of which discipline should be responsible for investigating the geographical complexes of past geological ages. We would be ready to offer this task, which is of a historical nature, to geology, mainly to the branch termed *paleogeography,* which could without any great difficulty expand its sphere of operation to comprise the whole perceived environment, provided that the material and trained staff needed for the examination of this object were available.

No matter how obvious the division of labor between geography and geology would seem to be from our point of view, the drawing of an exact chronological boundary between these disciplines would be difficult. This question is, nevertheless, sufficiently one of secondary importance that it cannot be expected to cause any dispute. A suitable borderline would be the first occurrence of human beings or artificial elements on the earth, for instance, since geography is devoted to examining the perceived *human* environment.

As mentioned above, we would rather regard the very controversial field of geomorphology as an independent discipline, in that its task is to examine landforms spatially and temporally regardless of the demands or desires of geography, which examines the perceived environment, or geology, which examines the past. It is true that geography needs a geomorphographic system and a nomenclature that takes landforms into consideration as phenomena in the environment, but this system is purely geographical, as are the systems for describing vegetation, water, and other phenomena which we have drawn up and need in our work. It is also true that we need data on the structure and composition of the earth's crust, and these we obtain from petrologists and geologists, unless we are so familiar with these disciplines that we can acquire the data ourselves in the field. In either case they are borrowed, of course.

From a human point of view, the time that separates the present from the geological past is a long one, so that the specialized disciplines of *archaeology* and *history* have divided the task of examining it between them. The question thus arises of whether these disciplines could examine the perceived environments of their periods, that is, promote the *prehistorical* and *historical geography* included in our definitions by means of direct research. It would be delightful if this were the case, but it seems more probable that geographers with an education in the natural sciences will be responsible for examining these areas more often than will historians.

6.3. Inclusion of the Psychosocial Environment

Most of our methodologists have regarded the proposal of Schlüter (245–52) that geography should be concerned with the perceived environment alone as too narrow. According to Mackinder and Sölch, we should also scrutinize and examine the psychosocial environment, which the former (156, cf. 278, p. 449) referred to earlier as the "community" and the latter (268) now terms a "cultural chora."

Hettner, whose standpoint has been particularly decisive in this matter, writes (123, pp. 11–12):

> Some geographers restrict . . . the task to tangible and visible things, which form the *external picture* of the landscape. I consider this point of view too narrow. A country or the whole surface of the earth can be examined in this way, but the presentation will easily become aesthetic. If such a limitation is to be placed upon geographical investigation, it will certainly become impoverished and depleted. This restriction will probably not cause any harm to physical geography, for the consideration of heat can be smuggled in through some back door, whereas the limitation is of crucial importance to human geography. If this part of geography were restricted only to changes in the visible landscape attributable to human agency, various significant branches of human geography would be excluded and its internal unity would disintegrate, not to mention the fact that such a principle would be impossible to implement in a strict sense . . . Whether a phenomenon belongs to the *essence* of a landscape rather than its *picture* should determine whether it is an object of study for geography or not.

It should be noted that, as far as we know, nobody—not even Schlüter—
has recommended that the visible environment alone should be the object of
study for geography, in the manner caricatured by Hettner, since we are also
concerned with the perceptions of the other senses, even if this is not always
emphasized clearly enough. The onesidedness of the criticism is a minor
point here, but I must express my opinion on the main issue, since I belong to
the group of geographers at whom the criticism is mainly aimed.

No matter how tempting it would be to include regional units with all
their psychosocial features in the geographical curriculum, this task would
not only be too vast for our science, which is oriented toward the natural
sciences, but also extremely hard to implement in practice, even if one were
to content oneself with as broad generalizations as possible and definitions of
regions that were based on estimates alone, without any detailed induction.

The features of the psychosocial environment are dependent on place in
an entirely different manner from those of the perceived environment, especially where the traffic network is dense and connections rapid. It is therefore
also doubtful whether they can be used for the purposes of defining regions
in the same manner as perceived phenomena. And what aspects from among
the vast group of these psychosocial phenomena should actually be examined? Should it be language, religion, literacy, superstition, use of the Grego-
rian calendar, health conditions, the relief of poverty, science, or the arts? We
obtain the answer: Consider only the essential things, those that belong to
the nature of the subject. This is naturally theoretically quite the correct line,
and one that can also be observed fairly easily in practice in the perceived environment, but when searching for things pertaining to the essence of the
psychosocial environment, it soon becomes evident how helpless one is.
Every ordinary geographer at least must arrive at this conclusion, while one
who is familiar with cultural studies may extract the essential features from
this motley group with skill and careful assessment and mark the regions
that are homogeneous in terms of their psychosocial environments on a map.
If, however, we are to place the same requirements on the definition of regions as we are entitled to place on conscientious, prudent, and maximally
objective scientific work in general, we would do well to abstain from such
tasks altogether.

It admittedly seems somewhat unjustified to raise the question of the delimitation of regions in this connection, in the sense that neither Hettner nor
his supporters regarded the environment as an object of investigation in the
way that we have done above. From our point of view, Hettner's geography is
chiefly a physiology of geography and attempts almost exclusively, at least in
theory, to examine causality and interaction.

In spite of this, I will allow myself to draw attention to certain difficulties
involved in the definition of regions, since Hettner certainly did not under-

rate the significance of this task, having studied the major regional entities of the earth in one of his investigations (121) and having himself used the term "geographical individual." We may, therefore, also have to consider the question of how the psychosocial environment should be taken into consideration in the definition of these individuals and units.

We would like to refute the accusation of the impoverishment and debilitation of geography, which has been directed at us as being ill-founded. The topics we exclude from geography will certainly be developed further and more deeply than we could have done by specialists under the auspices of separate disciplines, and this will also benefit geography to an increasing extent where the need arises. What remains as our special field is that which will be of crucial significance, a complete, integrated whole. The spatial and temporal nature of the field of vision, substrate, and medium should constitute a sufficient basis for the definition of geographical entities. This means that we can all undertake to define regions, thus leading to a more reliable result. If we also take the influence of the psychosocial environment into consideration in the *interpretation*—to which we and other natural scientists are fully entitled without having to resort to "back doors"—the internal, causal connection prevailing in the perceived environment will also have been discussed from all aspects.

6.4. Relationship of Geography to Sociology, Psychology, and Local Studies

The psychosocial environment is not among the objects of study of the natural sciences, and there are clear indications of the problem that if geography is to occupy this field, it will sooner or later end up in a tug of war with a certain discipline that apparently has better facilities for doing this. That discipline is *sociology,* the task of which is to study human society, not only coexistence but also human interaction and its variable aims, which are characteristic of this society (Stein 262, p. 15, Fischer 55, pp. 132–33). We can thus also assume that it is specially qualified to grasp that society scientifically and describe the psychosocial "phenomena" represented by its activities, partly as a complex that corresponds to our notion of the perceived environment. This should all the more be the case since it possesses a more intimate relationship and lively interaction with *psychology* than geography does.

In his discussion of "entity-forming" sciences, Neeff states (180, p. 106) that it is the task of sociology and social psychology to examine the entities of cultural formations and communities.

Where the geographer takes only the perceivable features into consideration when defining regional units and examines all the factors that bring about phenomena in the object of study only at the interpretation stage, but does not consider it his task to examine the effect of that object on people and human society, sociology could be taken as defining environments on the basis of psychosocial features and examining the manner in which the perceived entity influences this psychosocial complex.

We could thus cooperate with sociology as far as our framework permits, as this would encourage a valid discussion of the significance of the beauty of nature as a factor guiding and stimulating human activities, as convincingly illustrated by Younghusband (305), for instance, or, to take another example, of the powerful impact of perceived environments on literature. This latter question has lately aroused attention in France and the United States, and perhaps also in other countries, to the extent that special volumes of literary readings and even definitions of regions with relevant geographical discussions, have been drawn up with a view to achieving "local nuances" and "local color" (Gorceix 75, Ramsay 218, etc.).

If this division of labor were to be implemented some time, it would also mean that geography and sociology, being "spatially bound" in a similar manner and both being disciplines providing evidence of the power of space and time, would finding themselves examining people's *home areas,* understood in the broadest sense of the expression, and together forming a discipline of *local studies* or *human ecology.*[3] By this means we could elucidate our relationship with *Heimatkunde* ("home area studies"), which in Finland and Estonia is a kind of preliminary unifying and documenting stage in disciplines examining the natural environment and settlement of one's own country, but which in Russia now seems to have become a form of local science which also attracts academics and differs from the old Russian concept of geography, which groped in the direction of an encyclopedic form of knowledge, since the latter is more systematic, concentrating on smaller areas in a logical manner and is more intensely stimulated by an affection for local features.

If we regard a home area in the above manner as an entity consisting of perceived and psychosocial environments, we can entrust the scientific examination of this entity to geography and sociology. At the same time, with respect to the needs of this research into human ecology, the interest shown by the general public in local matters could perhaps be utilized in a more purposeful manner.

3. The term human ecology has been used by Barrows (14), an American geographer, of geography in general, although on different grounds.

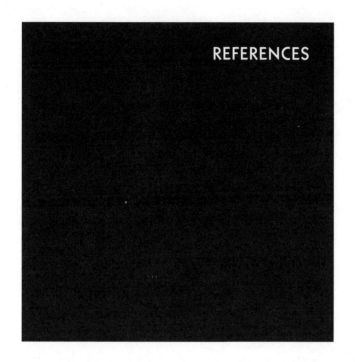

REFERENCES

1. Arstal, Aksel. Geografi og geologi. Medd. fra det Geogr. Inst. ved Univ. Kristiania, I. Oslo 1918.
2. Ahlmann, Hans W. Geomorfologien som modern vetenskap. Ymer, 1915.
3. ——. Om lagbundenhet i bebyggelsens utveckling i Italien, Danmark och Norge. Ymer, 1927.
4. ——. The geographical study of settlements. Geogr. Rev., 1928.
5. Andrée, K. Erscheinungs-, Zeit- und Raumwissenschaften. Aus der Natur, 1918–1919.
6. Auer, V. Iakttagelser rörande den akademiska geografiundervisningen i Skandinavien och Estland. Terra, 1923.
7. Banse, Ewald. Geographie. Pet. Mitt., 1912.
8. ——. Erdteile und Milieu. Pet. Mitt., 1915.
9. ——. Expressionismus und Geographie. Braunschweig 1920.
10. ——. Künstlerische Geographie. Die Neue Geogr., 1922.
11. ——. Lexikon der Geographie, I–II. Braunschweig 1923.
12. ——. Die Seele der Geographie. Braunschweig 1924.
13. ——. Landschaft und Seele. München u. Berlin 1928.
14. Barrows, Harlan H. Geography as human ecology. Ann. of the Amer. Geographers, 1923.

15. Becher, Erich. Naturphilosophie. Die Kultur der Gegenwart, III, 7. Leipzig 1914.

16. Beck, L. C. Die Aufgaben der Geographie mit Berücksichtigung der Handelsgeographie. Jahresber. d. Württenb. Ver. f. Handelsgeogr., 1884.

17. Berg, L. S. Predmet i zadachi geografii. Izv. Russ. Geogr. Obshch., 1915.

18. Bernhard, H. Die ländlichen Siedelungsformen. Geogr. Zeitschr., 1917.

19. Berthaut. Topologie, topographie et topometrie. Ann. de Géogr., 1912.

20. Blink, H. De geographie als wetenskap. Vragen des Tijds, 1886.

21. ——. Regionale geographie, natuurlijke landschappen en economisch geographische landschappen. Tijdschr. v. Econom. Geogr., 1920.

22. Bos, P. R. De plaats der aardrijkskunde in het systeem der wetenschappen. Groningen 1878.

23. Brandt, B. Die Landschaft an der Bucht von Santos. Mitt. d. Geogr. Ges. in Hamburg, 1919.

24. Braun, Gustav. Die nordischen Staaten. Eine soziologische Länderkunde. Breslau 1924.

25. ——. Zur Methode der Geographie als Wissenschaft. Ergänzungsh. z. 17./38. Jahresber. d. Geogr. Ges. Greifswald, 1925.

26. ——. Synthetische Morphologie. Jahrb. d. Pommerschen Geogr. Ges., 1928.

27. Brunhes, J. La Géographie humaine, I–III. 3 edition. Paris 1925.

28. ——. Géographie humaine de la France, I–III. Paris 1920, 1926.

29. Bryce, James. Geography in its relations to history. Rep. of the Proc. of the R. Geogr. Soc. in Ref. to the Improvement of Geogr. Education. London 1886.

30. Bucher, A. L. Betrachtungen über die Geographie und ihr Verhältnis zur Geschichte und Statistik. Leipzig 1812.

31. Chisholm, G. G. Economic Geography. Scott. Geogr. Mag., 1908.

32. Close, C. F. On the scope and position of Geography. British Association, 1911.

33. Cramer, W. Zur Geschichte und Kritik der Allgemeinen Erdkunde Carl Ritters. Progr. d. Realgymn. Gebweiler, 1883.

34. ——. Die Stellung der Geographie im System der modernen Wissenschaften. Mitt. d. Geogr. Ges. zu Metz, 1886.

35. Dantin Cereceda, J. Regiones naturales de España. Madrid 1922.

36. Davis, W. M. An inductive scheme of geography. The Journ. of Geogr., 1906.

37. ——. L'Esprit explicatif dans la géographie moderne. Ann. de Géogr., 1921.

38. ——. Die erklärende Berschreibung der Landformen. 2 edition. Leipzig 1924.

39. ——. A graduate school of geography. Commencement Address at Clark University. Clark Univ. Libr., 1922.

40. De Geer, Sten. Sveriges landsdelar. Ymer, 1918.

41. ——. On the definition, method and classification of geography. Geogr. Annaler, 1923.

42. ——. Sveriges geografiska regioner. Ymer, 1925.

43. ——. Norra Sveriges landformsregioner. Geogr. Annaler, 1926.

44. ——. Das geologische Fennoskandia und das geographische Baltoskandia. Geogr. Annaler, 1928.

45. Demangeon, A. L'Habitation rurale en France. Essai de classification des principaux types. Ann. de Géogr., 1920.

46. ——. La géographie de l'habitat rurale. Ann. de Géogr., 1927.

47. Dove, K. Methodische Einführung in die allgemeine Wirtschaftsgeographie. Jena 1914.

48. Dressler, Georg. Fusspfad und Weg geographisch betrachtet. Mitt. d. Ver. f. Erdk. Leipzig, 1905.

49. Dronke, Ad. Die Geographie als Wissenschaft und in der Schule. Bonn 1885.

50. Dörries, Hans. Zur Entwicklung der Kulturlandschaft im nordostschweizerischen Alpenvorlande. Mitt. d. Geogr. Ges. in Hamburg, 1928.

51. Filehne, W. Über die scheinbare Form der sogenannten Horizontebene. Arch. f. Anat. u. Physiol., Physiol. Abt., 1912.

52. ———. Über die scheinbare Form des Himmelsgewölbes und die scheinbare Grösse der Gestirne und Sternbilder. Deutsche Revue, 1912.

53. ———. Der absolute Grösseneindruck beim Sehen der irdischen Gegenstände und der Gestirne. Arch. f. Anat. u. Physiol., Physiol. Abt., 1917.

54. ———. Absolute Grösseneindrücke und scheinbare Himmelsform. Arch. f. Anat. u. Physiol., Physiol. Abt., 1918.

55. Fischer, Aloys. Soziologie, Sozialwissenschaften, Sozialpsychologie. Arch. f. d. ges. Psych., 1923.

56. Flahault, Ch. La géographie des plantes, avec la physiologie pour base. Ann. de Géogr., 1899.

57. Frenzel, Konrad. Beiträge zur Landschaftskunde der westlichen Lombardei mit landeskundlichen Ergänzungen. Mitt. d. Geogr. Ges. in Hamburg, 1927.

58. Friederichsen, Max. Ewald Banses "AFGeographisches Milieu." AF. Pet. Mitt. 1914.

59. ———. Moderne Methoden der Erforschung, Beschreibung und Erklärung geographischer Landschaften. Geogr. Bausteine, 6. Gotha 1914.

60. ———. Die geographische Landschaft. Geogr. Anz., 1921.

61. Friedrich, E. Anthropogeographie. (KENDE, Handbuch der geographischen Wissenschaft.) Berlin 1913.

62. Fröbel, Julius. Einige Blicke auf den jetzigen formellen Zustand der Erdkunde. Berghaus' Ann. d. Erd-, Völker- u. Staatenk., 1831.

63. ———. Über die Unterscheidung einer Erdkunde als eigentlicher Naturwissenschaft und einer historischen Erkunde. Berghaus' Ann. d. Erd-, Völker- u. Staatenk. 1832.

64. ———. Entwurf eines Systems der geographischen Wissenschaft. Mitt. aus d. Gebiete d. theoretischen Erdkunde, I. Zürich 1836.

65. Fröbes, Joseph. Lehrbuch der experimentellen Psychologie, I. 2 and 3 editions. Freiburg i. Br. 1923.

66. Gallois, L. Régions naturelles et noms de pays. Etude sur la région Parisienne. Paris 1908.

67. Geisler, Walter. Die deutsche Stadt. Stuttgart 1924.

68. Geistbeck, A. Grundlagen der geographischen Kritik. München 1918.

69. Gellhorn, Ernst. Beiträge zur Physiologie des optischen Raumsinnes, I–III. Pflügers Arch. f. d. ges. Physiol., B. 203, 1924, B. 208 and 210, 1925.

70. Gerland, Georg. Die wissenschaftliche Aufgabe der Geographie, ihre Methode und ihre Stellung im praktischen Leben. Beitr. z. Geophysik, I. Stuttgart 1887.

71. ———. Kant, seine geographischen und anthropogeographischen Arbeiten. Kantstudien, 10. Berlin 1905.

72. Giannitrapani, L. Il metodo degli studi di geografia regionale. Rev. Geogr. Ital., 1919.

73. Giessler, C. M. Zur Charakterisierung der phänomenalen Räume, insbesondere des Hörraumes. Arch. f. d. ges. Psych., 1923.

74. Girardin, Paul. Topologie et topographie. Ann. de Géogr., 1911.

75. Gorceix, Septime. Le Miroir de la France: Géographie littéraire des grandes regions françaises. Paris 1923.

76. Grabke, Hans. Über die Grösse der Sehdinge im binokularen Sehraum bei ihrem Auftreten im Zusammenhang miteinander. Arch. f. d. ges. Psych. 1924.

77. Gradmann, Robert. Das ländliche Siedelungswesen des Königreichs Württemberg. Forsch. z. Deutschen Landes- u. Volksk., Bd. 21, 1912.

78. ——. Geographie und Landeskunde. Geogr. Zeitschr., 1915.

79. ——. Wüste und Steppe. Geogr. Zeitschr., 1916.

80. ——. Pflanzen und Tiere im Lehrgebäude der Geographie. Geogr. Abende, 4. Berlin 1919.

81. ——. Die Erdkunde und ihre Nachbarwissenschaften. Internat. Monatsschr. f. Wiss., Kunst u. Technik, 1920.

82. ——. Das harmonische Landschaftsbild. Zeitschr. d. Ges. f. Erdk. zu Berlin, 1924.

83. Graf, Otto. Vom Begriff der Geographie. München u. Berlin 1925.

84. Granö, J. G. Maantieteellisen maakuntajaon perusteista. Maant. Yhd. Aikakausk., 1911.

85. ——. Erikoismaantieteellisestä aluejaosta. Helsingin Suomal. Tyttökoulun Jatko-luokkien Vuosiohj., 1917.

86. ——. Maantieteestä, sen asemasta yliopistossamme ja sitä meillä edustavista seuroista. Terra, 1920.

87. ——. Geografien vid universitetet i Dorpat. Terra, 1921.

88. ——. Eesti maastikulised üksused. Referat: Die landschaftlichen Einheiten Estlands. Loodus I, Tartu 1922.

89. ——. Ympäristö maantieteen tutkimusesineenä. Terra, 1924.

90. ——. Maisematieteen tehtävät ja maiseman muotojen järjestelmä. Terra, 1924.

91. ——. Maantieteen rajat. Terra, 1925.

92. ——. Die Forschungsgegenstände der Geographie, Acta Geogr., I, 2, 1927.

93. ——. Suomalainen maisema. Referat: Die finnische Landschaft. Terra, 1927.

94. ——. Geographical Regions. Atlas of Finland 1925. Helsinki 1929.

95. ——. Maantieteellinen Lounais-Suomi. Turun Ylioppilas, I. Turku 1929.

96. Grufman, J. Estniska republikens geografi. Ymer, 1923.

97. Gruner, P. Die Voraussetzungen und die Methoden der exakten Naturforschung. Himmel u. Erde, 1909.

98. Günther, Sigmund. Erdkunde und Mathematik in ihren gegenseitigen Beziehungen. München 1887.

99. Götz, W. Zeigt sich die allgemeine Erdkunde als Wissenschaft? Ausland, 1883.

100. Hahn, F. Die Klassiker der Erdkunde und ihre Bedeutung für die geographische Forschung der Gegenwart. Königsberger Studien, I. Königsberg 1887.

101. ——. Methodische Untersuchungen über die Grenzen der Geographie gegen die Naturwissenschaften. Pet. Mitt., 1914.

102. Hassert, Kurt. Wesen und Bildungswert der Wirtschaftsgeographie. Geogr. Abende, 8. Berlin 1919.

103. Hassinger, Hugo. Über einige Aufgaben geographischer Forschung und Lehre. Kartogr. u. schulgeogr. Zeitschr., 1919.

104. Haushofer, K. Politische Erdkunde und Geopolitik. Freie Wegevergleichender Erdkunde (Festschr. f. v. Drygalski). München 1925.

105. Haussleiter, O. Geographische Einflüsse im sozialen Geschehen. Kölner Viertel-jahrsh. f. Soziol., 4. Leipzig 1924.

106. ——. Wirtschaft und Staat als Forschungsgegenstand der Anthropogeographie und der Sozialwissenschaften. Weltwirtsch. Arch., 1924.

107. Heiderich, F. Geographisch-methodische Streiflichter. Zur Geographie der deut-schen Alpen (Festschr. f. Robert Sieger). Wien 1924.

108. Heim, Albert. Luft-Farben. Zürich 1912.

109. Hellpach, Willy. Die geopsychischen Erscheinungen. 3 edition. Leipzig 1924.

110. Henning, H. Der Geruch. 2 edition. Leipzig 1924.

111. Herbertson, A. J. The major natural regions: An essay in systematic geography. Ge-ogr. Journ., 1905.

112. Hermann, Conrad. Die Geographie und die teleologische Weltansicht. Das Aus-land, 1879.

113. Hesse, R. Die ökologischen Grundlagen der Tierverbreitung. Geogr. Zeitschr., 1913.

114. Hettner, Alfred. Die Entwicklung der Geographie im 19. Jahrhundert. Geogr. Zeitschr., 1898.

115. ——. Neue Äusserungen über Wesen und Aufgaben der Geographie. Geogr. Zeitschr., 1900.

116. ——. Das Wesen und die Methoden der Geographie. Geogr. Zeitschr. 1905.

117. ——. Das System der Wissenschaften. Preuss. Jahrb., 122, 1905.

118. ——. Die Geographie des Menschen. Geogr. Zeitschr., 1907.

119. ——. Über das Verhältnis von Natur und Mensch. Randbemerkungen zu Schlüters Vortrag. Geogr. Zeitschr., 1907.

120. ——. Methodologische Streifzüge, I–III. Geogr. Zeitschr., 1907, 1908.

121. ——. Die geographische Einteilung der Erdoberfläche. Geogr. Zeitschr. 1908.

122. ——. Geographische Anschauung. Geogr. Zeitschr., 1913.

123. ——. Die Einheit der Geographie in Wissenschaft und Unterricht. Geogr. Abende, I. Berlin 1919.

124. ——. Methodische Zeit- und Streitfragen. Geogr. Zeitschr., 1923.

125. ——. Die Geographie, ihre Geschichte, ihr Wesen und ihre Methoden. Breslau 1927.

126. Hult, Ragnar. Geografins uppgift och indelning. Finsk Tidskr., 1888.

127. ——. Finlands naturliga landskap. Geogr. För. Tidskr., 1895.

128. Huntington, Ellsworth. Geography and natural selection. Ann. of the Amer. Geog-raphers, 1924.

129. Hänninen, Kaarlo. Maantieteen opetus, I. Helsinki 1925.

130. Hözel, Emil. Das geographische Individuum bei Karl Ritter und seine Bedeutung für den Begriff des Naturgebietes und der Naturgrenze. Geogr. Zeitschr., 1896.

131. Jonasson, Olof. Agricultural regions of Europe. Econ. Geography, 1925–1926.

132. ——. Europas och Nordamerikas jordbruksregioner. Ymer, 1927.

133. Kan, C. M. De beoefening der aardrijkskunde als wetenschap. Tijdschr. v. h. K. Nederl. Aardr. Genotsch., 1889.

134. Kant, E. Maastik ja ümbrus. Prof. J. G. Granö' loengu referaat. Loodus, II. Tartu 1923.

135. ——. Tartu, linn kui ümbrus ja organism. Resumé: Tartu, étude de l'environnement et organism urbain. In 'Tartu'. Tartu 1927.

136. Kant, Imm. Schriften zur physischen Geographie. Kants sämtl. Werke, VI. Leipzig 1838–1842.

137. Kapp, Ernst. Philosophische oder allgemeine vergleichende Erdkunde als wissenschaftliche Darstellung der Erdverhältnisse und des Menschenlebens in ihrem inneren Zusammenhang. Braunschweig 1845.

138. Kirchhoff, A. Humboldt, Ritter und Peschel, die drei Hauptlenker der neueren Erdkunde. Deutsche Revue, 1878.

139. ——. Carl Ritter zum Gedächtnis. Gegenwart, 1879.

140. ——. Bemerkungen zur Methode landeskundlicher Forschungen. Verh. d. deutschen Geographentages in München, 1884.

141. Klein, J. Die Stellung der Erdkunde unter den Wissenschaften. Gaea, 1888.

142. Krebs, N. Die Verbreitung der Menschen über die Erdoberfläche. Leipzig 1921.

143. ——. Natur- und Kulturlandschaft. Zeitschr. d. Ges. f. Erdk. zu Berlin, 1924.

144. Krebs, W. Über Einteilung der Geographie. Deutsche Rundschau f. Geogr. u. Statistik, 1888.

145. Kries, J. V. Logik. Tübingen 1916.

146. Lautensach, Hermann. Allgemeine Geographie. Gotha 1926.

147. Lehmann, F. W. Paul. Herder in seiner Bedeutung für die Geographie. Wiss. Beil. z. Progr. d. Falk-Real-Gymn. Berlin 1883.

148. Lehmann, R. Die Einführung in die erdkundliche Wissenschaft. Leipzig 1921.

149. Leutenegger, Albert. Begriff, Stellung und Einteilung der Geographie. Gotha 1922.

150. Lüdde, Joh. Gottfr. Die Methodik der Erdkunde. Magdeburg 1842.

151. ——. Geschichte der Methodologie der Erdkunde. Leipzig 1849.

152. Lütgens, R. Spezielle Wirtschaftsgeographie auf landschaftskundlicher Grundlage. Mitt. d. Geogr. Ges. in Hamburg, 1920.

153. Løffler, E. Quelques réflexions sur les études géographiques, leur but et leur situation actuelle. Copenhague 1879.

154. ——. Geographie in Vorzeit und Jetztzeit. Letterstedtska För. Tidskr., 1888.

155. ——. Erwägungen über die jetzige Lage der Geographie. Zeitschr. f. wiss. Geogr., 1891.

156. Mackinder, H. M. On the scope and methods of geography. Proc. R. Geogr. Soc., 1887.

157. ——. The physical basis of political geography. Scott. Geogr. Mag., 1890.

158. Mager, F. Die Stellung der historischen Geographie im Rahmen der Gesamtgeographie. Geogr. Anz., 1923.

159. Magnus, Hagbart. Zur Siedelungskunde von Norwegen. Zeitschr. d. Ges. f. Erdkunde zur Berlin, 1898.

160. Marcus, Hugo. Die ornamentale Schönheit der Landschaft und der Natur. München 1912.

161. Marinelli, O. La divisione dell'Italia in regioni e provincie con partic. riguardo alle Venezie. L'Universo, 1923.

162. Markham, Cl. On the position which geography holds relatively with reference to the other sciences and positively as a distinct body of knowledge with defined limits. Adr. Brit. Ass. at Sheffield. Proc. R. Geogr. Soc., 1879.

163. Marthe, F. Begriff, Ziel und Methode der Geographie. Zeitschr. d. Ges. f. Erdk. zu Berlin, 1877.

164. ——. Was bedeutet Karl Ritter für die Erdkunde? Zeitschr. d. Ges. f. Erdk. zu Berlin, 1879.

165. Martiny, Rudolf. Die Grundrissgestaltung der deutschen Siedlungen. Pet. Mitt. Ergänzungsh. 197, 1928.

166. Martonne, Emm. de. Tendance et avenir de la géographie moderne. Revue de l'Univ. de Bruxelles, 1914.

167. ——. Les régions géographiques de la France. Paris 1921.

168. ——. Traité de géographie physique, I. 4 edition. Paris 1925.

169. Mathes, François E. Topology, topography and topometry. Bull. Amer. Geogr. Soc., 1912.

170. Matzat, H. Methodik des geographischen Unterrichts. Berlin 1885.

171. Maull, Otto. Zur Geographie der Kulturlandschaft. Freie Wege vergleichender Erdkunde (Festschr. f. v. Drygalski). München 1925.

172. Mayr, Rich. Die Stellung der Erdkunde im Kreise der Wissenschaften und der Schuldisciplinen. Zeitschr. f. Schulgeogr., 1880.

173. Meinardus, W. Luftkreis und Weltmeer im Lehrbereich der Geographie. Geogr. Abende, 3. Berlin 1919.

174. Meitzen, A. Siedelung und Agrarwesen der Westgermanen und Ostgermanen, Kelten, Römer, Finnen und Slawen, I–IV. Berlin 1895.

175. Meyer, Georg. Erdkunde, Geographie und Geologie, ihre Beziehungen zu einander und zu andern Wissenschaften. Strassburg 1889.

176. Michotte, P. L'orientation nouvelle en géographie. Bull. de la Soc. R. Belge de Géogr., 1921.

177. Mill, Hugh Robert. On research in geographical science. Address to the Geogr. Section. Brit. Ass. for the Advancement of Science. Glasgow 1901.

178. Moseley, H. N. Scientific aspects of geographical education. Report of the Proc. of the R. Geogr. Soc., 1886.

179. Müller, Georg. Die Unterschungen Julius Fröbels über die Methoden und die Systematik der Erdkunde und ihre Stellung im Entwicklungsgange der Geographie als Wissenschaft. Diss. Halle a. S. 1908.

180. Neeff, F. Der Geist der Wissenschaft. Wissen u. Wirken, 17/18. Karlsruhe 1925.

181. Nelson, Helge. Sveriges kulturgeografiska provinser. Ymer, 1918.

182. ——. Geografiska studier över de svenska städernas och stadslika orternas läge. Festskrift (Lunds universitets 250-års jubileum). Lund 1918.

183. Neuman, L. Die methodischen Fragen in der Geographie. Geogr. Zeitschr., 1896.

184. Niemeyer, Gertrud. Die südostspanische Steppe. Mitt. d. Geogr. Ges. in Hamburg, 1927.

185. Nowack, E. Über das System in der Geologie und die Beziehungen der Geologie zu den Nachbarwissenschaften. Der Geologe, 1922.

186. Oberhummer, Eugen. Die Stellung der Geographie zu den historischen Wissenschaften. Antrittsvorl. Wien 1904.

187. Obst, Erich. Eine neue Geographie? Die neue Geographie, I. Braunschweig 1922.

188. ——. Die Geographie der Zukunft. Deutsche Allgem. Zeitung., 1923.

189. ——. Die Krisis in der geographischen Wissenschaft. Preuss. Jahrb., 192, 1923.

190. Oppel, A. Landschaftskunde oder Physiognomik der gesamten Erdoberfläche in Skizzen, Charakteristiken und Schilderungen. Breslau 1884.

191. Oppenheim, Paul. Die natürliche Ordnung der Wissenschaften. Jena 1926.

192. Oppenheimer, Hans. Die Logik der soziologischen Begriffsbildung. Heidelberger Abh. z. Philos. u. Gesh., 5. Tübingen 1925.

193. Ostwald, Wilhelm. Die Farbenlehre, I–II. Leipzig 1919.

194. Overbeck, Hermann. Geographisch-methodische Zeitfragen. Schriften f. kaufm. Bildungswesen, 4. Leipzig 1925.

195. Partsch, Josef. Der Bildungswert der politischen Geographie. Geogr. Abende, 7. Berlin 1919.

196. Paschinger, Viktor. Versuch einer landschaftlichen Gliederung Kärntens. Zur Geographie der deutschen Alpen (Festschr. f. Robert Sieger). Wien 1924.

197. Passarge, Siegfried. Die natürlichen Landschaften Afrikas. Pet. Mitt. 1908.

198. ———. Physiologische Morphologie. Mitt. d. Geogr. Ges. in Hamburg, 1912.

199. ———. Physiogeographie und vergleichende Landschaftsgeographie. Mitt. d. Geogr. Ges. in Hamburg, 1913.

200. ———. Morphologischer Atlas, I. Morphologie des Messtischblattes Stadtremda. Mitt. d. Geogr. Ges. in Hamburg, 1914.

201. ———. Die Steppen-Flusstalung des Okawango im Trockenwald-Sandfeld der Nordkalahari. Mitt. d. Geogr. Ges. in Hamburg, 1919.

202. ———. Die Grundlagen der Landschaftskunde, I–III. Hamburg 1919–1921.

203. ———. Vergleichende Landschaftskunde, I–IV. Berlin 1921–1924.

204. ———. Landschaft und Kulturentwicklung in unseren Klimabreiten. Hamburg 1922.

205. ———. Die Landschaftsgürtel der Erde. Breslau 1923.

206. ———. Landeskunde und vergleichende Landschaftskunde. Zeitschr. d. Ges. f. Erdk. zu Berlin, 1924.

207. ———. Das Problem landschaftskundlicher Forschung und Darstellung. Mitt. d. Geogr. Ges. in Hamburg, 1927.

208. Penck, Albrecht. Die Physiographie als Physiogeographie in ihren Beziehungen zu anderen Wissenschaften. Geogr. Zeitschr., 1905.

209. ———. Beobachtung als Grundlage der Geographie. Berlin 1906.

210. ———. Der Krieg und das Studium der Erdkunde. Zeitschr. d. Ges. f. Erdk. zu Berlin, 1916.

211. ———. Die erdkundlichen Wissenschaften an der Universität Berlin. Rede z. Gedächtnisfeier d. Stifters d. Berliner Universität, König Friedrich Wilhelms III. Berlin 1918.

212. ———. Geographie und Geschichte. Neue Jahrb. f. Wiss. u. Jugendbildung 1926.

213. ———. Neuere Geographie. Sonderb. d. Zeitschr. d. Ges. f. Erdk. zu Berlin: Hundertjahrfeier 1828–1928. Berlin 1928.

214. Peschel, O., Neue Probleme der vergleichenden Erdkunde als Versuch einer Morphologie der Erdoberfläche. Leipzig 1869.

215. ———. Geschichte der Erdkunde bis auf A. v. Humboldt und C. Ritter. 2 edition. München 1877.

216. Philippson, A. Inhalt, Einheitlichkeit und Umgrenzung der Erdkunde und des erdkundlichen Unterrichts. Mitt. d. Preuss. Hauptst. f. d. naturwiss. Unterrichts, 2. Berlin 1919.

217. ———. Die Lehre vom Formenschatz der Erdoberfläche als Grundlage für die geographische Wissenschaft. Geogr. Abende, 2. Berlin 1919.

218. Ramsay, Robert L. Short stories of America. Boston 1921.

219. Rathjens, Carl. Morphologie des Messtischblattes Saalfeld. (Morphologischer Atlas, ed. S. Passarge, II.) Hamburg 1920.

220. Ratzel, Fr. Anthropogeographie, I–II. 2 edition. Leipzig 1899.

221. ——. Über Naturschilderung. 4 edition. München 1923.

222. Reiter, Hanns. Die Konsolidation der Physiognomik, als Versuch einer Ökologie der Gewächse. Mit Anhang: Das System der Erdkunde. Granz 1885.

223. ——. Der Entwicklungsgang der Wissenschaften von der Erde und sein Einfluss auf die Stellung derselben in der Gegenwart. Freiburg i. Br. 1886.

224. Richthofen, Ferdinand von. China, I. Berlin 1877.

225. ——. Aufgaben und Methoden der heutigen Geographie. Leipzig 1883.

226. ——. Triebkräfte und Richtungen der Erdkunde im neunzehnten Jahrhundert. Zeitschr. d. Ges. f. Erdk. zu Berlin, 1903.

227. Rickert, Heinrich. Die Grenzen der naturwissenschaftlichen Begriffsbildung. 3 and 4 edition. Tübingen 1902.

228. ——. Kulturwissenschaft und Naturwissenschaft. 4 and 5 edition. Tübingen 1921.

229. Ritter, Carl. Einleitung zur einer allgemeinen vergleichenden Geographie und Abhandlungen zur Begründung einer mehr wissenschaftlichen Behandlung der Erdkunde. Berlin 1852.

230. ——. Über das historische Element in der geographischen Wissenschaft. Abh. d. Akad. d. Wiss. in Berlin, 1834.

231. ——. Über räumliche Anordnungen auf der Aussenseite des Erdballs und ihre Funktionen im Entwicklungsgange der Geschichten. Berlin 1850.

232. Rosberg, J. E. Geografin och dess studium i Finland, särskilt i Åbo. Åbo Akad. Årsskr., 1918.

233. ——. Mitä on maantiede? Terra, 1919.

234. ——. Finska landskapstyper. Fennia, 40, 1919.

235. Rothe, K. C., und Weyrich, E. Der moderne Erdkundeunterricht. Wien 1912.

236. Ruge, S. Über das Verhältnis der Erdkunde zu den verwandten Wissenschaften. Progr. d. Annen-Realschule. Dresden 1873.

237. Rühl, A. Aufgaben und Stellung der Wirtschaftsgeographie. Zeitschr. d. Ges. f. Erdk. zu Berlin, 1918.

238. Sander, Erich. Ästhetische Geographie. Pet. Mitt., 1922.

239. ——. Geographische Renaissance. Wiss. Beil. d. Braunschw. Landesztg. 1923.

240. ——. "Rhythmus"–? Pet. Mitt., 1924.

241. Sapper, Karl. Geologischer Bau und Landschaftsbild. Braunschweig 1917.

242. Sauer, Carl O. The survey method in geography and its objectives. Ann. of the Amer. Geographers, 1924.

243. Schlüter, Otto. Die Formen der ländlichen Siedelungen. Geogr. Zeitschr., 1900.

244. ——. Die Siedelungen im nordöstlichen Thüringen. Berlin 1903.

245. ——. Die Ziele der Geographie des Menschen. München 1906.

246. ——. Die leitenden Gesichtspunkte der Anthropogeographie, insbesondere der Lehre Friedrich Ratzels. Arch. f. Sozialwiss., 22. Tübingen 1906.

247. ——. Über das Verhältnis von Natur und Mensch. Geogr. Zeitschr., 1907.

248. ——. Über einige neuere Werke zur französischen Landeskunde. Geogr. Zeitschr., 1910.

249 ——. Die Erdkunde in ihrem Verhältnis zu den Natur- und Geisteswissenschaften. Die Geisteswissenschaften, I, 1913–1914. (Also Geogr. Anz., 1920).

250. ——. Die Stellung der Geographie des Menschen in der erdkundlichen Wissenschaft. Geogr. Abende, 5. Berlin 1919.

251. ———. Über Inhalt und Aufgaben der Geographie. Erziehung u. Bildung, wiss. Beil. d. Preuss. Lehrerztg., 1920.

252. ———. Die analytische Geographie der Kulturlandschaft. Sonderb. d. Zeitschr. d. Ges. f. Erdk. zu Berlin: Hundertjahrfeier 1828–1928. Berlin 1928.

253. Schmidt, Peter Heinrich. Wirtschaftsforschung und Geographie. Jena 1925.

254. Schultz, Arved. Die natürlichen Landschaften von Russisch-Turkestan. Hamburgische Univ., Abh. aus d. Geb. d. Auslandsk., 2, 1920.

255. Sederholm, J. J. Den vetenskapliga geografins mål och medel. Fennia, 32, 1912.

256. Semenov-Tyan-Shanski, W. P. Tchto takoje geografiya? Izv. Russ. Geogr. Obshch., 1915.

257. Sieger, Robert. Geographische und statistische Methode im wirtschaftsgeographischen Unterricht. Geogr. Zeitschr., 1901.

258. ———. Forschungsmethoden in der Wirtschaftsgeographie. Verh. d. XIV. deutschen Geographentages zu Köln. Berlin 1903.

259. Spandau, Max. Staat und Boden. Zeitschr. f. Geopol., 1925.

260. Spethmann, Hans. Dynamische Länderkunde. Breslau 1928.

261. Steffen, Gustaf F. Sociologi, I–IV. Stockholm 1910–1911.

262. Stein, Ludwig. Einführung in die Soziologie. Philos. Reihe, 25. München 1921.

263. Stoltenberg, Id. Landschaftskundliche Gliederung von Paraguay. Mitt. d. Geogr. Ges. in Hamburg, 1927.

264. Stratil-Sauer, G. Nachkriegsgeographie in Breslau. Geogr. Anz., 1923.

265. Supan, A. Über den Begriff und Inhalt der geographischen Wissenschaft und die Grenzen ihres Gebietes. Mitt. d. Geogr. Ges. zu Wien, 1876.

266. ———. Über die Aufgaben der Spezialgeographie und ihre gegenwärtige Stellung in der geographischen Literatur. Pet. Mitt., 1889.

267. ———. Leitlinien der allgemeinen politischen Geographie. 2 edition. Leipzig 1922.

268. Sölch, Johann. Die Auffassung der "natürlichen Grenzen" in der wissenschaftlichen Geographie. Innsbruck 1924.

269. Tammekann, A. Prof. J. G. Granö maastiku- ja ümbruseteaduslised uurimised Valosaarel, Soomes. Loodus, II. Tartu 1923.

270. ———. Koillis-Viron rannikkolaakio-seutukunnan rajat. Terra, 1926.

271. ———. Die Oberflächengestaltung des nordostestländischen Küstentafellandes. Publ. Inst. Univ. Dorp. Geogr., 12–14, 1926.

272. Timmermann, A. Over den omvang der natuurkundige aardrijkskunde. Tijdskr. v. h. Nederl. Aardriksk. Genootsch., 1887.

273. Troll, Karl. Die natürlichen Landschaften des rechtsrheinischen Bayerns. Geogr. Anz., 1926.

274. Ule, W. Die Methoden der geographischen Forschung. Handb. d. biolog. Arbeitsmethoden, herausgeg. v. E. Abderhalden. X. 4. Berlin 1923.

275. Wagner, Hermann. Der gegenwärtige Standpunkt der Methodik der Erdkunde. Geogr. Jahrb., VII, 1878.

276. ———. Bericht über die Entwicklung der Methodik der Erdkunde. Geogr. Jahrb., VIII, 1881.

277. ———. Bericht über die Entwicklung der Methodik und des Studiums der Erdkunde. Geogr. Jahrb., X, 1885.

278. ———. Bericht über die Entwicklung der Methodik und des Studiums der Erdkunde. Geogr. Jahrb., XII, 1888.

279. ——. Bericht über die Entwicklung der Methodik und des Studiums der Erdkunde. Geogr. Jahrb., XIV, 1891.

280. ——. Lehrbuch der Geographie, I. 10 edition. Hannover 1920–1923.

281. Wagner, Paul. Methodik des erdkundlichen Unterrichts, I. 2 edition. Leipzig 1925.

282. Waibel, Leo. Lebensformen und Lebensweise der Tierwelt im tropischen Afrika. Mitt. d. Geogr. Ges. in Hamburg, 1913.

283. ——. Urwald, Veld, Wüste. Breslau 1921.

284. Vallaux, C. La géologie et la géographie physique. La Géographie, 1923.

285. Vannerus, Allen. Vetenskapssystematik. Stockholm 1907.

286. Weber, A. Die Standortslehre und die Handelspolitik. Arch. f. Sozialwiss., 32, 1911.

287. Werenskiold, W. Geografi. Norsk Geogr. Tidskr., 1926.

288. Vidal de la Blache, P. Le principe de la géographie générale. Ann. de Géogr., 1896.

289. ——. Leçon d'ouverture du cours de géographie. Ann. de Géogr., 1899.

290. ——. De l'Interprétation géographique des paysages. Compte rendu des Travaux du Neuvième Congrès Internationale de Géographie, III, Genève 1911.

291. ——. Des Caractères distinctifs de la géographie. Ann. de Géogr., 1913.

292. Wilhelmi, D. Ideen über Geographie, deren Bearbeitung, Verhältnis zu andern verwandten Wissenschaften und Methode des Unterrichtes in derselben. Von dem Verfasser von Wahl und Führung. Leipzig 1820.

293. Wimmer, J. Historische Landschaftskunde. Innsbruck 1885.

294. Windelband, W. Geschichte und Naturwissenschaft. Rektoratsrede. Strassburg 1894.

295. Winderlich, R. Das Ding. Eine Einführung in das Substanzproblem, I. Wissen und Wirken, 15. Karlsruhe 1924.

296. Wisotzki, E. Zur Methodik Carl Ritters. Progr. d. Friedr.-Wilh.-Schule zu Stettin, 1885.

297. ——. Zeitströmungen in der Geographie. Leipzig 1897.

298. Vogel, W. Politische Geographie. Leipzig 1922.

299. Volz, Wilhelm. Das Wesen der Geographie in Forschung und Darstellung. Schles. Jahrb. f. Geistes- u. Naturwiss., I. Breslau 1923.

300. ——. Der Rhytmus in der Geographie. Mitt. d. Ver. d. Geographen zu Leipzig, 1923.

301. ——. Der Begriff des "Rhythmus" in der Geographie. Mitt. d. Ges. f. Erdk. zu Leipzig, 1923–1925. 1926.

302. Wunderlich, E., Siche, K., Pax, F., Schultz, A., und Praesent, H. Beiträge zur polnischen Landeskunde. Zeitschr. d. Ges. f. Erdk. zu Berlin, 1917.

303. Wundt, Wilhelm. System der Philosophie. 3 edition. Stuttgart 1907.

304. ——. Logik, I–III. 4 edition. Stuttgart 1920–1921.

305. Younghusband, Francis. Das Herz der Natur. Leipzig 1923.

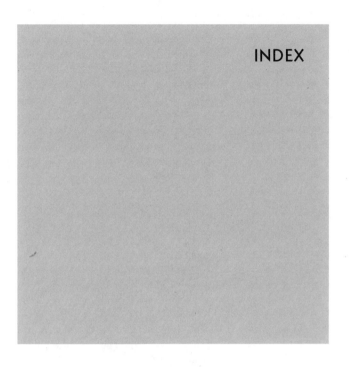

INDEX

Page numbers in italic denote illustrations.

LIBRARY OF CONGRESS CATALOGING-IN-PUBLICATION DATA

Granö, J. G. (Johannes Gabriel), 1882–1956.

[Puhdas maantiede. English]

Pure geography / Johannes Gabriel Granö : edited by Olavi
Granö and Anssi Paasi : translated by Malcolm Hicks.

p.   cm.

"Published in cooperation with the Center for American Places,
Harrisonburg, Virginia"–T. p. verso.

Includes bibliographical references and index.

ISBN 0-8018-5591-8 (alk. paper)

1. Physical geography–Study and teaching. 2. Physical geography–Estonia. 3. Physical geography–Finland. I. Granö, Olavi.
II. Paasi, Anssi. III. Title.

GB23.G6813   1997

910'.02–dc21   97-7649

                                                            CIP